ISSN 0025 3359

THE MARINER'S MIRROR

VOL. 82   NO. 4   November 1996

CONTENTS

PAGE

HENRY SECKFORD: SIXTEENTH-CENTURY MERCHANT, COURTIER AND PRIVATEER

By Susan Maxwell

Henry Seckford was from a Suffolk merchant family based at Seckford Hall, Woodbridge, on the Deben Estuary. He served Elizabeth I at court, centring his life around London and living at Woodbridge Hall, Clerkenwell, close to the docks east of the Tower of London.[1]

Henry's birth and early life are not recorded and he first comes to notice in the official records in the 1560s, when he held the offices of Groom of the Privy Chamber, Master of Tents and Pavillions (from 1560), these two offices supplemented in 1576 with the small sinecure of Master of Toils, held for life. Henry and his brother Thomas were appointed official victuallers to the Queen's troops in Ireland from 1574, Henry acting mainly as an organiser and transporter of goods ranging from gunpowder to corn and beef. He was suspected of fraud and illegally transporting corn intended for Ireland to Spain, where he had strong trading links. It is Henry Seckford's legal and shady mercantile dealings predating and postdating his Irish service which form the basis of this study.[2]

The earliest record of these dealings is found in 1565 when he was granted a licence for eighteen months to export a thousand ('100 dickers') tanned leather skins. He probably exported them from Liverpool, as in October 1566 a letter from Sir Richard Molyneux and the Mayor of Liverpool to the Privy Council mentions a delivery of 'leather and calf skins to William Aldersey for Henry Seckford's use'.[3]

In 1567 and 1568 he traded between Bordeaux and London using a variety of vessels to transport Gascony wine, a drink much in demand in England. These ships would have conveniently offloaded close to Seckford's London home at Vintner's Wharf, just below the Tower. The vessels were called the *Jonas* and *Robert* of Aldeburgh, Suffolk, the *Martin* of Newcastle, and the *Peter* and *Trinity Richard* of London, varying in size between 40 and 58 tons. These would have been coasting traders which frequented the comparatively short routes between London and the Atlantic seaboard (Antwerp to Spain). They had three masts, with a characteristic outline of square stern and bow, both sporting high upper works.[4]

Seckford's own two ships seem to have plied between England and Spain regularly, three instances having come down to us in 1563 (*Harry Seckford*) and 1566 (*Anne Seckford*). In two cases the outward route was similar; London to Spain or the Canary Isles via various ports of call (probably determined by the availability of goods for the return voyage at a suitable price) – Cadiz, Gibraltar and Velez Malaga (where there was a cape merchant, Richard Alcock as an agent), Marbella or Gran Canaria. Any change in the agreed route was made by consent of the merchants between them and the master and purser (HCA 13/66, fos 261-3). The return cargo would usually have been wine or dried fruit such as raisins.[5]

We have no evidence of a return voyage in either year in the London Port Books. In 1568, however, *Anne Seckford* brought back a cargo of Spanish raisins and her captain on this occasion was John Renolds, an Ipswich man. Was this the return part of the same voyage?[6]

Trade with Spain became increasingly more difficult because of the strained political and religious situation between Catholic Spain and Protestant, heretical England. There was no formal arrangement to guarantee the rights of English traders in Spanish ports. From 1568 until 1574 a trade embargo was in place due to the activities of pirates (often English) in the Channel. As a result Seckford had to seek either new markets or press for a changed Anglo-Spanish foreign policy. In fact he did both.

The Spanish merchants, including Seckford, grouped themselves into a Spanish Company, the Queen granting a patent of incorporation on 8 June 1577. All those who had been 'engaged in Spain and Portugal before 1 January 1568/9 together with their apprentices, may be a fellowship by the name of president, assistants and fellowship of merchants of Spain and Portugal'. It had the backing of numerous merchants, including Henry Seckford, to which was added the weight of Robert Dudley, Earl of Leicester, the Queen's favourite courtier. The company may have provided the backup needed for the merchants resident in Spain, but as it has been less noted in history than others (such as the Levant Company or the English East Indies Company) perhaps we could assume it was either less important or not particularly successful. The corn trade was the subject of an English embargo after 1585 (when war between England and Spain was semi-official) as was trade in goods beneficial to the Spanish war effort (tin and lead for munitions, for example). It could be that Elizabeth I was offering a sop to the merchants and backing trade with Spain officially, whilst secretly gaining more from the less legal form – privateering.[7]

Henry Seckford was hedging his bets too. From the evidence it seems he turned from the Spanish wine trade to more speculative ventures in less sure markets – and even further afield.[8] He invested in Martin Frobisher's second voyage to Cathay in 1577. His brother Thomas also invested £50. What, if anything, Henry received from this investment is unknown, but tales of riches and a route to fabulous new markets in China were enticing, and there was a group around the Hakluyts who were pressing the government to expand England's influence.

When Thomas Cavendish, also inspired by that same dream of untold wealth, looked for investors in 1585 for his Cathay voyage, it was only natural that he should turn to his own kinsmen and near neighbours in Suffolk, the brothers Henry and Humphrey Seckford. Their quests for new markets matched his own aspirations and there was the prospect of a quick return on their investment if he succeeded in opening up trade in the East.[9]

How this link was forged has already partly been told. In 1582 Thomas Cavendish came of age, inheriting all his dead father's estates in Suffolk and Lincolnshire. However his mother Mary Wentworth felt he was 'of younge yeres not sufficientcie experienced to make the best comoditie and profitt' of the estates and despite the 'speciall instance motion and intreatie' of her son 'as well for the motherlie reale affection and speciall care she shud of thadvauncement and preferment of her sonne' she set about arranging things so that he should receive an income but not have direct control of the lands. At first his cousin Augustine was manager, Augustine leasing the Lincolnshire lands by verbal arrangement, on condition that Thomas received the profits. Mary Wentworth received an annual income of £120 for the twenty-one years the lease ran. Everything ran smoothly until 1585. Thomas then 'for diverse great somes of money and for and in consideration of diverse bondes and other encumbrances entered into by Henry and Humphrey Sackford esquires' sold the lease to them. In August 1585 his mother did likewise and Augustine declared his trust discharged.[10]

The Seckfords were ideally suited to roles as land agents, owning Lincolnshire lands as Cavendish himself did. For example in 1573 Henry Seckford, jointly with Thomas Mawryson, obtained a third share in lands in Barlingh (Barlinges), Marche Chappell, Fullestowe, Sowth Inges, Waarmeholme, Garnethorpe Fenne, Garnethorpe Inges, Conisynges, Fullestowe Readyirges, Utterby Readinges and a 'free fishery' in Barlinges, from William Stanlye, Lord Montegle and George More. Five years later he surrendered his interest in the Barlinges property to Morryson (Mawryson) by deed of release, but kept his interest in the rest.[11] From there it would be easy to oversee both Seckford and Cavendish properties. That the Seckfords were chosen by Thomas Cavendish and his mother to tend the Lincolnshire lands rather than Augustine is significant, as we shall see.

Augustine lived in Woodthorpe Manor and on 4 January 1586, possibly before Thomas Cavendish returned from Virginia with Grenville's expedition, Augustine began to cause trouble over this manor. He objected to it being removed from his control by Cavendish and the Seckfords. The result was a summons by

> Mr Secretary Walsingham to answer such matters as shulde be objected against by Henry Sackford and Humphrey Sackford, esquires, deputies to Thomas Candysh, esquire, entered his apparaunce and was nevertheless enjoy(n)ed to give his attendance upon the Lordes and others for her Majesties pryvy council and not to depart without speciall lycence obtained in that behalf.[12]

Whether this was before or after the agreement the Seckfords and Cavendish together made with George Ognell, a rich London merchant, over Woodthorpe is unclear. Under this agreement Ognell paid the other three signatories £1,100 'in hand' and in trust for Thomas Cavendish and took possession of the manor. Cavendish no doubt used this money to good effect in preparation for his proposed Cathay venture later in the year. For the moment Henry Seckford's court connections had pre-empted trouble between the cousins and preparations continued.

Similar deals took place over the Suffolk estate in 1585, 1586 and 1591 when Cavendish needed money for his main voyages, and Cavendish relied heavily on the Seckfords' expertise and connections to raise money. They bought or mortgaged land in Suffolk in 1584-5 from him (e.g. manor lands of Stratton, Wenham Combust, Sweffling and Belton in Suffolk and Gapton on the Norfolk/ Suffolk border, purchased for a 'certain some' unless Cavendish redeemed them in London the following year for 20s. Henry Seckford held the Stratton Manor Court for Cavendish on 28 May 1585 too). This was Cavendish's fundraising activities towards the Grenville expedition to Virginia for which it is thought he contributed, fitted out or supplied the *Elizabeth*, a 50-ton vessel. It is conceivable but unproven that Henry Seckford provided the supplies.[13]

In early 1586 the Seckfords were involved in a series of Suffolk land deals (16 February): Cavendish sold Chasers tenement, Levington, to Humphrey Seckford for £300 and two days later it was conditionally mortgaged to John Foxe of Aldeburgh for

£318, to be void if the money was paid back by the Feast of the Annunciation, 1589, at the Market Cross in Ipswich. The sale was confirmed on 11 April.[14]

On 13 May a statute staple was concluded between Cavendish, the two Seckfords, John Foxe and Mary Cavendish concerning Chaunters, a second Levington tenement, the sale of which raised £2,000, and was used as surety for a bond of good behaviour (28 May) for the *Desire*. She was a new, 120-ton vessel specially commissioned by Cavendish which, along with the *Content* (60 tons) and *Hugh Gallant* (40 tons) had been in preparation for a month, an event which excited the interests of the exiled Spanish ambassador, Mendoza.[15]

The deals detailed above reveal the care with which Cavendish was guided by Seckford in raising large sums of money. Some no doubt went Seckford's way to victual the ships in London and Harwich: another area of his expertise. The Spanish reports show the small fleet was well prepared, armed and victualled.

When Cavendish returned to Plymouth in 1588 in the *Desire*, she carried what was a fortune in those days in booty and a handsome reward to the investors. Cavendish regained some lands sold unconditionally in 1586: paying Humphrey Seckford £500 for Stratton and Seabridge manors, Levington, on 1 May 1589 (holding the manorial court himself in March) and he paid off 'a certain some' to the Seckfords to regain Grimston Hall and lands in Trimley, possibly on 13 May.[16]

The same pattern of sales occurs in 1591 prior to Cavendish's last voyage. In 1587 Cavendish conditionally sold the manor of Wenham Magna, Washbrook, Suffolk, to Henry Seckford and others. On 14 April 1591 it was sold to Humphrey Seckford and John Wentworth under a grant of reversion from the Queen and in the same year a fine was levied on the manor of Humphrey Seckford against Cavendish. Three other manors, West Burfield (West Bergholt), Dernefield in Sweffling, and Gapton (both north Suffolk manors) were sold at the same time for £2,000. Some of this money went to buy two galleons, the *Roebuck* and the *Galleon Leicester*, and some to fit out the whole fleet which also included the *Desire*, the *Black Pinnace* and the *Dainty*.[17]

The *Black Pinnace* may have been Seckford's own ship, sometimes called the *Supply*, which he used as privateer in 1589 with Peter Lee as captain. (The *Supply* and the *Margaret* captured a 'fish leaguer'.) It has, however, also been identified as the *Black Pinnace* which brought Sir Philip Sidney's body home from the Netherlands. Neither identification is conclusive. The *Dainty* was a bark jointly owned by Adrian Gilbert (half-brother to Walter Ralegh) and John Davis, vice-admiral of the expedition.[18] Cavendish died en route to the Pacific Ocean and the expedition, in contrast to the circumnavigation, was a disastrous failure. Although Henry Seckford advanced £300 for victualling the fleet, some stores were stolen while being loaded, and the organisation was poorer than in 1586, as John Hawkins wryly noted.[19]

Trouble over Cavendish's will, proved in 1596, led to protracted legal proceedings between Tristram Gorges, the executor, Henry Seckford as land agent and Cavendish's mother, lasting at least until 1613. The final outcome is unknown.[20]

Cavendish's thoughts about Henry Seckford in his advice to his executor Tristram Gorges in 1592 stand as a pattern for the whole of Seckford's life: 'He is an hungry man and one that will seeke muche, use your discretion with him, he can clayme nothinge but as a parte vitler [victualler]. If any suche importunate men troble you comforte theym with the return of the other shippes, which trulie there is some hope of, if ever they returne, they cannot be but riche'.[21] It especially illuminates Henry Seckford's life as a privateer.

Privateering voyages began in the 1570s, perhaps as a way of recouping losses in the Spanish trade, and spanned twenty years or more. Seckford had seemingly acquired in 1576 two Dutch vessels arrested by the English and detained in Cornwall: the *Swanne* and the *Scoure Water*, both in danger of rotting. He may have subsequently used these for privateering, as often happened with impounded ships. About the same time he and other merchants had had 'losses susteyned by them through the arrest of their shippes and goodes of late made by Monsieur Lausac in France', and sought compensation of £2,000 from the Dieppe merchants.[22]

Here Seckford is the injured party, but more commonly his name is mentioned as the perpetrator of losses, and it is these cases we will examine in more detail.

Seckford appears in connection with a spoil case brought by the Danes originally in 1579 which dragged on through the courts until the 1590s, though it was never proved he was directly involved. A Captain Robert Holden, commanding the *Elephant*, attacked the *Maiden* of Copenhagen heading to Iceland some time before 1579. Two thousand pounds worth of goods (23 chests of sugar and 6 cast iron guns) were seized. The Danes claimed there were two other ships involved belonging to Henry Seckford. The Danish king wrote three times to Elizabeth and her council, and in 1586 the Danish Ambassador, Rammell, was ordered to deal with the matter. The High Court of Admiralty, involved from the start, extracted a confession from Captain Holden, who tried to blame Henry Seckford, producing letters without inscription or seal to prove his case. Seckford denied any complicity, stating the letters were forgeries. The Danes received some compensation but the matter did not rest there. The prosecutors had left England and the accused parties were missing. It was discovered that one of the other attackers was Thomas Clerke, a 'notorious pirate' whose name is frequently mentioned in official papers in connection with piracy. He was often sought but not caught! Sometimes his name is linked with Seckford's, so it is possible Seckford was involved too. However, Clerke had been slain near Dunkirk since the incident and subsequent enquiries, so could not answer any charges! Henry Seckford seemingly transferred the 'accused ship' (no name is given) to Sir Humphrey Gilbert, then preparing a long voyage to North America. Although he delivered two servants, David Drilling and John Code, to Danish custody they were released on hearing Holden's confession. The Danes failed to prove that spoil goods had come Seckford's way, or that he had participated in spoiling the *Maiden*, but their suspicions remained. Pursuance of their accusations was profitless: witnesses pertinent to the case kept disappearing, and Seckford's closeness to the Queen meant that accusing him was tantamount to an attack on Elizabeth. The matter was dropped in 1591.[23]

The merchants of Lubec were also unhappy with Seckford. William Van Dueton, Herman Elmanhurst and other merchants from Hamburg and Lubec complained to the Privy Council (it is thought in June 1580) that a ship belonging to Henry Seckford, together with another of Thomas Clerke's, had taken goods from one of their ships. The English vessels were possibly the *Bonaventure*, a 70-ton ship released from the port of London at the request of Seckford after 18 March, and the *Marigold*, a bark from Sandwich, 'to repare together'. Later, on 29 August 1580, the subject of the *Bonaventure* of London was discussed again at the Privy Council, perhaps after the attacks. Again

Seckford seems to have been clever enough and close enough to the Queen to stay clear of the law, or at least avoid punishment, whereas Clerke was not. Another Lubec merchant, Herman Van Oldinshed, was perhaps luckier in his case. One of his ships was attacked and spoilt by one of Seckford's but the crew was apprehended in 1583. The outcome is unknown.[24]

The French had cause for complaint too. In 1578 a 'flieboat belonging to Mr Henry Seckford, and brought into the haven of Cardiff and other portes in the west partes of his realme' had seized a ship belonging to William Rodier and John Pontcastle of Bordeaux and its 60-ton cargo of wine had been spoilt. There were demands for an enquiry and redress. Whether this was the underlying cause of the following sequence of events is unclear. At any rate, Beauvoir La Nocte, the French Ambassador in London, wrote on 12 July 1590 to Lord Burghley about Henry Seckford's promise to 'redress wrongs'. Seckford had kept wines belonging to John Thomas taken from an Engerville (French) ship. 'Other hard dealings' were mentioned too. If Seckford did nothing about the promised restitution Beauvoir threatened to inform the Queen and Privy Council. On 22 July Dr Aubrey wrote to Dr Caesar of the High Court of Admiralty about the complaints. Seckford refused to pay compensation or plead his case, so Beauvoir carried out his threat (29 July). This Engerville ship may have been the French prize taken in 1590 by the *Discharge* owned by Seckford under Thomas West's captaincy, which had a cargo including Canary wines and sugar. (After this voyage, incidentally, the *Discharge* changed ownership to Thomas Fenner and later to John Bird – 1591.) The *Discharge*, a pinnace of 50 tons, was frequently used by Seckford for reprisal raids, along with the *Supply* (or *Black Pinnace*) and the 60-ton *Return*.[25]

The *Discharge* figures in another long drawn out and complex Italian case, which we will examine now.[26]

The Italians were allowed to trade legitimately with England as long as they were not supplying the Spaniards. If it was suspected that they were carrying prohibited goods (e.g. cannon or corn) then they became legitimate targets for English attack.

Attention focused on the *Uggera Salvagina*, a large Venetian argosy, first heard of in 1587 when she arrived in Constantinople with an English 'Roman Catholic' aboard, who had left England at the end of May as a pilgrim to Jerusalem. Perhaps this unnamed man was one of Walsingham's spies?

We next hear of her in October/November 1589 when Henry Seckford's pinnace *Discharge*, heading south off the Spanish coast, was attacked by the *Uggera Salvagina*. A fierce fight ensued. The argosy fired 'all her great ordnance and small shot' damaging the *Discharge*'s sails, tackle, furniture and the hull, killing one crew member and endangering Henry Seckford's life. This was the beginning of an international incident which continued unresolved for years. The *Uggera Salvagina* became a legitimate reprisal target. She was seized at Muros before 31 March 1590 with two English pilots aboard and news of this was sent to Madrid. She was released by 11 April without caution money being paid. It is not known if the Englishmen remained with the ship or not.

By 19 September 1590 a report of an English fleet preying on all ships off the Algarve reached Spain. The *Uggera Salvagina* and another Italian vessel, the *N.S. de Loretto*, both ready to sail, remained in port fearing attack by these pirates. In this fleet were, amongst others, *Discharge* and two galleons, the *Samaritan* and the *Riall*, the *Discharge* presumably repaired after the earlier encounter. She had John Davies (or Davis) as captain and a complement of 44 crew. Was this Davies the same man who jointly commanded Cavendish's last voyage? Another Davis from Limehouse has been noted as a pirate and it could have been him. The crew almost certainly included men later named in Admiralty Court cases: Francis Lee of Liverne Stoke, Worcester, a yeoman; William Bendes of Limehouse (who may have been master as he served twice in this capacity on the *Discharge*); the Isle of Wight sailors Gideon Sanders (a privateering veteran) of Brading and William Irish; and Richard Die of Ratcliffe, a shipwright. They were all experienced in privateering.

The presence of two galleons would indicate a covert royal blessing on the raid, and they may indeed have been royal ships. There were two such named 'voluntary' ships paid for by Elizabeth in the 1588 Armada lists: the *Samaritan*, 250 tons and 100 crew, was from Dartmouth, and the *Golden Riall* (or *Ryall*), 120 tons, 50 crew, was owned by Thomas Middleton, a London merchant, and based at Weymouth. Seckford and Middleton seemingly often worked together. The presence of these vessels, and their part in the following action, sanctioned in whatever way by the Queen, would help to explain why the Italian's complaints took so long to be heard; the longer the case dragged on, the more chance Elizabeth had of retaining her spoils. But we anticipate!

The *Uggera Salvagina* eventually decided to sail from Cascaes on 26 October, against the advice of everyone in port. The *N.S. de Loretto* went with her. Two days later they were both captured off Cape St Vincent by an enlarged English fleet: now 36 ships and 8 galleons strong, according to the reports sent from Spain to the Venetian Doge. The *Loretto* fought and defended herself with cannon, but the larger argosy did not fire a shot. Was this because of the possible presence of English pilots aboard, and if so were they English agents?

In English reports the *Loretto* is often referred to as the *Mary Margery*. Prize ships were renamed and reused later for mercantile voyages or privateering raids. The *Loretto*'s captain was Francesco Bartoli, a Florentine, and the ship was laden at Lisbon for Leghorn with, amongst other goods, sugar, pepper and silk, to a total value of between 50,000 and 60,000 crowns. Some of the cargo belonged to Florentine merchants, as the bill of lading later showed, and the rest to friends and servants of the Grand Duke of Tuscany. The crew was landed in Spain, the vessel being brought to Weymouth by the *Samaritan* and the *Riall* amongst others. They had also been involved in the capture of the *Uggera Salvagina*, as the petition Seckford presented to the Privy Council shows. He states these ships left him to bring in the *Salvagina* to port alone.

This vessel was an even more important prize, having cargo valued at 100,000 ducats, according to reports which were sent to the Doge. The crew were kept on board at first as prisoners, although later some were landed in Spain and travelled to Lisbon. The officers were detained on board. The English sailors took 350 parcels of pepper into the flagship (unnamed), seizing two barrels of 'reals' destined for Leuta, and lightening the ship by jettisoning 100 sacks of corn. As Seckford states it was his ship alone which brought the *Salvagina* to England we can assume it was his crew which partially looted her. (It later transpired that her master too had looted jewels from the cargo and was later arrested in Venice for the offence.)

The Spaniards' response to the attack was to launch the 'Catholic Fleet' to clear the pirates. The Venetian and Florentine merchants urgently held a meeting to pay for an agent to go to England to recover the *Salvagina* and her cargo.

Meanwhile the *Discharge*'s crew under one 'Davyes' took the argosy to Plymouth and began to supervise her unloading. The discharge took ten weeks from October 1590, with Seckford sending down victuals costing £114 10s. 10d. to the *Salvagina* to release his ship's company. After the vessels docked, in early November, the Queen ordered an inventory of the cargo to ensure they and the 'furniture of those shippes' be kept and preserved. The Privy Council ordered West Country officials to carry this out urgently, aware of the partial looting of this important vessel. The Italian agents Philip Corsini (for the *Mary Margery*), Supio Borzini (for the *Uggera Salvagina*) and others were also present. 'Davyes', his ship and goods were to be arrested to answer Italian charges of embezzlement.

By the end of December Captain Lother had brought the *Mary Margery* into Weymouth as a prize vessel with cargo including pepper. On 18 January 1591 she too was impounded with her cargo, until charges of embezzlement, losses and the Italians' case could be heard. Captain Lother or others were 'put into such securitie by bond to the Judge of th'Admiraltie' to restore the value of goods 'if the same should not prove good and lawful prize as was ordered'.

This was the crux of the argument between the Italian merchants and English seamen, who disputed the value of goods until 1591. All this time pressure was exerted on the Queen by the Doge in Venice, the Venetian Ambassador in France and the Florentine merchants to quickly execute justice on the 'pirates' and reimburse the merchants. The English merchants in Venice had also been approached to pressure their sovereign to minimise damage to England's trade there.

It proved difficult to arrest John Davies (Davyes) as he returned to sea and by February 1591 was back in Falmouth, where 'he had a determination, indirectlie to make awaie and discipate 200 bags of pepper, divers jewels and other thinges of great value which he took out of an argosie'. Calls went out again for his arrest, which were repeated in April with a command to appear before the Privy Council because he had dispersed the spoils around the South West.

By February news reached the Doge that the *Salvagina* was guarded. Both crew and cargo were well treated in England, on the Queen's express orders. The Italians pressed for the ship to be moved to London for even better protection. The Queen agreed. Unfortunately, whilst the *Salvagina* was on tow from Falmouth to London she was wrecked. The governor of the fort near the scene took all the guns out of her and the crew was saved. Some were now in Lisbon telling of treachery, according to the Venetian Ambassador in Spain.

All the efforts of the Italian merchants had failed and they now faced ruin.

Some Italian sailors from the *Salvagina* complained to the Admiralty Court that their apparall and other goods were spoilt on seizure. The Court sympathised with their plight. As a humanitarian gesture 30 bags of pepper were sold to Walden, a London merchant, at 22d. per pound and £400 from this sale was distributed to the sailors. If any pepper remained it was also sold for the highest price so that Elizabeth 'maie no more be troubled with theire claymorous importunyties'. This clemency was not to prejudice the outcome of the proceedings which was growing more complicated.

As well as the disputed value of the lading, the Italians accused Thomas Middleton and Erasmus Harvey, London merchants entrusted with the care of the sequestered cargo, with 'uncasing and false marketing of 25 bags of pepper part of the greater lading from the ship as prize, and sequested by the Commissioners at Plymouth where it was landed'.

On 16 June 1591 the Privy Council informed the Admiralty Court of Henry Seckford's petition for reimbursement for offloading the *Salvagina*. They were ordered to inform interested parties of the request, and Seckford was to be compensated either from remaining goods or 'otherwise to be satisfied unto him'.

The legal disputes continued centring on the question of what was lawful prize. It depended on the origin of the goods carried in the vessel and whether the original merchants in Spain were Spanish citizens or Venetian and Florentine factors trading from Spain. If the merchants were Spaniards then on seizure of their goods by the English privateers this was 'good prize' in law. Where the merchants were Italians then the seized goods were 'not good prize' and they either had to be returned or compensated, as the English had no quarrel with Venice or Florence. However a third category provided a legal grey area: those who were Italians trading in Spain but who were regarded as naturalised. Was their cargo 'good prize' or not? Also there were goods not in sequestration which had been listed as cargo, and there were goods which had been sequestered but which had since disappeared!

After much wrangling an agreement of sorts was reached in April 1592. The prizers received £3,000 for 'good prize' equal to bonded goods in sequestration, but the Italians lacked jewels, pepper and other goods worth £5,000 which were missing. Philip Corsini, Thomas Cordell and William Garraway paid £12,000 by bond to Henry Seckford, Thomas Middleton and Erasmus Harvey in case goods from the *Salvagina* proved to be Spanish. This was to be paid at a rate of 2s. 2d. a pound for pepper, 26s. 8d. a hundredweight for white sugar, 26s. 8d. for pannells sugar, £4 10s. a hundredweight for elephant's teeth (tusks), 5s. a pound for refined camphor, and 2s. a pound for unrefined camphor, independently assessed by Robert Cobb and Andrew Jones.

The English were not the only looters: the master of the *Salvagina* was imprisoned in Venice for selling stolen jewels from her, and the purser was thought to have pilfered many jewels too, but had not returned to Venice in January 1592 to answer the allegations. The temptation to steal such a rich, exotic cargo was too much for any sailor of whatever nationality at this time; wage rates even on privateers were poor to say the least. Seckford, as always, profited!

Henry Seckford continued his activities as a merchant into James I's reign. He had served Elizabeth as a courtier in office until she died, and continued his service in charge of tents and pavillions for the new monarch until his own death. The legal quarrels occasioned by the demise of Thomas Cavendish in which he was involved as the land steward continued after his own death, and were taken up by the representatives of his son and heir, Henry. Henry Seckford was a vigorous, thrusting and quite ruthless merchant and businessman, always seeking the best route to personal profit whilst at the same time serving others. If his wealth was not able to be won legitimately he was not averse to more questionable ways. In the Elizabethan age he was certainly not alone in this course of action, but unlike others he did not lose the Queen's favour or his own head as a result. Henry Seckford's life is an interesting microcosm of much that typifies

Elizabethan life and attitudes, and we are fortunate in having such a wealth of documentary material to draw on to complete a verbal picture. It is a shame that there is no portrait to complement this study.

References

1 V.B. Redstone, 'The Seckfords of Seckford Hall', *Proceedings of the Suffolk Institute of Archaeology IX*, 359-69 [thereafter Redstone].

2 For Seckford's Irish service, see the relevant volumes and pages in *Calendar of State Papers, Domestic*, 1547 onwards (Kraus reprint, 1967) [thereafter *CSPD*]; *Calendar of Patent Rolls, Elizabeth I* 1558 onwards (HMSO, 1939) [thereafter *CPR*]; *Calendar of State Papers, Ireland, 2* (1574-85) (Kraus reprint, 1974) [thereafter *CPSI*]; *Calendar of Carew Papers in Lambeth Library (Ireland)*, I, (1515-74), II (Kraus reprints, 1974) [thereafter *CCP Lambeth*]; *Acts of the Privy Council, New Series, 8*, (1571-5) (London, 1894) [thereafter *APC*].

3 *CPR*, 3, (1563-6) (HMSO, 1960), p. 283, no. 1139; *CSPD* (1547-80, ed. R. Lemon, 1856), p. 276, no. 76.

4 Brian Dietz (ed.), *The London Port Books, the Port and Trade of Elizabethan London, Exchequer of Queen's Remembrancer's* (London Record Society, 8, [1972]), 17ff, (return loadings only) [thereafter Dietz]; J. Bird, *The Geography of the Port of London* (1957), 30ff; D.B. Quinn, *England and the Discovery of America, 1481-1620* (London, 1974) 199ff.

5 Dietz, 17, 40, 70; *Chancery Proceedings 2, Series 2* (1579-1621) (HMSO, 1983) bundle 283, no. 66; *APC* 10 (1577-8), 408; *APC* 11 (1578-80), 15; Pauline Croft, 'English Mariners Trading to Spain and Portugal, 1558-1625', *M.M.*, 69 (1983), 252-4; Pauline Croft, 'England and the Spanish Inquisition, 1558-1625', *English Historical Review*, 7 (1972), 246-61.

6 Dietz, 41.

7 *CPR*, 7 (1575-8) (HMSO, 1982), 317; Pauline Croft (ed.), *The Spanish Company* (London Record Society, 9, 1973), 95.

8 *Calendar of State Papers, Colonial (East Indies)*, 2 (1513-1616) (ed. W.N. Sainsbury, 1862), 17, 24.

9 See D.B. Quinn, *The Last Voyage of Thomas Cavendish, 1591* (University of Chicago/London, 1974), introduction, for brief biography of Cavendish [thereafter Quinn, 'Last Voyage').

10 G. Dyke, 'The Finances of a 16th Century navigator, Thomas Cavendish of Trimley in Suffolk', *M.M.*, 44 (May 1958), 108-15 [thereafter Dyke, Finances]; P.R.O., Chancery Proceedings, Elizabeth C2/CC7/42; G. Dyke, 'Chronology of Thomas Cavendish' (unpublished manuscript); S. Jennings, 'Thomas Cavendish' (unpublished A-level thesis, 1971) [thereafter Jennings, 1971]; P.R.O., Court of Requests Proceedings, REQ 2/26/21.

11 *CPR*, 6 (1572-5) (Kraus reprint, 1974), 66, 115. Spellings of names are taken from this edition.

12 *APC*, New Series 14 (1586-7) (ed. J.R. Dasent, 1897), 276 (a marginal note on the manuscript referred to in the calendar), 299.

13 Bury and West Suffolk Record Office [thereafter WSRO], E1/36, 9 March, 1584-5; East Suffolk Record Office [thereafter ESRO], 50/3/115; Jennings, 9, 10; Quinn, 'Last Voyage', 8; D.B. Quinn, *The Roanoke Voyages*, Hakluyt Society Publications, Series 2, 104 (1955), 2 vols, 121, 158, 230.

14 ESRO 50/22/1/22 (1); ESRO 312/252; ESRO 512/256; Dyke, Finances, 110; Jennings, 1971, 6. John Foxe was MP for Aldeburgh from 1584 when Cavendish sat for Shaftsbury. He was also a shipping merchant and trader with Spain.

15 Dyke, Finances, 110; British Library Additional Manuscript 12504/301, surety bond for *Desire*, 28 May 1586; R. Hakluyt, *Principal Navigations...*, 11 (Glasgow, Maclehose, 1903-5), 290-347 (Francis Pretty's account of the Circumnavigation 1587); *Calendar of State Papers (Spanish)*, 3 (1580-6) (ed. Hume, 1896), 578, 11 May [thereafter *CSPS*].

16 Dyke, Finances, 112.

17 Copinger (ed.), *The Manors of Suffolk V*, 9 [thereafter Copinger]; Copinger VI, 109; Dyke, Finances, 114.

18 K.R. Andrews, *Elizabethan Privateering, 1585-1603* (Cambridge, 1964), 248 [thereafter Andrews, *Privateering*]; Quinn, 'Last Voyage', 19ff; see Samuel Purchas, Hakluytus Posthumus... (Glasgow, Maclehose, 1905-7), 16, 151-95, and R. Hakluyt *Navigations* (1598) for complementary narratives of the 1591 Voyage; Quinn, 'Last Voyage', for Cavendish's own version and Quinn's discussion of it.

19 Quinn, 'Last Voyage', 19ff; J.A. Williamson (ed.), *The Observations of John Hawkins* (London, 1933), 20.

20 Dyke, Finances, 115.

21 Quinn, 'Last Voyage', 56.

22 *APC*, New Series, 9 (ed. J.R. Dasent, 1894), 307; *APC*, new series 10 (ed. J.R. Dasent, 1895), 129.

23 *Calendar of State Papers, foreign (North and East Europe)* (ed. A.I. Butler, 1904) (1579-80), 19 and 42; *APC* 11 (1578-80), 173; for Clarke see relevant *CSPD* volumes for 1575-9.

24 *CSPD* I (1547-80), 663; *APC*, new series, 11 (1578-80), 423; *APC*, new series, 12 (1580-1), 183; Redstone, 363; *CSPD* II (1581-90), 148.

25 *List and Analysis of State Papers, foreign,* 2 (ed. R.B. Wernham, 1969) (July 1590-May 1591); *APC*, 2 (1578-80), 44, 99; *APC*, 19 (Kraus reprint, 1974), 333; Andrews, *Privateering*, 248.

26 The following paragraphs are a reconstruction of the early part of the story based on the following sources (I have not followed all the trial process as it is long-winded and very complicated):

Calendar of State Papers (Venetian), 8 (1581-91) (London, 1894), 324, 484-5, 504, 509-11, 523, 535, 538, *HMC Report on the Westmoreland Manuscripts* (1892), 4; Chancery Papers in the possession of the Marquess of Salisbury, Petition 588 (Letter, Henry Seckford to the Privy Council, undated); Wernham, 399; *APC*, 19 (1590), 77-78; *APC*, 20 (1590-1), 223, 282; *APC*, 21 (1591), 39-40, 173, 207-8; *CSPD* 3 (1591-4, Kraus reprint, 1967), 214-6; *List and Analysis of State Papers, foreign* (London, 1980) (June 1591-April 1592), 433; Calendar of State Papers (Royal Letters), Venice, LXIV; K.R. Andrews, (ed.), *Elizabethan Privateering Voyages to the West Indies, 1588-95*(Hakluyt Society, second series, 8 [1959]), 143, 151, 156, 159, 163.

Susan Maxwell is a primary school supply teacher. Graduating in history from Durham University, she has continued private research into the life of Thomas Cavendish, a sixteenth-century circumnavigator, ever since. The preceding paper is the first published offshoot of this interest.

The Mariner's Mirror Vol. 82 No. 4 (November 1996), 398-408

PARLIAMENTARY NAVAL POLITICS 1641-49

By M.L. Baumber

At the time of outbreak of the Civil Wars the official head of the Navy was the King but since the reign of Henry VIII it had become customary for him to delegate his powers to a Lord High Admiral. The Lord High Admiral had three distinct functions. He was the commander-in-chief of the fleet, he was the head of the High Court of Admiralty, and he was responsible for the naval administration. The fees obtainable from cases in the Admiralty Court made the office one of the most lucrative and sought-after in the monarch's gift, so the incumbent was usually an important court figure. Often he would be a soldier, rarely did he have much knowledge of the sea prior to his appointment.[1]

This was not as disastrous a recipe as it might appear on the surface. When he commanded in person, the Lord High Admiral had a council of captains to advise him on naval matters and he usually heeded their advice, only taking the lead when there was actual fighting to be done. Often the Lord High Admiral did not go to sea at all but appointed a vice-admiral from among the sea officers to command in his place. Nor did he have to have a detailed knowledge of maritime law. Cases in the High Court were heard by judges, who were specially appointed.

The naval administration was run by a board of four professional officers: the treasurer, who was responsible for the financial side of the business, the surveyor, who looked after the ships and the Royal dockyards, the clerk, who dealt with the correspondence and the comptroller, who kept parallel books to the other three to make sure they were doing their jobs properly. In addition they met weekly and acted jointly in advising the Lord High Admiral on setting out the fleet, maintaining the dockyards, preparing estimates of expenditure, preparing contracts, hiring, paying and feeding the seamen etc. There was no necessity for the Lord High Admiral to attend Navy Board meetings and by the time the Civil Wars broke out he was not even entitled to.[2]

These four officers, often known collectively as the Navy Commissioners, together with Trinity House, the merchant captains' guild, would be ready with advice on the appointment of suitable men as captains for the royal ships. Problems would only arise if an ignorant Lord High Admiral attempted to exercise the theoretical powers which he possessed.

When the Long Parliament met in November 1640 the MPs hostile to Charles I found that they were unable to influence either naval policy or the appointment of officers in the fleet, dockyards and Admiralty directly at all. The changes in the naval administration between then and 1649 are a history of the struggle by Parliament and, particularly the House of Commons, to assert its authority over a jurisdiction originally quite independent of it.

The first move was to strike at the financial roots of the Navy. Ship money had been a major grievance and in 1641 it was abolished. Instead the Commons decided to use the Customs revenue for the support of the fleet. Alleging that Charles had spent the money previously on improvements to Whitehall, the Commons set up a Committee of Navy and Customs to investigate the accounts of the Customs Commissioners. The allegations proved to be quite false but they served to establish the right of the Commons to keep a watch on the finances of the Navy. The committee, chaired at first by Sir John Culpepper but later by Sir Henry Vane senior, had become a permanent standing committee by the time the First Civil War broke out.[3]

However, to begin with, the Committee of the Navy and Customs played little part in policymaking. To influence that, Parliament had somehow to assert its authority over the Lord High Admiral. At the outbreak of the First Civil War he was Algernon Percy, Tenth Earl of Northumberland. He had been appointed by the King in 1638, largely because his influence in the north of England was thought to be crucial to Charles's plans to coerce the Scots. At first he was a supporter of Strafford but he was estranged from the court by a quarrel with Hamilton and by 1642 he had become sympathetic to the Parliamentary cause.

In March 1642 a large summer fleet of 19 state ships and 23 armed merchantmen was planned, largely because of the rebelllon in Ireland. The list of captains was compiled in the usual way and when the King saw it, he approved Northumberland's selections without comment. Northumberland then submitted the list to Parliament. Why he took this action is not clear because constitutionally he had no obligation to do so. Perhaps it was his innate sympathy with the Parliamentary cause or he may have received a broad hint that the necessary money would not be forthcoming unless the MPs were allowed a say.

Whatever the reason his action created a dangerous precedent and the Commons took advantage of the opening. Every captain was discussed and voted on separately. Two were rejected. Most important of all the Commons objected to the commander-in-chief. Northumberland did not plan to go to sea himself and he had named Sir John Pennington as his vice-admiral. The choice was a logical one. He was experienced and popular and he was the commander of the winter guard, which the new fleet was designed to replace. Unfortunately he was also a known Royalist, so the Commons substituted the name of the Earl of Warwick. After hesitating for over three weeks Northumberland bowed to Parliament's wishes.[4]

Charles was naturally extremely angry with Northumberland but he too hesitated and it was not until the end of June that he decided to dismiss him and use the power in his prerogative to reappoint Pennington directly.[5] As with everything that he did the King's action was counterproductive. The three months' delay had allowed Warwick time to consolidate his hold on the fleet and Parliament quickly confirmed his position as their vice-admiral, so that when a revolt took place among the ships anchored in the Downs, he was able to neutralise it.

The dismissal of Northumberland also allowed Parliament, and particularly the Commons, to get its hands on the whole naval administration. At the outbreak of the war the members of the Navy Board were Sir Henry Vane junior and Sir William Russell, joint treasurers, Captain William Batten, surveyor, Captain George Carteret, comptroller, and Thomas Barlow, clerk. By the end of July 1642 Carteret had joined the King and Batten was at sea with the fleet. Both Russell and Barlow ceased to perform their duties, leaving Vane the only active officer. On 5 August he was appointed the sole treasurer, and the Committee of the Navy, whose chairman was his father, was empowered to take all the decisions necessary for the smooth running of the fleet.[6]

Even Vane must have recognised that this arrangement could only be a temporary expedient but he made sure that when a proper administration was set up he remained in control. In September 1642 a new Navy Commission came into existence. There were 12 members. Six were MPs – Sir Henry Vane junior, Giles Greene, John Rolle, Samuel Vassall, Alexander Bence and Squire Bence. Six were professional men – Captain William Batten, Captain Richard Crandley, Captain Roger Tweedy, Captain John Morris, Captain Phineas Pett and John Hollond. Vane remained treasurer and Hollond performed the duties of the clerk. Pett took responsibility for Chatham. The offices of comptroller and surveyor were abolished. As Batten spent most of his time at sea the remaining responsibilities were divided between Crandley, Morris and Tweedy. Vane, Batten, Crandley, Tweedy, Pett, Morris and Hollond were to be paid.[7]

Nothing was done about the question of the Admiralty until Warwick returned from sea. Northumberland's hope that his office would be restored was to be disappointed. A Committee of Admiralty and Cinque Ports was set up on 18 October to exercise the powers of the Lord High Admiral, composed of three members of the House of Lords, Northumberland, Warwick and Holland, and six members of the House of Commons, Sir Henry Vane senior, Sir Henry Vane junior, Sir Robert Pye, Giles Greene, Henry Marten and John Rolle. Northumberland's secretary, Thomas Smith, was appointed Secretary to the Committee. On 2 December three more MPs were added. They were Samuel Vassall, Alexander Bence and Squire Bence. The net result was that Vane was on both bodies and was also Navy Treasurer. Five of the other MPs – Giles Greene, John Rolle, Samuel Vassall, Alexander Bence and Squire Bence – were also on both the Navy Commission and the Committee of Admiralty and Cinque Ports.[8]

To begin with there was no direct clash between Warwick and Vane over naval affairs because Warwick was only vice-admiral of the fleet and therefore ultimately subject to the control of the Committee of Admiralty and Cinque Ports on which Vane's supporters had a majority. But as a member of the Lords, Warwick resented Vane's attempts to bring all the machinery of the state under the control of the Commons. He was also at loggerheads with him over the Post Office .

During 1642 Warwick had managed to seize the entire fleet but in 1643 Parliament lost the initiative at sea. Although Hull and Plymouth both held out with assistance from the fleet, everything went wrong elsewhere. Parliament fared disastrously in the South West. Dartmouth and Bristol were lost without Warwick being able to render any assistance and his attempts to relieve Exeter were unavailing. Jersey was also secured for the King by Sir George Carteret. To make matters worse, when the Parliamentary squadron in the Irish Sea turned for home in October, there were no ships ready to replace it, leaving the way wide open for the King's army in Ireland to be shipped over to help his cause in England.

John Pym, the Parliamentary leader, was well aware of the difficulties the Navy faced and he knew the reverses were not Warwick's fault. He believed that two things were needed if the fleet was to function properly. The first was an adequate supply of money and the second was strong leadership. From the beginning of the war Parliament had appropriated the Customs revenue to the use of the Navy. No separate account exists for 1643 but a calculation based on the consolidated total for January 1643 to May 1645 suggests a sum of around £250,000, £200,000 from the Customs and another £50,000 from other sources. The Navy Commissioners estimated the cost of the ships set out in 1643 at £332,000. Some ships did not get to sea, but £320,000 seems to have been spent.[9]

As early as May 1643 the rumour was going round that the Parliament, '...to form a fund for the support of the fleet are beginning to tax food, a course formerly greatly abhorred by the English'. It was true but the pill was so bitter that Parliament did not swallow it until 8 September and even then no part of the money was earmarked for the Navy.[10] Two more months were allowed to pass before the excise on flesh and salt were reserved for the supply of the fleet. Late though the grant was, Warwick was greatly relieved. Work could begin on fitting out the winter guard and the preparation of a new Irish Seas fleet.

Pym was convinced that the firm leadership he wanted could only be secured by Parliament appointing an effective Lord High Admiral. The Commons were reluctant to see their grip on the Admiralty broken but the misconduct of members of both the Admiralty Committee and the Navy Commission served to underline the need for change. The High Court of Admiralty had come under heavy attack in the early days of the Long Parliament, from those who detested prerogative government in any shape or form, and from common lawyers, who disliked the civil law procedures used there. While Northumberland was Lord High Admiral, the work of the court went on unmolested but after his dismissal there was trouble. The salaries of the judges were not paid[11] and contracts became more and more difficult to enforce. On one occasion the Marshal of the Admiralty was himself arrested for restraining goods according to the High Court's order. In theory the Committee of Admiralty and Cinque Ports could act as a check but in practice the members proved unable or unwilling to do anything.

Even more glaring were the shortcomings of the Navy Commission. At the beginning of September Warwick was complaining about the way ships captured as prize were being released. On 31 October Lord Say alleged that the Commission had allowed 140 ships to sail, despite the embargo in force. This was a serious accusation. The embargo was imposed to ensure that the fleet was fully manned. Exemption conferred two advantages on the lucky captains and owners: they could recruit a full crew and gain a considerable start over their trade rivals.[12]

An investigation was ordered and the following day a conference was held between the two Houses, at which Giles Greene, the chairman of the Navy Commission, was closely examined. The questioning must have shown that the merchants on the Commission or their friends had shares in the ships concerned or goods laded on them, because on 2 November the Commons ordered a drastic change. The Navy Commission was dissolved. The MPs on it were added to the Committee of Navy and Customs and the professional officers reconstituted as a Board of Navy Commissioners on the old pattern. As late as September 1647 Greene was having to deny that he took bribes while chairman of the Navy Commission.[13]

This was a great improvement but not a complete solution. Some of the Navy Commissioners themselves were shareholders, both in ships engaged in normal trade and in armed merchantmen hired for the state.[14] The behaviour of the Committee of Admiralty in its dealings with those trying to subvert the High Court of Admiralty gave small grounds for believing that it would exert the firm control the Navy

Commissioners needed. On 13 November Warwick complained that Joseph Pett, Robert Moorcock and Robert Warwick had not been admitted to their places at Chatham.[15] The committee to investigate what had happened was also charged with considering the question of Mr Smyth, which seems to imply that he was responsible for the obstruction.

Vane had been absent negotiating the alliance with the Scots between August and November and he cannot have been pleased with what he found on his return. He thought that the Admiralty should remain in commission and the fleet be commanded by a professional officer, subject to Parliamentary control, but the confusion into which maritime affairs had fallen cut the ground from under his feet. The paramount need for the moment was to win the war. Warwick had already proved himself a capable commander and he had Pym's ear. Reluctantly Vane agreed to back him for Lord High Admiral, secretly resolving to get rid of him again at the first available opportunity.

The ordinance creating Warwick Lord High Admiral was introduced into the Commons on 28 November. Warwick's Peace Party opponents managed to delay its passage for a week but the progress of the war clinched the issue. On 6 December letters were read from Sir William Brereton, the Parliamentary commander in Cheshire, announcing that the first reinforcements for the King from Ireland had landed near Chester. The ordinance passed the Commons the same day and was approved by the Lords the next morning.[16]

The piloting of the ordinance through Parliament was Pym's last achievement. By the end of the year he was dead and once his restraining hand was removed, the split in the Parliamentary leadership became plain for all to see. The campaign of 1644 served only to make Vane and the radicals in the Commons more determined than ever to bring both the Army and the Navy under proper Parliamentary control. The Earl of Essex, as Lord General, asserted that his office rendered him independent of Parliament's Committee of Both Kingdoms, which was supposed to be co-ordinating the movements of the various English armies with those of the Scottish army, which marched to the aid of Parliament in January 1644. When the Committee attempted to instruct him to combine with Sir William Waller against Oxford, he defied it and went off on his own campaign in the West. This action was partly responsible for the collapse of Waller's army after the battle of Cropredy Bridge and ended in Essex's own defeat at Lostwithiel, events which between them neutralised the great Parliamentary and Scottish victory in the north at Marston Moor.

There were fears that if Essex had been successful he would have tried to negotiate a peace with Charles on his own terms, in which he would have figured as a sort of Lord Protector, quite independent of the House of Commons, with his friends in the House of Lords monopolising all the great offices of state. It was for just such a plot that his father had been executed in 1601. In the winter of 1644-5 Parliament passed the famous Self Denying Ordinance. All army or navy officers, who were members of either House of Parliament, were ordered to surrender their commissions within forty days. Parliament would then reappoint those it thought appropriate. Essex, Waller and Manchester, the warring commanders, were all forced to surrender their commissions, leaving the way open for the appointment of Sir Thomas Fairfax as the commander of the New Model Army. He was an excellent professional officer but he was subject to the orders of Parliament.

The same Ordinance forced Warwick to surrender his office of Lord High Admiral. Vane was as determined as ever to bring the Navy, as well as the Army, under the control of the Commons. All the summer of 1644 the Commons had been restive and attempts had been made to take advantage of Warwick's absence at sea, by using the Committee of the Navy to interfere in the running of the dockyards, disciplinary matters and the operation of detached squadrons of the fleet, about whose movements London often learned more quickly than Warwick did. But for Vane this was not enough and the events in Cornwall gave him valuable ammunition in his campaign to reassert effective Parliamentary authority. Warwick had not blotted his copybook in the same way as Essex and he had never openly defied the Committee of Both Kingdoms but he was Essex's cousin; his son-in-law, Lord Robartes, had been chiefly instrumental in persuading Essex that he would get support in Cornwall and the final decision to campaign in the west had been taken at a conclave on board his flagship, the *James*, off Lyme Regis. Like Essex, he was suspected of trying to keep the great offices of state in the hands of the House of Lords.

Vane's position was strengthened by divisions among the Lords themselves. Say had always been with the radicals and they could now count on Northumberland as well. He had played a leading part in the peace negotiations in 1642-3 but he had been greatly offended when the King refused to promise him reappointment as Lord High Admiral. He was even more bitterly disappointed when Pym preferred Warwick to him in December 1643. From that point onwards he appears to have adopted a moderate independent stance. In 1645 his manoeuvres bore fruit. He was made governor of the royal children and if the office of Lord High Admiral was out of his reach, he was in a position to make sure Warwick did not retain it either.

Consequently, despite considerable lobbying, Parliament did not reappoint Warwick, and Batten was sent to sea as vice-admiral with powers similar to those of Fairfax. Mindful of what had happened in 1643, Parliament did not revive the mixed Navy Commission, nor would it have anything to do with Hugh Peter's utopian scheme for the privatisation of the administration and dockyards, which would have left the Navy wide open to exploitation by city merchants. Instead the Committee of Admiralty and Cinque Ports was revived to exercise the powers of the Lord High Admiral.[17]

Although Warwick, Northumberland and Vane all had seats on it the traditional proportions of one Lord to every two MPs ensured that the Commons would usually get their way. The day to day business was run, as under Warwick, by an old-style board of professional officers. The work of Navy Treasurer had been done by Vane's deputy, Richard Hutchinson, for some time but he still officially held the office and could attend the board when he wished. Batten remained surveyor but, as before, his absence at sea threw most of the work onto Crandley, Morris and Tweedy, who looked after things in London, and Phineas Pett, who was responsible for Chatham. Now that the Commons had reasserted its control, the Committee of the Navy and Customs relapsed into the obscurity from which Warwick's appointment as Lord High Admiral had rescued it. Vane had learned that his purposes were best served by more traditional methods.

The events of 1646-9 were in many ways almost a rerun of the First Civil War in reverse, beginning with control of the Navy in the hands of a Committee of Admiralty assisted by a board of professional Navy Commissioners. This was followed by a second period when Warwick was Lord High Admiral. In 1649 the Admiralty was again put in commission and the mixed Navy Commission had a second period of notoriety.

An analysis of attendances and signatures to letters shows that the bulk of the administrative work on the Committee of Admiralty and Cinque Ports from 1646 to 1648 was done by Warwick, Giles Greene, Alexander Bence and John Rolle,[18] but this blanket total disguises a number of important changes. Once the First Civil War ended, the alliance between the Independents led by Vane and St. John and the War Party Presbyterians dissolved, leaving the latter in a majority. Warwick was therefore able to re-establish a large part of his authority. An attempt to destroy his position as Governor of the Plantations and Islands in 1645 by reinstating the Earl of Carlisle's patent was overturned and Warwick successfully established his claim to the revenues of the foreign post.[19] The building programme, which led to the construction of three new frigates in 1646 and four more in 1647, was undoubtedly his work too.

The summer of 1647 brought a sharp change. In August the Army seized London. Warwick was among those who thought that the behaviour of Parliament had forced Fairfax[20] to do what he did, but the result was a remodelling of the naval administration which he did not like. Captain John Morris appears to have died late in 1646. In April 1647 John Bence was proposed as his replacement but never approved, his nomination falling a victim to the continual clashes between the Lords and the Commons, which characterised the interwar period. The dispute was not resolved until the Army occupied London, when a revamped Committee of Admiralty, on which the Independents had a majority, substituted Thomas Smith.[21] As he had been one of those charged with corruption in 1643 Warwick cannot have been pleased at his return. His appointment was undoubtedly the work of Northumberland, whose secretary he had been.

Ironically the upshot was a confrontation between Smith and another former Northumberland nominee. One of the first moves of the reconstituted Committee had been to propose the replacement of Batten as vice-admiral by Colonel Thomas Rainsborough. Batten had become surveyor in 1638 through Northumberland's influence but he was now under suspicion of disloyalty, because he had provided the transport that allowed ten of the eleven MPs most hostile to the Army to escape to France. He later described how he was called before that 'false man' Mr Smith and given an ultimatum. He must voluntarily resign the position of vice-admiral or he would be dismissed both from it and from the office of surveyor.[22] What Warwick's attitude to Batten's removal was is not recorded but we do know what he thought about his successor, Colonel Thomas Rainsborough. He detested the man both personally and because of his Leveller opinions. He played a major part in obstructing the confirmation of Rainsborough's appointment for over three months.[23]

The gap between Warwick and the Army-dominated Parliamentary leadership widened as a result of the revelation that while Charles had been negotiating with Parliament for peace he had been secretly making a treaty with the Scots on quite different lines. Scandalised, Parliament passed the Vote of No Addresses on 3 January 1648, which bound members not to negotiate with the King again until he assented to a number of basic propositions. When the resolution came before the Lords, Warwick not only voted against it but also entered a protest.[24] It was not that he had suddenly become a Royalist, rather that he believed any lasting peace depended on an agreement with the King however obstructive he might be.

Hostility to the Army was widespread in the Navy, so when a rebellion broke out in Kent in April 1648 it quickly spread to the fleet. Pett was besieged in Chatham dockyard by the insurgents and a mutiny in the Downs fleet led to Rainsborough being turned off his flagship. The plan of the Kentish gentlemen and the officers of the *Constant Reformation*, who were behind the revolt, was that Batten should be invited to replace him. Had that happened there can be little doubt that the whole fleet would have gone over to the Royalists. Smith had been right, from the Army's point of view, to get rid of him because he had been in communication with the Royalists for over a year. At the crucial meeting, however, Captain Penrose, of the *Satisfaction*, crossed their plans by proposing Warwick instead, a suggestion taken up by all the other officers present.[25]

The mutiny coming on top of revolts in Kent and South Wales was a profound shock to Parliament and when Penrose arrived with news that the mutineers would accept Warwick, the Committee at Derby House, which had replaced the Committee of Both Kingdoms, hastened to close with the offer. Warwick was more cautious. He was prepared to serve despite the Vote of No Addresses because he still believed that Parliament was the lesser of the two evils but he flatly refused the place of vice-admiral, insisting that he should be restored to the office of Lord High Admiral.

The financial advantages conferred by the position of Lord High Admiral were detailed at the beginning but it would be insulting to Warwick to assume that his insistence on the revival of the office was simply due to a desire to line his pockets, though pamphleteers were to allege just that, in attempts to blacken his character later in the year. If Warwick had accepted the position of vice-admiral, after having been Lord High Admiral in the First Civil War, his subordinates would have concluded that Parliament did not fully trust him, with damaging results. As vice-admiral he would not have the power of martial law, which was essential if he was to act quickly to suppress the trouble. Nor could he give orders directly to the Navy Commissioners or the dockyard officials.

Warwick was also concerned once again about the chaos into which maritime law had descended as a result of the way the Commons had continued to obstruct the settlement of the High Court of Admiralty. On 9 January 1647 the Lords heard that because the court was unsettled, indebted persons daily went to sea and mariners and owners had no way of recovering their money. There were reports of how 'for want of legal Proceedings in those Cases violent Possession of ships have been taken and divers Persons wounded'. In February there were complaints from foreign ambassadors that trade was hindered, from captains that they could not maintain discipline over their crews, and from owners that they could not remove erring captains, who were also part owners, by action at common law. On 23 April Lord North reported a paper setting out the daily complaints of mischiefs, inconveniences and failures of justice for want of a settlement of jurisdiction.

July 1647 brought a petition from Solomon Smith, the Marshal of the Admiralty, that when he attempted to execute the warrants of the court, actions were brought against him in the Common Law Courts. Three times the Lords tried to persuade the Commons to pass an ordinance settling the jurisdiction of the court and each time they failed.[26] Whether the Presbyterians or the Independents held sway, the common lawyers still won the day. Only the appointment of a Lord High Admiral could resolve the impasse. The MPs liked the solution no more in May 1648 than they had in April 1645 but they were in a weak position. Even so the ordinance, which passed both Houses on 29 May, contained no grant of martial law, an omission which was to hamstring Warwick's best efforts.[27]

Warwick went to work with vigour but he was only able to contain the revolt, not suppress it. His refusal to endorse the Kentish petition for a Personal Treaty led the Downs mutineers to reject his authority and declare for the King.[28] Fortunately the Kentish rebels were defeated by Fairfax at Maidstone, which enabled relief to be brought to Pett at Chatham and gave pause to the mutinous elements among the crews at Portsmouth. However the situation was still tense. The revolt spread to Essex. Members of Trinity House presented a petition for a Personal Treaty in defiance of the Vote of No Addresses. There were defections even among the Navy Commissioners. Batten and Crandley absconded, taking the *Constant Warwick* with them. They were welcomed with open arms by Prince Charles. Although Lord Willoughby of Parham was the nominal head of the Royalist fleet, it was really Batten, as his second in command, who made all the decisions for the next three months.

With Fairfax occupied in Essex and Cromwell employed in dealing with the invasion of a Scottish Army designed to assist the English Royalist risings, the moderate elements in Parliament had more room for manoeuvre. On 3 August they succeeded in getting the Vote of No Addresses rescinded, a move which enabled Warwick to appeal more effectively to the disaffected in the Navy. On 19 August he was at last given the power of martial law, though even now two commissioners, Walter Strickland and Alexander Bence, were sent to monitor how he exercised his authority.[29] The defeat of the Scots at Preston ended the Scottish threat, the capture of Colchester terminated the Essex revolt and the withdrawal of the mutinous ships to the United Provinces enabled Warwick to follow and blockade them in Goree.

As the position of Parliament grew stronger its need for Warwick's services declined and deliberate efforts were made by the radicals to undermine his position, so that an excuse could be made for putting the Admiralty in commission again at the earliest possible moment. There is not a scrap of evidence to justify the claim that he was about to surrender his fleet to Prince Charles. Indeed the reverse was the case. All eyes were on the negotiations now taking place between Charles and the Parliamentary Commissioners in the Isle of Wight, headed by Northumberland. If the negotiations were successful, the combined fleets would come out in support of the treaty; if Charles proved intransigeant Batten would have a good reason to return to his Parliamentary allegiance.[30] When the abortive attempt of 17 October to rescue the King became known, with the implication that the negotiations had failed, Prince Charles had to dismiss Batten and replace him by Prince Rupert.[31] Even so disaffection was rife, three of the royal ships were secured by Warwick, and Rupert was forced to immobilise the rest up Helvoetsluis sluice out of his reach.

The fleet returned to England on 23 November to find all outstanding military business cleared up and the Army leaders back in London debating what to do next. As late as 5 December Warwick was still in the Army camp, because he publicly justified Colonel Pride's purge of the House of Commons.[32] Ironically one of his fiercest critics during the blockade, Alexander Bence, was among those purged! But the course of events was now beyond his control. He had always struggled for a constitution based on King, Lords and Commons, so he could not condone the trial and execution of the King. Nor did he support the abolition of the House of Lords.

The radicals, now in complete control, demanded that all those wishing to hold office under the Commonwealth must publicly disown the action of Parliament in rescinding the Vote of No Addresses and the negotiations at Newport. With this demand Warwick could not comply, as he was on record as having protested at the Vote in January 1648. The position of Lord High Admiral was abolished in February 1649[33] and any remaining sympathy Warwick might have had for the new regime was extinguished when his brother, the Earl of Holland, was executed for his part in the abortive rising in Middlesex in July 1648.

The radicals marked their triumph in the Navy by reviving the mixed Navy Commission of 1642, showing very clearly that it was a device to ensure close parliamentary control over the Navy. Yet for a second time its effective authority lasted no more than a year, before renewed allegations of corruption against the merchants provoked complaints from the Generals at Sea. The result was that the Commonwealth government once more shifted the merchant MPs to the Committee of the Navy and Customs.[34] The professional Navy Commissioners were again left to go about their business subject to the Committee of Admiralty and Cinque Ports, which was at that time a sub-committee of the Council of State.

References

1 See J.R. Tanner's editorial note in *Tracts of Sir William Monson*, vol iii (NRS xliii 1893), 425-7. An article by W.C. Perrin in *M.M.* (1926), 128 has a precis of Buckingham's patent. It consists mainly of a list of jurisdictions and fees. The command of the fleet is only mentioned in passing.

2 *Monson* iii, 398-402, gives a more detailed rundown.

3 For an account of these early committees see M.L. Baumber, 'The Navy during the Civil Wars and the Commonwealth', 1642-51', MA thesis (Manchester, 1967), 5-9.

4 For Parliamentary consideration of the list see *Commons Journals* [*CJ*] ii, 474b and 478a. For Northumberland's change of mind see *Lords Journals* [*LJ*] iv, 697a.

5 For the King's action see letter to Warwick of 28 June, *LJ* v, 178.

6 *CJ* ii, 705.

7 *LJ* v, 356.

8 *CJ* ii, 872b and iii, 283a. Firth and Rait, *Acts and Ordinances of the Interregnum* I, 29-30.

9 P.R.O. E351/2285. Vane's enrolled accounts also show that in May 1645 the Navy still owed £130,000. Navy Commissioners figures

can be found in Bodleian Library (Bod) Rawlinson Papers A223.

10 *Calendar of State Papers (Venetian)* [*CSPV*] 1642-3, 277. Firth and Rait I, 278-9.

11 *LJ* v, 558a.

12 *CJ* iii, 381, and *LJ* vi, 284.

13 *CJ* iii, 284, 298 and 299. British Library [BL], Thomason Tracts [TT] E405 No. 8.

14 Notably Smith and Crandley, see P.R.O. Admiralty Bill Books 1-4 various.

15 *CJ* iii, 309-10.

16 Historical Manuscripts Commission [HMC], *Portland* I, 153. *CJ* iii, 331, and *LJ* vi, 330.

17 Warwick's Vindication of his conduct BL TT E278 No. 5 10 April 1645.

18 The Committee Book has survived in three pieces at Bod. Rawlinson C416, P.R.O. Adm. 673 and BL Add. MS 6305. The analysis can be found in Baumber (1967), Appendix 1 Tables (a)-(c).

19 For hearings on the Plantations see Bod. Rawlinson C94. For the Post Office see *LJ* viii, 424a, 438a-b, 568b-569b, 579b-581a. BL Add. Charters 71792.

20 For Warwick's attitude see HMC *Egmont* I, 440, and *Clarke Papers* I (Camden Society New Series vol. 49 1891), 137 and 225.

21 Bence, *LJ* ix, 136b 17 April 1647. Smith, *CJ* v, 285. It is not quite certain that this is the same Thomas Smith. There was a Thomas Smith who was one of the Prize Commissioners. They could have been the same man or two different people. My own belief is that they are the same man. Crandley had also been a Prize Commissioner (*LJ* vii, 347). A second Navy Commissioner, Phineas Pett, died at the end of September 1647. There was no argument over the appointment of his son, Peter Pett, in his place, who was able to weather all the political changes until his downfall in 1657.

22 Batten's removal took place on 13 September 1647. Batten's version can be found in BL TT E460 No. 13.

23 Rainsborough appointed, P.R.O. Adm. 673, 13 August 1647. Blocked in Lords, *LJ* ix, 433. In the end the Commons forced his appointment, the Lords refusing to recognise him to the last.

24 R. Ashton, *The English Civil War*, 315.

25 BL TT E445 No. 32.

26 For High Court of Admiralty disputes see HMC *Portland* I, 445, *LJ* viii, 663, ix, 150 and 332.

27 *LJ* x, 290b-291a, gives Warwick's appointment.

28 *LJ* x, 297-300, for Warwick's negotiations.

29 *LJ* x, 446. There had been a dead heat a week earlier on the issue, see p. 435.

30 For Royalist views of the situation see Bod. Carte Papers vol. 22 fos 363, 369, 378 and 569.

31 Bod. Carte vol. 22 fo. 360.

32 BL TT E476 No. 21.

33 *CJ* v, 138a.

34 This is the committee described by William Reid FSA in his article 'Commonwealth Supply Departments within the Tower of London and the Committee of London Merchants', *Guildhall Miscellany* ii, 319-52. Unfortunately he does not recognise Richard Hutchinson, at whose house the meetings were held, as Vane's deputy as Treasurer of the Navy. (He succeeded him in 1650.) Nor does he realise that the non-voting members he lists are actually the professional members of the Commission. He has a very rose tinted view of its activities, which was not shared by others. See John Hollond's *Discourses*, particularly pp. 126-7, for a different picture. See *CSPD* 1649-50 p. 48 for the *Elizabeth* hoy incident. BL Rawlinson A224 fo. 26, 24 February 1649, for disputes with the Generals over the appointment of captains and *CSPD* 1649-50 p. 34 for permission by the Council of State to the Generals to reinstate officers they think the Commission victimised.

Michael Baumber has been a frequent contributor to *M.M.* on early seventeenth-century naval history and is the author of *The General at Sea: Robert Blake and the Seventeenth-century Revolution in Naval Warfare* (1989).

THE *LURCHER* CUTTER IN THE SEVEN YEARS WAR
1761-1763

By Carol D. Greene

His Majesty's Cutter *Lurcher*[1] entered service in February 1761 through purchase of a captured French vessel.[2] She served in the Dover Strait and the North Sea on convoy and patrol duties until March 1762. She was then dispatched to the West Indies, where she took part, as the only cutter under the command of Admiral Pocock and Commodore Keppel, in the Capture of Havanna; and in other services in the waters adjacent to Cuba and Jamaica. A record of her purchase[3] states:

> Admiralty Order 16th Jany 1761 to Purchase two good Sailing Cutters. Cutter of 6 guns Countess De' Ayen Carvel Built. Admiralty Order 13 Mar 1761 to Name her the Lurcher & to Establish on her 6 carriage guns of 3 Poundrs & Swivels & 30 Men. Admty Odr 3rd Febry 1762 to increase her Comt to 35 men.

> Survey afloat at Sheerness the Feb 1761 Found fit for the Service. Burthen 81 57/94 Tuns

Officers Valuation for the Hull	£163.0.0
Mast & Yds	£ 17.1.4
	£180.1.4

> On the 26th Feb 1761 The Board Agreed for her at the above valuation

Her dimensions were recorded as 54 by 19½ feet, depth of hold 8 feet. Draught is not known.[4] No lines seem to have been taken off in the survey, since there are no draughts of her in the National Maritime Museum at Greenwich.

A catalogue of her rig and gear has been derived from log entries which described sail combinations, casualties to rig and hull, and evolutions such as rowing and anchoring. Her rig appears to have been that of a typical cutter of the period, such as illustrated in the works referenced 4(b), 4(c) or (5) below. Fore and aft sail inventory consisted of the main sail with four reefs, a trisail set in place of the main in heavy weather, a foresail with at least two reefs; and first, second, third, fourth and storm jibs set to the bowsprit. Square sails included the crossjack with a least one reef, topsail, topgallant sail and studding sails.

Spars consisted of the main mast, topgallant mast, main boom and gaff; and the bowsprit, which was hove in or out to suit the jib selected for the prevailing weather conditions. She crossed a crossjack yard, a topsail yard, and although not mentioned in the logs, a topgallant yard and studding sail yards. A 'spread yard' also appears in a log entry. Chapman[5] depicts a cutter with a yard slung below the crossjack yard to spread the foot of the topsail. This may be the spread yard.

The *Lurcher* was armed with six 3-pounders and a number of swivel guns – ½-pounders. A log[6] entry after a period of service in the North Sea states, 21 November 1761, 'Drew ye guns and found Dammaged 4 three pr & 3 swivels'. Assuming symmetry, at least four swivels may have been carried. The ship also carried a complement of small arms as stated in many log entries: 'exercised great guns and small arms'. Apparently, her armament was increased to eight guns in the West Indies, for she is identified twice in Admiral Pocock's correspondence[7] as 'Lurcher 8'. Anchoring gear included a 'Best Bower', a 'Small Bower' and a kedge with associated cables. Sounding leads and lines, as well as speed log and lines appear in journal entries when these items were lost in use. She had a boat which was not further described. Log entries indicate that she was fitted with oars: 13 November 1762:[8] 'at 8 Weigh'd the Anchor and Gott the Oars Out', and another makes reference to nettings. At least some ballast was iron:[9] 9 October 1761, 'Took 10 piggs of iron ballast on board'; 7 February 1762, 'People employ'd in shifting the iron ballast'.

Lurcher was a frail vessel with which to face the rigours of the North Sea or tropical squalls. She suffered numerous casualties to her spars and sails, for example: 'sprung head of mainmast (twice); spread yard in slings carried away; main topsail yard in slings carried away; main boom and gaff carried away; sprung topsail yard and fished it; sprung the topgallant mast', etc.[10,11] Every sail, except the trisail, storm jib and studding sails, required repair or replacement at some time during her short history. These were all weather casualties. In the West Indies she lost two masts, sent the bowsprit to the yard in Havanna, and had the usual blown sails. She experienced hull damage as well: 23 October 1761, 'at 11 Sprang a leak in our upper works and made a great deal of water'. However, she continued convoy duty until a lay period in Harwich from 24 November 1761 to 8 December 1761, during which time she hove down to scrub her bottom and boot tops; then had carpenters caulking decks and topsides for several days. Frequent anchoring also took its toll, for in January 1762 in Harwich, carpenters came on board to overhaul the windlass. The bowsprit bitts were repaired in Havanna. Her journals enlighten us on many details of oft repeated minor maintenance which burdened her crew: 'cleaning vessel; scrape and grease mast and bowsprit; tar masthead and blocks; heeled and scrubbed; overhauling and setting up rigging; reeving new halliards; restowing the hold; people drawing and knotting yarns', etc.[12,13,14]

Initial fitting out in February 1761, and a subsequent refit in July of 1761 at Sheerness, accumulated total costs of £881 8s. 7d.[15] Preparation at Portsmouth in February 1762 for her voyage to the West Indies cost £195 9s. 2d., and repairs at Plymouth, after an encounter with a privateer which damaged her mast, spars and rigging, cost £12 12s. 4d.

Finally, wind, sea and service had taken such a toll of the *Lurcher*'s fabric that Commodore Keppel wrote to the Admiralty from the Edgar in Port Royal Harbour on 5 April 1763:[16]

> Sir
>
> The Lurcher Cutter being in a Crazy Condition and requiring such continual Repairs of all Kinds, and being very much eat by worms, I have ordered her to be dismantled and sold. Captain Truscott and his officers returned home by the first ships bound to England, and her people I have turned over into the ships here in order to assist in Manning the late Spanish Ships at the Havanna.
>
> I am Sir Your very humble Serv.t G. Keppel

EMPLOYMENT – DOVER STRAIT AND THE NORTH SEA

Captain James Walker[17] took command of the *Lurcher* at Sheerness on 12 May 1761. John Hicks, Master, reported on 27 May 1761. Manning, rigging and provisioning of arms and stores continued until 3 June 1761, when she acted on her first orders: 'Took over Convoy the Naval Transports & Supply for the Downs. Fir'd a gun as a signal to the Mas^tr of the Vessels to Come & Receive Orders. A.M. Fired a gun as a signal for weighing & came to sail'.

Lurcher carried out convoy and patrol duties in the Dover Strait between Folkestone, Dover and Deal, and the blockading fleet stationed off the French coast between Dunkirk and Calais. Her log of 18 July 1761 records a particularly active twenty-four hours:

> Fresh Gales & Squally W^r in Company the Alarm Cutter, at 2PM saw 2 Sails to Windw^d gave chace fir'd 3 guns at them: they were a Dutch Brigg & a fishing Boat at 4 spoke wth a Dutch East Indiaman [the *Voorland*] in Distress sent our Boat & pilot on board-at 5 she struck on the Clift at 8 she got off & Anchor'd in 16 f^m Water-Graveline Steeple SW 4 or 5 Lg^s at 9 strong Gales of Wind Saw a sail to the W^stW^d gave chace at 11 carr^d away the Spread Y^d in the slings cut it away with Braces & Halyard gave over chace & stood to the W^d at 2 spoke W^th the Alarm at 4 sent the Boat on b^d the Dutch E^st Ind Man & lay by the ship at 6 brought on board from them 7 Englishmen fir'd a gun & Hoisted a signal to the Alarm at 8 she join'd us & we stood to the E^stW in 4 f^m Water Dun^k Steeple NE 3 or 4 M^ls.

Over the next few weeks *Lurcher* patrolled the Dover Strait, usually operating in company with the *Alarm* cutter. She chased and challenged a variety of vessels while on this station. Between patrols she anchored periodically, either in the Downs on the English side, or off Dunkirk on the French side, usually in company with other English warships operating in this area,[18] typically 12 July 1761:

> Fresh breezes & squally W^r S^th Foreland NNW Dist 3 or 4 Lg^s at 3PM Calais Steeple SSE Dist 2 or 3 Lg^s at 4 Carr^d away the M. Boom & Gaff at 5 saw the Fleet off Gravlin [Gravelines] at 7 Join'd them & came to anchor wth the small B^r in 11 F^m water & veered to 2/3 of a cable Calais Steeple WSW Dist 3 or 4 Lg^s Gravelin Steeple SBE 6 or 7 M^l found riding here His Maj^s Ships Tweed, Unicorn, Biddeford & Baltimore.

Short-legged *Lurcher* needed these periods at anchor to replenish provisions, and for repairs to spars, sails and rigging. Lying close to the English coast, however, provided opportunities for the men to run: 26 June 1761, 'Sent the Boat on shore at 12 fir'd a gun for the Boat to come on b^d Two men left her'; 27 June 1761, 'Sent the Boat on shore for provis^n & one man left her...at 1AM the Q^rMas^r & Boatsw^n having charge of the watch, took the Boat & six of the people wth them and carr^d off the boat'.

On 27 July 1761 *Lurcher* sailed for Sheerness for a refit. Guns, powder, sails and stores were offloaded before she hauled into the dock. On 3 August 1761 she sailed again to the Nore to begin the second phase of her career as escort for the mail[19] packets and other trade between Harwich, Yarmouth and the Dutch port of Hellevoetsluis.[20,21] *Lurcher* made over 30 voyages in this employment, frequently in company with the *Swan* sloop, 14.[22] They usually escorted one or more of the mail packets *Dolphin*, *Catherine and Harriot*, or *Prince of Orange*.[23] The packets were not immune from *Lurcher*'s chronic personnel shortage either,[24] for on 24 September 1761 'enter'd 3 Volunteers from the p^nce of Orange Packet'. French privateers operating in these waters also drew the attention of *Lurcher*, but without success: 22 September 1761, 'at 9 got into Sheveling [Schelde?] Bay hoisted out the boat & sent on board some Dutch fisherman who gave us intelligence of a French Privateer that was gone to Texel[25] but the day before at 11 made Sail and turn'd to windward'. The next day: 'anchored in Helvock Road [Hellevoetsluis] people employed Heeling and scrubbing the vessel at

11 weighed & run off Goree pier head to look for a French privateer we had heard was there found no vessel there but a small fishing boat at 12 Stretch'd toward Helvok again'.

Although *Lurcher* often anchored or moored to a buoy in Harwich harbour, or in the roadstead at Hellevoetsluis, she frequently shifted to an outside anchorage; and always anchored off Lowestoft, Felixstowe and Yarmouth roads when at these ports. It cannot have been very comfortable aboard such a small vessel at these locations through a North Sea winter. Besides shifting anchorage and ship's work, her need for speed added another labour in port, for she was heeled and scrubbed every five weeks on average during the autumn and winter of 1761-2.

The Dover Strait patrol carried the responsibility to chase and bring to unidentified vessels. Their rigs and routes give an interesting picture of shipping: a Dutch brig – Amsterdam to London, a Dutch hoy – Dunkirk to Bordeaux (gave up the chase when the main topsail yard carried away), a Dover packet for Flushing, three more Dutch hoys, an English sloop – Cork to Rotterdam, a Dutch ship for Dunkirk, a ship from Lisbon to Riga (pressed three men out of her), two English vessels, a Dutch snow from Bordeaux, two Danes – one from Portsmouth for Norway, and a Dutch ship from Amsterdam. Packet escort was also interrupted to chase: a Dutch galliot – Rotterdam for London, a Spanish snow – Amsterdam to Carthegena, a ship – Leghorn for Rotterdam, a sloop – Rotterdam to London, a dogger – Rotterdam to London, Dutch fishing boats, a vessel – Rotterdam to Rouen, a snow, two Dutch doggers – Shetland to Rotterdam; and she pressed three men from some coasters. Twice, *Lurcher* escorted a bilander in her convoy. No mention is made of seizing those vessels trading with French ports, since presumably these were neutrals.

In mid January 1762 she escorted a last convoy to Holland and another back to Harwich before sailing on the 31st for Portsmouth, and thence to the West Indies. Only a day out, however, she almost added her bones to many others on Goodwin Sands: 1 February 1762,

> at 5PM hard squalls Coming on at WNW caused the vessel to drive hove up and found the cable stranded [she had anchored due to winds from SSW] at 1/2 past 5 Endeavoured to run into ye downs sounded 6 fath^m to 2 & a 1/2 w^r at 8 Bro^t up wth ye b Bower ye pilot not being able to discover any marks and made the signal of Distress at 10 came on bo^d a Pilot from Ramsgate who thought proper to cut ye cable to keep clear of the Breakers and sound^d from 9 to 6 fath^m wat^r Sandown Castle NWBW S^o foreland SSW Dist 4 m^ls at 9 ye Ramsgate Boat brought on board our anchor and cable at 10D^o made the signal for the Mast^rs of Merch^t vessels to receive orders.

This convoy was escorted to the Isle of Wight. *Lurcher* arrived in Portsmouth on 4 February 1762 to spend a month in repair and provisioning for sea, for much of the period alongside the *Yarmouth*[26] or *Plymouth* hulks; or in drydock. Carpenters and caulkers came on board to caulk her decks and upper works. The people were employed washing ballast, overhauling the rigging, pointing and splicing the cable, and other work. She sailed on 2 March to Guernsey, where on the 7th 'at 2PM hove up and came to sail in Company with His Maj^s Ship Mercury[27] [sixth rate, 20] & Fredrick and Willm Tender'. The *Frederick William* was carrying the wine for the West Indies fleet.[28] At noon the next day *Lurcher* made the signal of distress,[29] having carried away the main gaff, and then at 4a.m. 'fell in with a Dogger privateer which Engaged us for some time but our having rec^d much Dammage in our Mast and Rigging she got clear off'. The convoy ran into Torbay and then into Plymouth Sound for repairs to the *Lurcher*, but heavy seas prevented pulling the mast from the *Mercury*, so *Lurcher* hauled into Plymouth alongside a sheer hulk for a new mast and for rigging repairs.

EMPLOYMENT – ATLANTIC CROSSING AND WEST INDIES

Finally, on 17 March 1762, in strong gales with snow, the *Mercury* made the signal to get underway. The convoy, averaging a bit over 100 miles a day, sailed across the Bay of Biscay, along the Spanish coast, and westward of Madeira and the Canaries before picking up the Trades to the West Indies. At 24 degrees North, with Barbadoes estimated S57W, 1,940 miles, *Lurcher* chased a sail to the NE. On 4 April 1762 'at 4PM fired a 3 Pounder at yᵉ Chace which Prov'd a Pollacko [polacre?] at 6 Dᵒ not being able to speak yᵉ Chace left off & Endeavoured to join the Mercury'. *Mercury* tells a slightly different story, however: 'Saw a sail to yᵉ NE standing to westward at 9 made the sails to be a Pollaco at 10 all boats manᵈ & armᵈ to tow the Lurcher Cutter to the Pollaco at noon in chace'. This is only one of several chases recorded by *Lurcher* on this passage.

Mercury and *Lurcher*, on 9 April 1762, fell in with a convoy of five sail of transports[30] from England carrying troops which had become separated from Admiral Pocock's fleet. Then on the 15th the *Lurcher*'s log under Captain Walker[31] abruptly ends with the notation in large flowing script 'Captain Dead'. *Lurcher*'s journals are missing from this date until 22 June 1762, when Lieutenant John Carey[32] took command of her. In fact, Captain Walker was still alive and in command at this date. The *Lurcher* accompanied the convoy to Barbadoes, where she joined Admiral Pocock[33] and the fleet on 23 April 1762. It was possible to track the *Lurcher*'s movements with the fleet, and in action near Havanna, from the logs of other ships.[34]

Mercury anchored in Port Royal, Martinique,[35] with Admiral Pocock's fleet on 26 April 1762 and notes that *Rose*, 24, *Alarm*, 32, and *Lurcher* sailed at noon. *Lurcher* joined the fleet for Havanna.[36] She is presumed to be one of the small vessels sent by the Admiral with the *Bonnetta* and a pilot[37] 'to lay them upon the Keys on both sides of the channel and shall procede tomorrow with all the fleet'.[38]

The fleet was standing off Havanna when Admiral Pocock ordered *Lurcher* into the most significant action of her career:[39]

> accordingly the 10th [June 1762] in the evening I ordered Captain Knight of the Belle Isle to go in and Batter the Castle of Chorera, and sent the Cerberus, Mercury, Bonnetta and Lurcher with Her to keep firing in the woods in the Night, and embarked all the Marines in the boats. The next Forenoon the Enemy quitted the Fort.

It fell calm, so at 5p.m. on the 11th the group anchored half a mile from the fort[40] and began to engage until 8p.m., at which time they warped further in. At 10:30p.m. *Lurcher* went in with armed boats from the *Belle Isle* and a barge from the *Mercury* to cut out a brig which lay anchored under the fort. They were fired at from the castle both with great guns and small arms.[41] At 8a.m. the fort seemed to be silenced, so the ships fired grapeshot at the enemy in the woods. The fort later fired grapeshot at *Belle Isle*, which caused damage and casualties. Firing on the fort was resumed, with the fort taken as noted.

It is now that we learn the fate of Captain Walker. Admiral Pockock writes peevishly in his letter:[42] 'On the 13th of last month [June 1762], Captain Walker of the Lurcher Cutter, on going up Chorera River out of mere Curiosity, was killed by the Enemy'.

The surgeon, George Craig, was also killed, and the boat crew presumably taken, since mention is made of men returned after the truce. Two men died of wounds on 18 August.

The Admiral ordered *Cerberus, Sutherland* and *Lurcher* to patrol off Matanzas and reconnoitre the bay. *Lurcher*, assisted by a barge and a lieutenant from the *Sutherland*, spent the rest of June sounding that bay. Lieutenant Carey came on board while in this employment, but only until 1 July, when he was relieved by Peter Clark.[43] The log is again missing until 17 August, when Lieutenant William Truscott took command. She was not idle during this period, for she cruised off Port Mariel, assisted in raising the block ships sunk by the enemy in the mouth of that port, and made a trip to Havanna to bring additional purchase to assist in raising those ships.

Lurcher made other trips to Havanna from Port Mariel, finally sailing to Havanna with a convoy on 29 August. She remained in Havanna engaged in ship's work, including replacing the mast and bowsprit, caulking, clearing the limbers and washing the hold, and[44] 'hove out Breemd and Paid, with Terpentine, Brimstone and Tallow'. On 14 October she sailed with the fleet[45] under Commodore Keppel for Port Royal, Jamaica. The fleet passed north up the Florida Strait[46] to Latitude 27N, East around the Bahamas, turned in through the Caicos Passage, through the Windward Passage and thence to Port Royal on 5 November.

Lurcher remained there until 7 December, for a time lending her men to shift stores from a store ship to a storehouse on shore. She then sailed with *Deptford* (fourth rate, 60), a merchant ship and two brigs westward along the south coast of Jamaica. She parted company off Negrile Point on the west end of Jamaica and turned east. Then, on 14 December,

> Saw a sail to the E[t]ward Standing towards us, made Sail towards her. At 10 being about 3/4 of a mile from her Observ'd her to be a Schooner of much Superior force and an Enemy Haul'd our wind and made what sail we could from her, She tackt and Stood after us, Not thinking it Prudent to Engage a Vessel of such Superior force we Run into Beckfords cove then Moord with Ropes to the Shore.

The next two days, taking advantage of their position, they wooded and watered, heeled and scrubbed, then rowed out of the cove. On return eastward to Port Royal they spoke a brig privateer, and gave chase to a sail inshore believed to be an enemy privateer, but lost her and returned to port.

This action may have prompted Commodore Keppel to write:[47]

> the Enemies small Privateers have been excedingly troublesome about the Island for these two months past, I detached such ships as were clean in quest of them, but without much success and was under the necessity of ordering the Lurcher Cutter, the only small cruizer under my command to sea. I can't say her force or condition such as to expect much from her, and as her short Complement and want of Officers rendered her less fit for the purpose of cruizing upon the Picaroons, in case of falling in with two of them together, I thought it indispensibly for the good of the King's Subjects and the Credit of the King's Colours to increase her complement twentyfive men and appoint a Lieutenant, as any accident in action to the Captain, would of course left the vessel to a destiny disgraceful to the service. The applications to me from the Merchants and Planters upon this Island to keep small cruizers at sea, they are made sensible has been out of my power. I had promised if no sloops arrived from England to have purchased two of the best sailing vessels in these seas as Guard Coasts to the Island, but the certain approach of Peace will, of course, make that expense unecessary.

Lurcher lay in Port Royal through mid January 1763, her people again handling stores ashore, replacing another mast (which sprung as soon as she was at sea), and again heeling and scrubbing. The next weeks were spent on patrol in and out of bays along the southwest coast of Jamaica; and in chasing suspicious sails, one of which was a schooner from Montego Bay from which *Lurcher* took three men who had run from ships of the fleet. She sailed from Port Royal on 20 February, on which day Captain Truscott read the proclamation of peace to her people. This squally voyage (split the mainsail and second jib) took her via the Cayman Islands, the Isle of Pines, around the west end of Cuba, to Havanna on 3 March. One reason for this voyage seems to have been to transport Robert Brown, 'Land Officer', and his servant Peter George,[48] to Havanna.

After provisioning and repairs to her sails and rigging, *Lurcher* returned to Port Royal, Jamaica, retracing the northern route she had previously taken with the fleet. On this passage she carried supernumeraries: 6 March, 'Rec'd on b^d a Serjeant (Army – Robert Gordon) & 10 Negroes'.[49] The blacks, identified in the depersonalised manner of slavery by their first names only (Negro Bob, Negro Quaskey, Negro Oliphant, etc.),[50] were carried on two-thirds rations.

Lurcher arrived at Port Royal on 29 March. This was her last service to the Royal Navy. On 3 April 'such Stores as was found useful for His Maj^s Service' were offloaded, and all pursers' stores and powder were transferred to the *Richmond*. *Lurcher* sailed up to Kingston, where sadly, on 13 April 1763, Captain Truscott's *Lurcher* journal closes: 'AM Hauled the Pendant & sent all the People pe^r Order on Board His Majesty's Ship Edgar. [signed] Wm Truscott'.

PROVISIONING

Initial provisioning of the *Lurcher* in Sheerness dockyard consisted of '11 bags bread, 21 barrl beer, 2 barrl beef, 1 barrl pork, 2 1/2 hghd pease, 1/2 hghd oatmeal, 60 lb butter, 93 lb cheese; 4 butts, 6 barrl and 6 1/2 hghd water'. Thereafter, most frequently mentioned are fresh beef, beer, peas, bread, butter, cheese, and of course, water. *Lurcher* frequently drew provisions from other ships with which she lay at anchor or operated, most often in home waters the sloops *Swan* (280 tons), *Hound* (267 tons), and *Happy* (141 tons). Victuals were occasionally received in Harwich from 'Ben Powland', presumably a contractor. She took water and provisions from the *Mercury* (433 tons) on the Atlantic crossing. It is interesting that accounting was occasionally kept of the number of iron hoops on the casks received and returned empty. The journals from the West Indies are less revealing than the records from home waters, but beer, bread, butter, fresh beef, pork and water were still staples. Rum first appears in supplies from Havanna.

OFFICERS AND MEN

Captain James Walker commissioned the *Lurcher* and served as commanding officer until his death in Cuba on 13 June 1762. Lieutenant John Carey from the *Namur* was then appointed commander on 14 June, but was not able to join the cutter until 22 June, as noted. He was relieved by Lieutenant Peter Clark, who was in turn relieved on 17 August by Lieutenant William Truscott.[51] Truscott is a model for sea officers who rise from a tiny command to flag rank. His progression in rank was Lieutenant 1757,

Commander (*Lurcher*) 1762, Captain 1778, Rear Admiral of the Blue 1795, Rear Admiral of the White 1797; he died in 1798. The deficiency in officers noted by the Admiral was rectified by the appointment of Lieutenant Farmery Epworth from 24 December 1762 until 29 March 1763; then by Lieutenant William Dixon until decommissioning. Each captain brought aboard two servants who left with the captain (Captain Walker's were discharged), and each lieutenant brought one servant.

A total of 96 seamen and rated men served on the *Lurcher* at various times. Of these, 32, or one-third, ran. They ran whenever they could get a foot ashore (or in the boat). They ran at Sheerness, Harwich, Folkestone, Deal, Hellevoetsluis, Portsmouth, Havanna and Kingston. Ratings, seamen and landsmen were all runners. As a result, advancement in grade was rapid on the chronically shorthanded *Lurcher*. One, John Williot, impressed on 2 June 1761 from the *Princess Royal* as an ordinary seaman, rose on 8 June to Able Bodied Seaman, and then on 1 August to Quartermaster to replace this rating who stole the boat. This was his undoing, however, for he had the boat when Captain Walker was killed, and died of his own wounds later.

Lurcher carried a surgeon, a quartermaster, a bos'n, a gunner and a carpenter. Surgeons, gunners and carpenters were appointed by warrant. Turnover here was high, with six surgeons, three quartermasters, three gunners, and six carpenters transferring in or making the rating, and then transferring out. Two men were appointed Clerk, with the style and penmanship in Captain Walker's log changing at the time Joseph Silvia made clerk. Pilots were carried (as supernumeraries in the muster book) when in unfamiliar waters, such as to Sheerness, on the Dutch coast, at Plymouth and in the West Indies. A 'Chaplin's Servant' was aboard *Lurcher* in her last days. *Lurcher* was frequently visited by the 'Clerk of the Cheque' to muster her people when she was in home waters. On the whole, *Lurcher* was a healthy ship for wartime service in that era, with only six deaths, four from combat, and very few sent to hospital.

Only one punishment was recorded in home waters: 24 September 1761, 'Read the Art[l] of War & Abstract of y[e] Act of Parlimen[t] to y[e] Shipp's Company Flogg'd Pat[k] Murphy for Quarreling & fighting'. A long idle period in Havanna in September 1762 bred indiscipline. 'Punnished Peter Bolden with two Dozen Lashes for Mutiny, Disobedience of Orders and treating his Officer with the Utmost Contempt', and three days later, 'Punnish'd John Miles, Jam[s] bell and Den[s] Trout with one dozen each for Desertion'. Then, in November in Port Royal: 'Punnish'd Will[m] Miller, Patrick Murphy and John Miles with one Dozen Each for Drunkenness and Quarrelling'. Frequent reading of the Articles of War and Act of Parliment for the Encouragement of Seaman seemed to have had little effect.

Lurcher's muster books[52] also record expenditures made by the men throughout their service for necessities and tobacco. Forty-four men drew 'Slops and Cloaths' from the Navy at amounts ranging from 3s. 10d. to £2 6s. 9d. Nineteen required beds, usually at 11s. 6d., and five men purchased 'Dead Mens Cloaths' for 10s. to 19s. 8d. Twenty-one bought tobacco for 3s. 2d. to 12s. 8d. Patrick Murphy, able seaman, in addition to drinking and quarrelling, was the ship's spendthrift, expending £2 6s. 9d. for 'slops and cloaths', 11s. 6d. for 'beds', 15s. for 'dead mens cloaths', and 12s. 6d. for tobacco.

On 13 April 1763, 28 men remaining of the *Lurcher*'s complement were transferred to the *Edgar* (fourth rate, 60) to return to England. The fate of John Hicks, Master, who had fitted out, navigated, jury rigged and nursed the *Lurcher* from her first days to her last, and whose crabbed signature had appeared under that of her four captains to authenticate the muster book entries, is recorded in the Journal of the *Edgar*.[53] On a night, 300 miles off the northern coast of Florida, when *Edgar* lay slatting in a calm in which she had made only 10 miles in twenty-four hours, on 20 July 1763, 'at 2AM departed this life W[m] [*sic*] Hicks formerly Master of the Lurcher Cutter'.

EPILOGUE

Lurcher compressed into slightly less than two years' service all the patrol, convoy, combat and messenger duties which can be demanded of a small, fast vessel in wartime. And she performed these in two theatres an ocean apart. The Royal Navy did not forget her, for a second *Lurcher* cutter (83 bm, 50 x 20) was launched at Deptford later in 1763. Thereafter, the name *Lurcher* appeared again on other small patrol vessels of the Royal Navy throughout the next century.[54]

References

1 'LURCHER: (3) One who loiters or lies hidden in a suspicious manner; a spy. (4) A cross-bred dog, properly between the sheepdog or collie and the greyhound; largely used by poachers for catching hares and rabbits'. *The Compact Edition of the Oxford English Dictionary*, Book Club Associates, Oxford University Press (London, 1979), .

2 J.J. Colledge, *Ships of the Royal Navy*, David & Charles (Newton Abbot, 1969).

3 Public Records Office, London (hereafter P.R.O.), Adm. 180, Progress and Dimensions Book Index, Lurcher, Book 2, 590, 684; Book 3, 23.

4(a) D. Lyon, *The Sailing Navy List* (London, 1993), 208.

4(b) Claude S. Gill (Certified Master Mariner), *The Old Wooden Walls: Their Construction, Equipment, etc. Being an Abridged Edition of Falconer's Celebrated Marine Dictionary*. Edited and arranged, with an introduction, by W. & G. Foyle (1930).

4(c) Arranged, with an introduction, by Claude S. Gill (Master Mariner), *Steel's Elements of Mastmaking, Sailmaking and Rigging* (from the 1794 edition), Edward W. Sweetman (New York, 1932).

5 Fredrik Henrik af Chapman, *Architectura Navalis Mercaturia*, Adland Coles (London). Rig Plate LXII, No. 15, English Cutter.

6 P.R.O. Adm. 51/559, Part VI, Lurcher Cutter, Journal by Captain James Walker, from 12 May 1761 to 14 April 1762.

7 P.R.O. Adm. 1/237, Admiralty & Other Letters, etc., Jamaica 1762 to 1765, Admirals Sir George Pocock and Hon[ble] Aug[st] Keppel.

8 P.R.O. Adm. 51/559, Cap[t] Truscott – Lurcher Cut[r], A Journal of Proceedings On Board His Majesty's Cutter Lurcher 17 Aug[t] 1762 to 13 April 1763.

9 P.W. King, 'Iron Ballast for the Georgian Navy and Its Producers', *M.M.*, Vol. 81 No. 1 (February 1995).

9(a) P.R.O. Adm. 51/550, Cap J[n] Carey Lurcher Cutter Amm[d] Vessel, A Journal Kept on Board His Majesty's Cutter Lurcher from the 22 of June 1762 to the 1st day of July 1762.

10 P.R.O. Adm. 51/559, Part VI, Lurcher Cutter, Journal by Captain James Walker, from 12 May 1761 to 14 April 1762.

11 P.R.O. Adm. 51/559, Cap[t] Truscott – Lurcher Cut[r], A Journal of Proceedings On Board His Majesty's Cutter Lurcher 17 Aug[t] 1762 to 13 April 1763.

12 P.R.O. Adm. 51/559, Part VI, Lurcher Cutter, Journal by Captain James Walker, from 12 May 1761 to 14 April 1762.

13 P.R.O. Adm. 51/559, Cap[t] Truscott – Lurcher Cut[r], A Journal of Proceedings On Board His Majesty's Cutter Lurcher 17 Aug[t] 1762 to 13 April 1763.

14 P.R.O. Adm. 51/550, Cap J[n] Carey Lurcher Cutter Amm[d] Vessel, A Journal Kept on Board His Majesty's Cutter Lurcher from the 22 of June 1762 to the 1st day of July 1762.

15 P.R.O. Adm. 180, Progress and Dimensions Book Index, Lurcher, Book 2, 590, 684; Book 3, 23.

16 P.R.O. Adm. 1/237, Admiralty & Other Letters, etc., Jamaica 1762 to 1765, Admirals Sir George Pocock and Hon[ble] Aug[st] Keppel.

17 D. Syrett and R.L. DiNardo (eds), *The Commissioned Sea Officers of the Royal Navy 1660-1815* (Navy Records Society Occasional Publications, 1994), 454.

18 H.M. vessels noted in these anchorages by *Lurcher* were (Colledge, *Ships of the Royal Navy*): *Alarm*, cutter, 4, *Amazon*, 26, *Arethusa*, 32, *Argo*, 28, *Arrogant*, 74, *Baltimore*, 14, *Beaver*, 14, *Biddeford*, sixth rate, *Boscawen*, cutter, *Dispatch*, 14, *Enterprise*, tender, 10, *Escort*, 14, *Flamborough's Prize*, 14, *Fly*, 8, *Fortune*, 18, *George*, sloop, ?, *Grace*, cutter, *Happy*, 8, *Hazard*, 8, *Hind*, 24, *Lancaster*, 66, *Lynx*, 10, *Maidstone*, 28, *Melamp*, 36, *Mercury*, 20, *Minerva*, 32, *Newark*, 80, *Nottingham*, 60, *Pamona* (?), *Princes Royal*, packet, *Richmond*, 32, *Scarborough*, 22, *Success*, 24, *Syren* (?), *Tweed*, 32, *Unicorn*, 28, *Winchester* (?), *Wolf*, 10

19 Alan Robertson, *The Maritime Postal History of the British Isles*, Pardy & Son (Printers), The Triangle, Bournemouth; Alan W. Robertson, *A History of the Ship Letters of the British Isles* (An Encyclopedia of Maritime Postal History). 'During periods of war which totalled 17 years, the Dover-Calais service was suspended. Main packet communication was via Harwich.'

20 Henry Benham, *Once Upon a Tide*, George B. Harrap (London, Toronto, Wellington, Sydney, 1955). 'Hellevoetsluis and Brill (Brielle) were throughout the 17th and 18th centuries the Dutch terminus from Harwich...'.

21 Admiralty Chart 1406, 7 May 1982, Dover and Calais to Orfordness and Sheveningen. This chart shows access to Hellevoetsluis blocked by a dyke. However, a chart of the mid eighteenth century displayed at the National Maritime Museum at Greenwich, England, shows that access existed at that time. *Lurcher* often anchored off this town.

22 P.R.O. Adm. 51/3989, Sloop Swan, a Journal Commencing the 6th December 1760 to the 5th December 1761.

23 Benham, *Once Upon a Tide*: 'During the Spanish War of 1762-1763 there were four 70-tonners: Dolphin, Carteret and Harrison, Prince of Wales and Prince of Orange, with crews of sixteen, and each armed with one swivel and one carriage gun. These were big wartime crews, for the usual establishment of a packet was captain, mate, eight able bodied seaman and one ordinary seaman'.

24 *Ibid.*: 'Packet men were, however, protected from impressment...'. Note that Captain Walker was careful to enter the men as 'volunteers', probably induced by the bonus offered for that act.

25 Admiralty Chart 1408, Feb. 1978, North Sea, Harwich to Terschelling and Cromer to Rotterdam.

26 Colledge, *Ships of the Royal Navy*..

27 P.R.O. Adm. 51/4258, Mercury Capn Goodall, Remarkable Transactions on b[d] His Majest's Ship Mercury Between the 17 of Jan 1762 & the 26 of March 1763.

28 See Ref. 7: *Namur* off Chorera River near the Havanna, 14 July 1762, 'as the Frederick William Tender which brought out the Wine was Leaky...'.

29 P.R.O. Adm. 51/4258, Mercury Capn Goodall, Remarkable Transactions on b[d] His Majest's Ship Mercury Between the 17 of Jan 1762 & the 26 of March 1763.

30 See Ref. 7: Admiral Pocock notes the arrival of *Lurcher* and convoy in his letter of 26 May 1762 from *Namur* off Cape Nicholas, Haiti, where he lay to gather the fleet. Of the warships in his fleet named in the margin and an enclosure with this letter, *Lurcher* is the only cutter. The ships named in the margin were *Namur, Valiant, Culloden, Belle Isle, Orford, Edgar, Rippon, Hampton Court, Marlborough, Mercury, Alarm, Basilisk* bomb, and *Lurcher*.

31 P.R.O. Adm. 51/559, Part VI, Lurcher Cutter, Journal by Captain James Walker, from 12 May 1761 to 14 April 1762.

32 P.R.O. Adm. 51/550, Cap J. Carey Lurcher Cutter Amm[d] Vessel, A Journal Kept on Board His Majesty's Cutter Lurcher from the 22 of June 1762 to the 1st day of July 1762.

33 See Ref. 7: Admiral Pocock notes the arrival of *Lurcher* and convoy in his letter of 26 May 1762 from *Namur* off Cape Nicholas, Haiti, where he lay to gather the fleet, etc.

34 Logs referenced were: (a) P.R.O. Adm. 51/4258, *Mercury*, sixth rate, 20, Capt. Goodall, 17 Jan. 1762-26 Mar. 1763, (b) P.R.O. Adm. 51 180, *Cerberus*, sixth rate, 28, Capt. Charles Webber, 1 Feb. 1762-27 Sept. 1762, (c) P.R.O. Adm. 51 3783, *Belle Isle*, third rate, 64, Capt. Joseph Knight and P.R.O. Adm. 52 1170, J.W. Thresher, Master, 10 Sept. 1761-9 Sept. 1762, (d) P.R.O. Adm. 51 295, *Echo*, sixth rate, 24, John Lendrick Commander, 29 Apr. 1762-5 Jun. 1763, (e) P.R.O. Adm. 51 266, *Defiance*, fourth rate, 60, (f) P.R.O. Adm. 51 351, *Ferrett*, sloop, 14, Capt. James Almes, 9 Jun. 1762-16 Aug. 1762, (g) P.R.O. Adm. 51 3994, *Trent*, sixth rate, 28, Capt. John Lindsay, 1 Jun. 1760-30 Jun. 1762, (h) P.R.O. Adm. 51 300, *Edgar*, fourth rate, 60,

Capt. William Drake, (?)-23 Sept. 1763, (i) P.R.O. Adm. 51 3756, *Alarm*, fifth rate, 32, Capt. James Alms, 27 Oct. 1761-9 Jun. 1762; and P.R.O. Adm. 51/3757, Capt. Charles Whosley, 20 Jul. 1762-11 Jul. 1763.

35 Admiralty chart 3273, 16 Sept. 1983, The West Indies.

36 See Ref. 7: Admiral Pocock notes the arrival of *Lurcher* and convoy in his letter of 26 May 1762 from *Namur* off Cape Nicholas, Haiti, where he lay to gather the fleet, etc.

37 P.R.O. Adm. 1/237, Admiralty & Other Letters, etc., Jamaica 1762 to 1765, Admirals Sir George Pocock and Honble Aug^st Keppel.

38 See Ref. 7: Admiral Pocock notes the arrival of *Lurcher* and convoy in his letter of 26 May 1762 from *Namur* off Cape Nicholas, Haiti, where he lay to gather the fleet, etc.

39 See Ref. 7: Admiral Pocock on *Namur* off Chorera River near the Havanna, 14 Jul. 1762.

40 P.R.O. Adm. 51/3783, *Belle Isle*, third rate, 64, Capt. Joseph Knight and P.R.O. Adm. 52 1170, J.W. Thresher, Master, 10 Sept. 1761-9 Sept. 1762

41 *Ibid.*

42 See Ref. 7: Admiral Pocock on *Namur* off Chorera River near the Havanna, 14 Jul. 1762.

43 Syrett and DiNardo, *The Commissioned Sea Officers...*, 83-4.

44 P.R.O. Adm. 51/559, Capt Truscott – Lurcher Cut^r, A Journal of Proceedings On Board His Majesty's Cutter Lurcher 17 Augt 1762 to 13 April 1763.

45 See Ref. 7: Admiral Pocock, *Namur*, 9 Oct. 1762, 'to sail the 11th for Jamaica to go to Rear Adm'l Rodney, Valiant 74, Timeraire 74, Orford 64, Alcide 64, Edgar 60, Nottingham 60, Pembroke 60, Trent 28, Richmond 32, Lurcher 8'.

46 Admiralty chart 3273, 16 Sept. 1983, The West Indies.

47 See Ref. 7: *Valiant*, Port Royal, George Keppel.

48 P.R.O. Adm. 36/7213 and Adm. 36 7214, 'Lurcher Cutters Complete Muster Book'.

49 *Ibid.*

50 See Ref. 7: There was correspondence with the Admiralty regarding employment of 'free negroes and slaves' to assist the troops in Cuba. They were not provided by the planters 'until the Proprietors are certain of being paid for them in case of death &c'. In the end, about 600 plantation labourers did serve the forces on Cuba. Of the ships which operated with *Lurcher*, *Cerberus* carried 40 and *Sutherland* carried 33 to Havanna. The other seven blacks named on the *Lurcher* were Quegu, Quamino, Ben, Pompey, Johnny, Cuageo and Jimmy.

51 Syrett and DiNardo, *The Commissioned Sea Officers...*, 445.

52 P.R.O. Adm. 36/7213 and Adm. 36/7214, 'Lurcher Cutters Complete Muster Book'.

53 See 34, logs referenced.

54 Colledge, *Ships of the Royal Navy.*

Mr Carol D. Greene holds a BS in Electrical Engineering. He has served in the U.S. Navy as an engineering officer, on a cruiser in the Korean War, has worked in submarine shipbuilding, the offshore oil industry, and the space industry. Now retired, he cruises aboard his own sloop on Puget Sound.

200 YEARS OF ADMIRALTY CHARTS AND SURVEYS

By Roger Morris

In the eighteenth century there was no central organisation for publishing charts for the Fleet, and the captains and masters of His Majesty's ships had to provide themselves with what charts they could find and afford. Though some ships were sent out with special instructions to make surveys, there was likewise no system for publishing their work on their return. The manuscript charts were stowed away in the attics of the Admiralty building, and if they were engraved and printed it was by the personal arrangement of the surveying officer, and at his own expense. This was a highly unsatisfactory state of affairs, and at last it was decided that something had to be done.

A memorial was put to the King by Their Lordships of the Admiralty, and on 12 August 1795 George III signed an Order in Council setting up a Hydrographic Office for the Royal Navy. Alexander Dalrymple, already Hydrographer to the Honourable East India Company, was appointed Hydrographer, and his salary was fixed by an Admiralty Order of 11 September at £500 a year. His task was solely to provide charts and other navigational information for the ships of His Majesty's Fleet. He was not a Naval officer, and was not empowered to give instructions for particular surveys, nor was there any intention of making Admiralty charts available beyond the Navy.

Fig. 1. The seal of the Hydrographic Office as introduced by Dalrymple, from a chart of 1808.

Dalrymple's first task was to sift through the attic cupboards and to see just what he had inherited from the clerk in whose nominal charge the manuscript charts had been. This took him some time, and it was not until 1800 that he published his first chart – of Isle Houat in Quiberon Bay. He introduced the 'Seal of the Hydrographic Office', the badge which, in a form directly evolved from his original, still appears on every Admiralty chart (**Fig.** 1). A scientific cartographer, Dalrymple was meticulous in everything he undertook. His charts were models of clarity and elegance, and as accurate as the surveys on which they were based. But they were produced very slowly, and Their Lordships became impatient.

In May 1807 Dalrymple was ordered to purchase a set of all charts published in Great Britain, to make a selection of the most useful, and to arrange for these to be issued to the Fleet. He made the purchase, more than 1,000 charts at a cost of £168, but he pleaded that he lacked the experience to make any judgement of the relative merits of the various charts, and recommended the setting up of a committee of sea officers to make the selection.

The Committee was duly set up in November, and made its first report in February 1808. From the first they had clashed with the Hydrographer – even their terms of reference were disputed by Dalrymple. The most serious difference, though, came when the Committee wanted to make use of the surveys of the French explorer D'Entrecasteaux, which had been captured and passed to the Hydrographer, to correct the charts of the South West Pacific. Dalrymple resisted this, saying that he looked upon them as a sacred and secret trust, and could not be used until the French had a chance to publish them. He was overruled, and when new plans were formulated to increase the output of the Hydrographic Office he was told that great and continual exertion would be required on the part of the Hydrographer which could not be expected of him at his advanced age (he was then seventy-one), and he was dismissed in May 1808. Bitterly mortified, he died three weeks later.

He left an office where the organisation for drawing, engraving, and printing the Admiralty charts to a high standard of accuracy and presentation had been firmly established, and where production of those charts was being achieved in a steady, albeit not very broad, stream. He can justly be considered the father of the Admiralty Chart.

He was succeeded by Captain Thomas Hurd, who had been a member of the Chart Commission – a little bit of skulduggery, possibly, here. Hurd was the first of an unbroken line of seamen Naval officers as Hydrographers, of which the current, Rear Admiral Nigel Essenhigh, is the 23rd (or the 24th Hydrographer from Dalrymple).

Hurd had done some surveying himself, both of the islands of Bermuda and in the approaches to Brest, and had experience of the Office when ashore drawing up the results of his Bermuda surveys. As a naval officer he was in a much stronger position than Dalrymple to commission surveys of areas where information was lacking, and as early as 1809 William Chapman, in the brig *Sorlings,* was sent to make surveys of the dangers in the Thames Estuary and off the east coast.

Chapman died in 1810, and was replaced by George Thomas as surveyor, and a new ship, the *Investigator*, was commissioned for surveying. When her master, one Mr Triskey, asked who was to be in command he was told to 'obey Mr Thomas in all things'. Thus was made official for the first time the practice which has been followed ever since of having surveying ships commanded by the officer in charge of the surveys. Hurd quickly went further. He recommended to Their Lordships that a corps of officers well acquainted with the science of maritime surveying be formed along the lines of the Royal Engineers of the Army. This was approved, and in 1817 specialist surveying pay was established for these officers. At 20s. for commanders and 15s. for lieutenants and masters in addition to the pay of their rank this was generous, and bearing in mind the inflation since that time has never been matched in later days.

Hurd also recommended that, when sufficient copies of charts had been printed for the needs of the Naval service, additional copies be pulled and sold to the maritime public at large to help defray the costs of his office. This too was approved, though the first sales were not brought to account until the year of his death. The princely sum of £72 appears in the accounts for 1823 as received from the sale of charts. The first catalogue of charts for sale was published two years later.

Hurd's successor, W.E. Parry, is generally known as the absentee Hydrographer. A noted Arctic explorer, he was away in the Canadian Arctic when Hurd died. The office was kept vacant for him until his return in October 1823, and he only accepted the post on condition that he be allowed to go back to the Arctic. In fact he went back twice, once from May 1824 to November 1825, and again in 1827. In all, of the six years of his reign as Hydrographer he spent almost three away in the north.

For most of his time in office he had to fight the parsimony and centralising control of the Secretary to the Admiralty, John Croker. Two things helped him in his fight. First, Croker was amenable to persuasion, if it could be shown that what was being asked for was both cost-effective and necessary for the Navy's efficient operation. Charts were self-evidently necessary, and with the small amount of money allowed to the Hydrographer could not have been called expensive. Second, Croker's Second Secretary, John Barrow, was himself a geographer of some distinction and a broad-minded man of science and letters who was a good friend to successive Hydrographers.

Even with his absences and his battles with bureaucracy, Parry continued the progress towards the Hydrographic Service we know today. As well as producing the first sales catalogue of charts, he directed that surveyors were to write up sailing directions for the areas they were working in, and he had a Naval assistant appointed to the Office specially to edit and publish Sailing Directions. The first volumes were produced in 1827.

But so sedentary, and at times so frustrating a job could not hold as active a man as Parry, and he resigned in May 1829. His connection with the Hydrographic world continued, though, when he became Comptroller of Steam Machinery in 1837. He was instrumental in backing his successor's bid for steam surveying ships, and was a useful friend at court in the higher circles of the Admiralty board. Finally, he was the only Hydrographer so far to found a dynasty, his grandson John Parry being Hydrographer throughout the Kaiser War.

Francis Beaufort, Parry's immediate successor, was the longest serving Hydrographer so far. When he was appointed in May 1829 he already had twenty-five years of sea service behind him, including surveying in the River Plate and his great hydrographic and archaeological survey of the south coast of Asia Minor. He was Hydrographer for twenty-five years, and built up an unrivalled authority in matters far beyond his official responsibilities – though these increased considerably during his long reign. His advice was even sought on behalf of Queen Victoria to find somewhere on the Isle of Wight where Her Majesty could land to get to Osborne without being stared at by the trippers in Cowes.

Soon after Beaufort took office Croker retired, and though he remained Second Secretary John Barrow became the virtual administrative chief of the Admiralty. The formation of a Scientific Branch comprising not only the Hydrographic Office but also the two astronomical observatories at Greenwich and the Cape, the Nautical Almanac Office and the Chronometer Office, and the placing of budgetary responsibility for the whole branch with the Hydrographer also greatly strengthened Beaufort's hand.

When Beaufort came to the Office there was no way a chart, once printed, could be kept up to date. Even today it is a problem persuading chart users that their charts should be amended, but in those days there was just no way of amending a published chart, and a chart might be in issue for a hundred years or more and never be modified. In 1832 Beaufort published *The Nautical Magazine,* a monthly journal funded partly officially and partly apparently with Beaufort's own money. The main purpose was to promulgate to subscribers new information of navigational significance before it was incorporated on the charts. It also contained articles of more general marine interest, and this aspect soon became so popular that in November 1834 the chart corrections were removed and published separately as *Notices to Mariners*. Both *The Nautical Magazine* and *Notices to Mariners* are still being published today.

So far we have been looking at the evolution of the services provided by the Hydrographer and his people from the Office, and have only looked in passing at the ships and surveys, and I want now to look in more detail at what was going on at sea.

With the defeat of Napoleon in 1814 there was an upsurge in world trade, and a surplus of Naval vessels and personnel. First Hurd and then his successors were not slow to take advantage of this, and in the years after the war the foundations of the worldwide Admiralty chart series were well and truly laid. The logic behind the expansion, which even Secretary Croker accepted, was that wherever British ships traded the Royal Navy might have to go to protect them, and wherever either went they needed charts to navigate safely. By and large we did not survey the waters of the major European maritime nations, but everywhere else, even in the waters of what were then lesser powers in Europe like Greece, Turkey, and Austria, British surveying ships were active and welcomed. The only instance of refusal for British surveys that I have been able to find is when the Emperor of Morocco peremptorily required Boteler in the *Hecla* to break off work in his waters in 1828.

Let me touch on some of the more remarkable of the nineteenth-century surveyors, their ships and their work.

The Hydrographer was, as one might expect of a scientific officer, at the forefront of technical progress. The first surveying ship planned for steam propulsion was the *Congo*, built specially for the River Congo expedition of 1816. Unfortunately trials showed that her engine was so underpowered as to be useless, and she actually sailed for West Africa as a sailing ship. The first survey carried out under steam seems to have been made by Richard Owen in 1828 of the Gambia River in the paddle gunboat *African*. By 1841 the Hydrographer had no less than six paddle steamers engaged in surveys in home waters. Sail lasted longer for overseas surveys because of the difficulty of finding coaling stations in the far-flung areas where surveying ships were expected to operate.

One of the greatest surveys, and certainly one of the most costly in terms of lives lost, was Owen's survey of Africa. Captain William Fitzwilliam Owen sailed from England in 1821 with the ship sloop *Leven* and the brig *Barracouta*. From 1822 to 1825 the crews of these two ships surveyed the whole east coast of Africa from the Cape of Good Hope to Cape Gardafui on the horn of Africa. They were riven by fever, what we would now call malaria, and it was only after they had been advised by a Frenchman at St Marys in Madagascar to dose themselves with quinine that mortality was brought within bounds. Even then dysentery claimed many lives. A later Hydrographer, Washington, said that the charts of the Great African Survey might have been drawn in blood, so many men had died to complete them. Even when recalled home in October 1825 the work of the two ships was not over. His instructions ordered Owen to survey the west coast from the Congo to the Gambia River. Being a dedicated surveyor, Owen decided that as the ships were going north anyway, they should conduct a running survey of the coast from the Cape to the Congo, which the ships duly did.

With the Spanish colonies in South America breaking away from the parent country the restrictions on trade with them, one of the causes of their discontent, were lifted. British capital and trade flooded into the continent, and as always trade needed ships and ships needed charts. In 1826 an expedition of two ships, the *Adventure* and the *Beagle,* was sent to survey the coast from the River Plate southward, through the Straits of Magellan, round to the island of Chiloe on the Chilean coast. The *Adventure* was commanded by Phillip Parker King, and the *Beagle* by Pringle Stokes.

The Straits of Magellan must be one of the worst places in the world to try to carry out a survey under sail. Beautiful on the few fine days, for most of the time there are fierce squalls of irregular direction, fogs, strong currents, the whole as if designed by nature to keep the secrets of the channels hidden from the prying surveyor. By June 1828 Pringle Stokes was worn out, disheartened by the endless struggle. The *Beagle*'s surgeon, Mr Bynoe, insisted on fourteen days' break from surveying, which was spent in a sheltered anchorage called Port Otway. Stokes could not summon up the energy to resume work, and when the ship sailed it was under the direction of the First Lieutenant, William Skyring. Stokes shot himself a few days later, and was buried at Port Famine, just south of where Punta Arenas now stands. His grave was still tended by the Royal Navy's Antarctic Patrol Ship at least until fairly recently – I visited it myself from the *Protector* in 1960.

Skyring had hoped to succeed to the command of the *Beagle,* but when she met up with the Commander-in-Chief in Rio de Janiero the Admiral appointed his flag lieutenant, one Robert Fitzroy, to the command. It says much for Skyring's loyalty that he supported Fitzroy throughout the remainder of the commission. The South American survey was almost complete when the ships went home to refit, and when the *Beagle* came out again in 1831 a young man, Charles Darwin, sailed in her as naturalist, with the result we all know.

This taking of scientists in surveying ships was a regular practice – even taking young men who were destined for other things and who became hooked on biology was by no means unique. T.H. Huxley, for instance, served as surgeon-naturalist in the *Rattlesnake* in New Guinea in the 1840s and was diverted from medicine to marine biology.

Most of the surveying and charting in the first half of the nineteenth century was more in support of trade than of military matters. But in 1854 the Russian War broke out, and Beaufort at once attached surveyors to both the Baltic and the Black Sea fleets. In the Baltic Sulivan, in the paddle survey ship *Lightning,* could be seen as the contemporary equivalent of the modern spy satellite. He made surveys and drew views of the strongpoints on the Finnish coast which the fleet had to take if they were eventually to bring pressure on St Petersburg itself. He first charted and drew views of the passages into and the forts at Bomarsund (**Fig. 2**). Then he guided the fleet through the tortuous archipelago to positions from which they could bombard the forts. The archives at Taunton have similar charts and views of Sveaborg and of Kotlin Island and Kronstadt. It is arguable, to put it no stronger, that the threat to St Petersburg which Sulivan's appearance off Kronstadt foreshadowed was more responsible for bringing the Tsar to the negotiating table than the fall of Sevastopol.

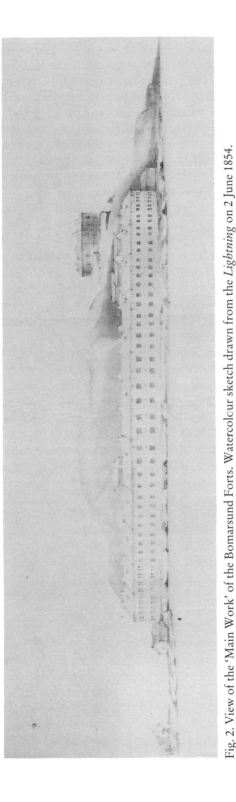

Fig. 2. View of the 'Main Work' of the Bomarsund Forts. Watercolour sketch drawn from the *Lightning* on 2 June 1854.

In the Black Sea, too, the work of the surveyor, Thomas Spratt, was vital to the maritime side of the war. It was marked at the war's end by his promotion to post captain and the award of the CB.

It was perhaps timely that events should make it so clear that, whatever the needs of commercial shipping, the Hydrographic Service's principal responsibility was, and is to this day, the support of the Fleet.

Though he is arguably the greatest of all the 24 Hydrographers, Beaufort was not always happy in his choice of men. He continued the tradition of polar exploration started by Parry, though he never went to the Arctic himself. His choice of Sir John Franklin to command the expedition which left Chatham in May 1845 to search for the North West Passage was, with hindsight, flawed. Though he had been a notable Arctic explorer in his youth, Franklin was, by 1845, sixty years old. Moreover, his early work had been by sledging and boat trekking along the shore, not in ships at sea among the Canadian Arctic Archipelago. His ships, the *Erebus* and *Terror,* were trapped in the ice for more than two years, halfway through which Franklin himself died. The expedition never returned, and for many years its fate was unknown. Beaufort formed an 'Arctic Council' to co-ordinate the search for Franklin. Much of the mapping of the Canadian Arctic over the next twenty years was achieved by expeditions searching for the Franklin team.

The command of one of those expeditions was given to another of Beaufort's less successful protegés, Sir Edward Belcher. Belcher was a tyrannical martinet who made every ship he commanded a floating hell. After one episode where he had placed all his officers under arrest and courtmartialled most of them the Admiralty decreed that he should never be given sea command again. Beaufort persuaded Their Lordships to rescind this ban, and Belcher went to sea again. But a more unsuitable man to lead an Arctic expedition, where sensitive man-management is essential for success, could scarcely be imagined. Not disaster, but farce, was the result. Three of his ships, the *Assistance,* the *Pioneer* and the *Resolute,* were beset in the ice, and against all advice Belcher abandoned them and embarked on a small sloop, the *North Star,* to return to England. The farcical element now takes over. A year after Belcher's return an American whaler found the *Resolute,* put a crew on board her and sailed her back to New London where the U.S. Government bought her, refurbished her, and returned her to Britain with their compliments! The story has a happy ending – when the *Resolute* was finally broken up, Queen Victoria had a desk made from her timbers and presented it to the President of the United States, and in later years both Presidents Kennedy and Clinton have used it.

A year into the Russian War Beaufort, by now over eighty, deaf, going blind, and with his memory going, was allowed to retire, a year after he had first requested to be released. By the end of his time in office the Admiralty Chart series was truly worldwide, with some 2,000 charts covering every sea. In his last year 140,000 copies were printed for sale or issue to the Fleet. They were being corrected by hand up to the date of sale or issue. And they were backed by supporting publications in the shape of Sailing Directions, Light Lists and Tide Tables. All the services provided today for the mariner, saving the advances in technology since his day, were now being supplied.

The method of producing the charts was, given the changes in technology, much what it is today. The Hydrographic Office cartographers made a compilation of all the available data in the area of a chart in a drawing on paper – effectively a shorthand sketch of the desired chart – with everything in the right place but not as neat and artistic as the finished product. This compilation drawing was then engraved in reverse on a copper plate, in the proper styles of lettering and line quality. The first pull from the copper was checked rigorously by one of the naval assistants for errors or omissions. Only when it had been passed as correct in all respects were publication copies printed. When amendments were required the copper was hammered up from behind, smoothed out, and the new detail re-engraved on the smoothed patch, the engraver carefully blending the new work in with the old. The main chart engraving had for some time been contracted out, and in November 1855, some ten months after Beaufort retired, printing was contracted out to Messrs Malbys, in whose hands it remained until it was brought back in house in 1922. Experiments were carried out with drawing charts on lithographic stones, which it was hoped would be cheaper than copper engraving, but the method showed little advantage. Some lithographed charts were produced, though, in parallel with copper engraving, throughout the rest of the century.

Surveying went on throughout the century, at home mainly in small, specially built paddle steamers, the last of them, the *Research,* built at Chatham and entering service in 1889. For foreign surveys the hydrographers had to make do with a very scratch collection of former sloops and gunboats. Perhaps the worst of these was the stinking *Stork,* a composite gunboat so ancient and so malodorous that, when working on the east African coast in 1890 she met the station flagship at Zanzibar, she was made to anchor downwind of her to avoid offending the Commander-in-Chief's nostrils as she

Fig. 3. The *Challenger* anchored off St Thomas, in the Virgin Islands, in March 1873.

stank worse than a slave dhow! In the Pacific, with coaling stations few and very far between, and in the West Indies a succession of pretty little schooners were built or bought for surveying. The last wholly sailing surveying vessel was the schooner *Sparrowhawk,* condemned and paid off as unfit for further service in May 1889.

A notable feature of the middle and later years of the century was the co-operation of the Hydrographer's ships with the scientists engaged in the then infant science of oceanography. Early work in first the *Lightning* and then the *Porcupine* in the waters between Scotland and Iceland were followed by the fitting out of the steam corvette *Challenger* for a world oceanographical cruise which lasted from December 1872 to the middle of 1876 (**Fig. 3**). The results of the voyage were published in some 50 volumes, the last of which came out in 1895, though it used to be said as late as the 1960s that there were still cases of samples from the voyage in the cellars of the Natural History Museum which had never been worked on.

The last Hydrographer of the nineteenth century, Wharton, held office for twenty years, from 1884 to 1904, a tenure only exceeded by Beaufort. He was a theorist as well as a practical surveyor, author of many books, Fellow of the Royal Society, the Royal Geographical Society and the Royal Astronomical Society. He should hold a particular place in the affections of the Society for Nautical Research as one of his books was *A*

Short History of HMS Victory. Beaufort had issued the first edition of General Instructions for Hydrographic Surveyors, but under Wharton these were completely revised and re-organised to produce detailed instructions on how to carry out every hydrographic operation, and on how the results should be rendered into Office. He also wrote and published privately a more general manual called *Hydrographical Surveying*, which went into many editions and was not superceded until the advent of the Admiralty Manual of Hydrographic Surveying in 1938.

The size and expenses of the Office had grown. For the financial year 1900-01 the total of Vote 6, the Scientific vote which included the Hydrographic Office and the other organisations for which the Hydrographer was responsible, but not the running costs of the ships nor the pay of the serving Naval officers, stood at £66,900 – a far cry from Dalrymple's £650 a hundred and five years earlier. There were now 3,089 charts in the sales catalogue, and a standard double-elephant sized chart sold at 2s. 6d. As well as standard navigational charts, from 1895 a series of quarterly and later monthly current charts of the major oceans were published, and in 1899 a similar series of wind charts. Sales were still conducted through Potters as principal agents, with a network of sub-agents – in 1901 there were 52 in home waters and 44 abroad. In 1898, when war broke out between the United States and Spain, Edward Potter asked whether sales to the belligerent countries should be stopped. Wharton argued that anything which caused other nations to depend on us to get about the world was to Great Britain's advantage, and the Board agreed that sales charts should be made freely available to both sides in the war.

By the time that Wharton retired the clouds of war were gathering over the North Sea, and accurate surveys and charts of this area became a high priority. A converted salvage tug, the *Hearty,* was employed on surveying the Dogger Bank and the waters to the south and west. To assist her, mainly by acting as large floating beacons, she was given four old third-class cruisers, later superceded by two surveying trawlers, the *Daisy* and the *Esther,* bought on the building slips and completed with accommodation and chartrooms where the fish hold and the trawl deck would have been.

As war broke out in 1914 John Parry, the grandson of absentee Parry, took over as Hydrographer. He was immediately faced with the problem of providing all the navigational information that the ships, both warships and merchant ships, of Britain and her allies needed to go about their business safely, but denying anything that might be of use to them to the enemy. The information itself was much more complicated than normal peacetime requirements – minefields (both ours and the enemy's) and the swept channels through them needed to be charted. Wrecks became much more numerous, and their positions and identities were, of course, sensitive. Lights and buoys were altered, or only exhibited at certain times. A system of radio and printed *Notices to Mariners* was set up, with series graded in security classification. The distribution of sales charts was strictly controlled, though it was recognised that it was not possible to be sure that no normal navigational charts would ever get into the wrong hands. Special charts of suitable classification were produced for particular operations, or for ports and harbours of special significance, and the distribution of these was very tightly controlled. By and large the system as it evolved during the war worked. It was repeated in the Second World War, when many of the people who had operated it the first time round were still around to set it up and run it again.

When the Dardanelles operation was being planned hydrographic support was called for. The *Endeavour,* which had been built specially for surveying by Fairfields in 1912, was sent out to the Mediterranean with full printing equipment and was based at Mudros.

By 1917 it was clear that the war was going Britain's way, and Parry began to think about how to get the Service going again after the end of hostilities. Both on the surveying side and with chart maintenance, the need to give the highest priority to operational requirements had led to a backlog of work on the worldwide navigational chart series. For the charts he hoped to be allowed to retain most of the extra staff taken on for war work. For the surveys he asked for a new fleet of surveying ships, suitable small vessels for home waters and larger ships for overseas work. At the end of 1918 it was agreed that six of the *Aberdare* class minesweepers surplus to requirements after the war should be completed as surveying ships. For overseas surveys the *Endeavour* was to be backed up by recommissioning the three sloops *Fantome, Merlin* and *Mutine* which had been paid off and laid up on their foreign stations when war broke out, much to Parry's disgust, as these ships had been obsolete when they had been built at the turn of the century.

The best laid plans of mice and men, and even of Hydrographers, usually 'gang agley', and these were no exception. The financial squeeze which was imposed in 1919 cut the Office staff from 367 in December 1918 in stages to only 118 by the end of 1923. Of the six *Aberdares* only four were commissioned into Britain's own service. One, *Crozier,* was given to South Africa and became the first of a line of *Proteas* in their naval surveying service, while the sixth, *Collinson,* was commissioned for trials only in 1919, then paid off and was sold in 1922 without ever entering service.

The old sloops were soon in trouble. Living conditions in them were intolerable, particularly in the tropics where all three were working. Both in the surveying ships and in their general service sisters serving in the Persian Gulf there were disciplinary incidents, and representations were made about the need to replace them. For once Their Lordships took decisive action quickly. Four of the *24* class of Fleet Sweeping Sloops (they were named after famous racehorses, but the class was called *24* because there were 24 of them and to avoid confusion with the *Racecourse* class of paddle minesweepers) were made available for conversion. They were ungainly craft, but when they were rebuilt they became seemly ships which gave good service, though they were coalburners, and coaling ship at frequent intervals was apt to interfere with chart drawing as coal dust would get everywhere. *Ormonde, Iroquois* and *Herald* entered RN service between November 1923 and March 1924, while *Silvio* was transferred to the Royal Australian Navy to become the first *Moresby* in 1925.

The first step in the electronic revolution took place in 1921, when an experimental echo-sounder was fitted in the *Kellett,* one of the home waters *Aberdares.* By 1927 the Hydrographer was writing to assure ships that there was no reason not to use echo-sounders to obtain depths in regular surveys, though up to 1932 soundings taken with echo had to be inked in on the sounding sheets in burnt sienna ink to distinguish them from the 'proper' lead-line soundings inked in in black. In shallow water or close inshore the ship's boats were used for sounding, and in them the echo-sounder did not arrive until much later.

Oceanography again became one of the surveying service's special interests between the wars, this time principally in conjunction with the Ministry of Agriculture and Fisheries. The sloop *Rosemary* was sent into the eastern North Atlantic in the summers of 1929 and 1930 to carry out a programme of surveying and oceanography. These cruises were so useful that it was agreed that a ship should be specially built for this work, to be paid for by the Min. of Ag. and Fish. but to be operated by the Hydrographer. A new *Challenger* was designed and built at Chatham, but by the time she completed in 1932 the great slump had hit the national finances, the Min. of Ag. and Fish. could no longer pay for her, and she was commissioned as a surveying ship pure and simple, the *Iroquois* being paid off to compensate.

Ashore one very significant development was the return of chart printing in house with the setting up of an Admiralty Chart Establishment at Cricklewood in 1922. At first the ACE was run by the Stationery Office, but in 1929 it was brought under the Hydrographer's direct control. With printing firmly under his eye Edgell, Hydrographer from 1932 to 1945, started investigating more modern and efficient methods of printing than the old flat-bed presses from which charts were still being pulled. It was decided in 1938 to convert to the rotary offset process, printing not directly from the coppers but from a zinc plate copied from the copper. This, once set up on the press, printed much faster than the old flat-bed method. By the outbreak of war the whole 4,000 charts of the worldwide series had been converted to this system. Without it there is no way that the demands of the wartime fleet could have been met.

By the time that war broke out the coal-burning converted minesweepers and sloops provided for surveying at the end of the Kaiser War had been replaced by ships built from the outset for surveying but on standard minesweeper and sloop hulls. Four fleet minesweepers of the *Halcyon* class were completed as surveying ships for work in home waters. The three sloops, larger ships for foreign surveys, were to be of the *Bittern* class, but in the event only the first, the *Stork,* was completed as a surveying ship. With warclouds gathering it was decided that it did not make sense to complete escort vessels of the latest class without armament. The last two ships were completed as escort sloops, and two older sloops taken in hand to convert for surveying. *Scarborough* just managed to squeeze in one season's surveying off the west coast of Malaya in 1939 before being rearmed, while *Folkestone* was still in dockyard hands at Hong Kong when war broke out and she was speedily rearmed as an escort.

The Office ashore was by now scattered across London. The Hydrographer and his staff were in the Admiralty. Chart Branch, which compiled the charts, was in Cornwall House, at the station end of Waterloo Bridge. The Chart Establishment, where they were printed, was out at Cricklewood, and the chart supply organisation was at Park Royal. Edgell badly wanted to concentrate all his operations at one site. But none of the occupied sites had room to take the others, while to start from scratch on a new site anywhere in the London area would be prohibitively expensive. Fortunately, in the late 1930s the government was looking at the need to disperse any activities which did not need to be in the capital out of reach of enemy bombing, and it was agreed that the Hydrographic Office was one such. Approval was given for a new HO to be built on a green-field site, and Taunton was selected. Office legend has it that the Chief Civil Assistant, Llewellyn, paid down his own cheque as a deposit on the land. Be that as it may, the other tale that he selected Taunton because he wanted to retire to Somerset is

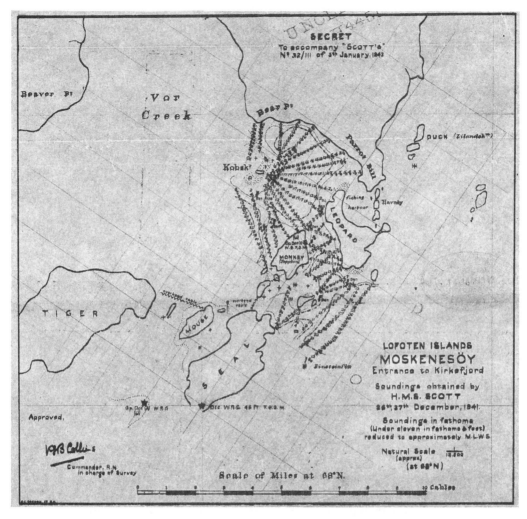

Fig. 4. Fair Chart of the survey of the entrance to Kirkefjord in the Lofoten Islands, done by *Scott* on Boxing Day and the following day in 1941.

not true – it was selected because it has good road and rail communications with the two main south coast naval bases, Devonport and Portsmouth, and had no industry to attract bombers. Approval was given in December 1939, and the printing works were in operation by June 1941. Not least of Llewellyn's services to his successors was to buy a good large parcel of land, so that in the subsequent expansions on the site the HO has never had to ask for funds to buy more land – even for car parks!

On the outbreak of war all but a nucleus of staff from Chart Branch and the Hydrographer's inner London offices were evacuated to Bath, where they camped in schools and offices until in November 1941 they moved into hutted accommodation above the town at Ensleigh. Ironically both in Bath and at Exeter, where chart printing was carried out until the Taunton building was completed, the buildings used by the HO were bombed. Luckily in both cases they had been vacated by the time the bombs fell. The Chart Supply Organisation which stayed at Cricklewood had a charmed life throughout the war, despite being alongside the railway marshalling yards, and never had a bomb hit.

As in every war, operations happen in unexpected places, and surveys are needed for them. One little-known affair was the attempt in December 1941 to establish a base in the Lofoten Islands to harass German coastal shipping. The *Scott* went in with the force engaged in Operation ANKLET. Her job was to survey the entrance to Kirkefjord so that the ships of the force could enter, and most importantly the force's oiler could get in so that the others could fuel from her in sheltered water. She made the survey on Boxing Day and the day after (**Fig. 4**). Not unexpectedly the force had to withdraw after only a few days when German air power began to mass against them.

With the biggest of all the operations of the war, the invasion of Europe, the Hydrographic Office was closely involved. In the planning stage the Staff Hydrographic Officer on Admiral Ramsey's staff had to control the issuing of charts so that the area being considered was not revealed by the number of staff officers calling up charts of the Bay of the Seine. All the ships employed in the invasion used Admiralty charts and publications. In the last days before D Day 30,720 packets of charts and publications, most of them classified SECRET or above, were sent out from Taunton to over 6,000 different recipients. In fact, older inhabitants of Taunton still refer to 'that secret Admiralty place'.

After the invasion, and also in the south of Europe as the Allied armies advanced through Sicily and Italy, surveyors went into newly captured ports close behind the assault troops, went straight to the docks and charted the wrecks and obstructions, assisted in the clearance, and issued plans to the first shipping to enter.

With the return of peace, as at the end of the Kaiser War, the backlog of charting and surveying had to be tackled. The ships that had survived the war were augmented by four Bay-class frigate hulls, which were completed for surveying abroad. Two brand new ships, designed for surveying, were planned, but as always financial stringency struck, and only one, the *Vidal*, was actually built. *Vidal* had a number of unique features – she was the first small ship to be designed to carry a helicopter, she was the first small ship to have cafeteria messing, and she was the testbed for the Admiralty Standard Range Diesel engines. This last was her Achilles' heel – the gearing to couple eight engines to two shafts gave a great deal of trouble in her early years, and as automatic watchkeepers had not been developed the engine-room staff needed to keep watch on the engines was very large.

Between the wars the technological revolution was in depthfinding, with the advent of the echo-sounder. Immediately postwar there was an equal revolution in position fixing. Fairly primitive electronic position fixing was developed during the war, and was used for clandestine surveys off the Normandy beaches before the invasion. After the war progress was rapid. The Decca navigator was being tested by the *Franklin* as early as 1945, and as the Decca chains spread round the coast trials became a feature of ships' programmes. The problem with all such systems is to compare the position given by the system with the position as obtained by visual fixing to real objects, and to determine the errors of the electronic system. Of course, as the electronic systems become more precise, they become more accurate than the visual fixing used to check them, and the check becomes more one against gross errors than one of real accuracy.

Fig. 5. Ships of the *Hecla* and *Bulldog* classes in the Mediterranean, January 1979. From left to right: *Herald, Hydra, Fawn, Fox*.

While Decca was good in the centre of its cover, all too often the area needed to be surveyed was in an area of poor Decca cover. The answer, developed by the mid 1950s, was to make a portable Decca chain with the master station in the ship which could be set up to give accurate results in the survey area – and so Two Range Decca was borne. Over the years there has been a steady refinement of such systems, and now, of course, satellite navigation has done away with the need for cumbersome shore stations.

A number of factors arose in the mid 1960s which affected the Hydrographic Service. The ships commissioned after the war were getting older, and the ones which had survived the war were at the end of their economic life. And the first generation of deep-diving true submarines were about to enter service. It was realised that the submarines would be heavily handicapped in their operations if a great deal more about the environment in which they were to operate was not known. By this I mean not just the shape of the seabed, but also the composition of and movements in the water they were passing through. And lastly inertial navigation was being developed, and for that to be effective the variations of the earth's gravity field needed to be known.

Pulling all these things together it was decided to build a new fleet of surveying ships, designed to be as cheap to build and operate as possible, and not to have any war role. Two classes would be designed, one for oceanic work, which would be equipped to measure gravity and magnetics, and to make oceanographic observations, as well as for conventional surveys, and the other of simpler and smaller ships for coastal work. They became the *Hecla* and *Bulldog* classes (**Fig. 5**). They have both been very successful in service, and are themselves now over twenty years old and in need of replacement.

Ashore in 1945 the Hydrographer had hoped to be able to concentrate at Taunton, as had been planned from before the war. This, though, was not to be. In the immediate aftermath of war there were higher building priorities, and it was not until 1968 that the second major building at Taunton was completed and the inefficient division of chart production between Cricklewood and Somerset ended.

The worldwide Admiralty Chart series had over the years grown, like Topsy, and in much the same undisciplined way. In the mid 1960s it was decided to take a hard look at the system, both the chart cover and scheming, and the design of the charts themselves, which had only slowly evolved from the first style set by Dalrymple 180 years before. At the same time the Wilson administration decided to take Britain into the metric system, and metres were already the preferred depth units of many overseas Hydrographic offices and the International Hydrographic Bureau. Taking the two together, it was decided to rearrange the Admiralty chart in a modern style, and at the same time to 'go metric'. The new style, with yellow land and blue washes indicating shallow water, is immediately and obviously different from the old, with its hachured or grey land and more ornate lettering. From the outset, all charts produced in the new style had their depths and heights in metres, and no metric charts were produced in the old style. There was also a bold legend in magenta saying what the units were, but it was hardly necessary after a short while.

With the new charts came a new step in printing. Four-colour printing machines were introduced. This was vital to being able to print the new-style charts quickly and accurately.

In the 70s and 80s the revolution was in plotting, both afloat and ashore. In the ships automatic data logging was introduced at first to deal with the complicated calculations needed to convert the gravity observed from a moving ship to the anomalies which the inertial navigation systems need to use to navigate. It was soon found that a system which logged all the surveying parameters to calculate the gravity anomalies could do much more with the data than just crunch numbers. Soon it was plotting the ship's track, drawing borders and lattices for fair charts and plotting sheets – any number of useful things. The days of the surveyor bending over the chart table on the bridge plotting a fix every minute or two have gone for ever. A fully automated surveying system, SIPS, was fitted in the latest surveying ship, the *Roebuck*, built by Brooke Marine at Lowestoft in 1985, and has been retrofitted in the other ships.

Ashore in the office automatic plotting was first used to draw the complicated graduations on the borders of charts, and to plot Decca lattices. It soon progressed to doing the simpler tasks formerly done by the reproduction draughtsman – the man who turned the cartographer's shorthand sketch of a new chart into a drawing from which a printing plate could be made. Now practically all the compilation drawing – the shorthand sketch – is digitised and the printing plates produced that way.

The final development is the production of charts and other publications for the mariner in digital form. The international hydrographic world has moved fast to draw up standards for digital data, though the production of fully capable navigational systems to use such data (as opposed to simple units for special users like yachtsmen and fishermen) is not proving as simple as some manufacturers thought at first. But at this year's Boat Show the Hydrographic Office introduced the Admiralty Raster Chart System, the first worldwide digital chart cover available commercially.

We have come a long way in 200 years. How we will survey, and what form the charts we produce will take in the future, is anyone's guess, but that we will be surveying and producing them for many years to come I have no doubt, and I wish my successors well in the task.

Sources

Rather than give specific references for what is by its nature a very broad brush canter through the history of the Hydrographic Service, I end by listing some of the more accessible sources for further and more detailed information.

The primary source must be the bound volumes of Admiralty surveys since 1851 held at Taunton and the printed annual reports of the Hydrographer of the Navy, produced continuously since 1879, the latter with a variable amount of information, being particularly thin between 1926 and 1953.

Of published works the three successive volumes of 'official' history, Commander L.S. Dawson's *Memoirs of Hydrography* published in two volumes in 1885 and reprinted by the Cornmarket Press in 1969, Vice Admiral Sir Archibald Day's *The Admiralty Hydrographic Service 1785-1919* published by HMSO in 1967, and my own *Charts and Surveys in Peace and War* also published by HMSO, in 1995, and carrying the history down to 1970, give the bones of the story. Rear Admiral G.S. Ritchie's *The Admiralty Chart*, originally published in 1967 and reissued in a revised edition for the bicentenary in 1995, deals with the surveys and surveyors of the nineteenth century in a very readable way. Biographies of Beaufort (*Beaufort of the Admiralty* by

Alfred Friendly, published in London in 1977) and Owen (*Captain Owen of the African Survey* by E.H. Burrows, published in Rotterdam in 1978) tell the stories of two of the hydrographic giants of the last century, while Ritchie's own autobiography *No Day Too Long – A Hydrographer's Tale*, published by Pentland Press, Durham, in 1992 gives the flavour of surveying and the Hydrographic Office in the middle of this century.

This article was the E.G.R. Taylor Lecture for 1995 given at the Royal Geographical Society on 29 November 1995.

All pictures are from the Hydrographic Office archives.

Rear Admiral Roger Morris is a former Hydrographer of the Navy. A complementary article to the present 'Surveying ships of the Royal Navy from Cook to the Computer Age' appeared in *M.M.*, 72 (1986), pp. 385-410 and his book *Charts and Surveys in Peace and War* was published in 1995.

436 The Mariner's Mirror Vol. 82 No. 4 (November 1996), 436-450

COOPERS AND CASKS IN THE WHALING TRADE
1800-1850

By Mark Howard

Whaling began in various parts of the world at different dates, and the people involved on those occasions no doubt stored any whale oil they kept in whatever liquid-tight storage containers were readily available in their area at the time. In some areas these were probably large ceramic jars, which would have been ideal for storage purposes, but less than perfect if the oil had to be moved from one place to another. Wooden casks probably came into their own when the start of commercial whaling created the need for a more robust container in which to transport the oil to market. Other factors promoting their use were the discovery of new offshore bay whaling grounds and the start of deep-sea whaling, both of which called for a more sturdy container than clay jars for carriage on ships at sea.

The first people to use whale oil casks on a regular basis may have been the Basques who commenced whaling in the Bay of Biscay some time before the twelfth century.[1] They were certainly using them by the middle of the sixteenth century when Basque whaling vessels sailed each year across the Atlantic to the coast of Labrador where they established temporary bay whaling settlements that usually included a cooperage.[2] Vessels were sometimes lost on these voyages and the underwater excavation of one such wreck site off the coast of Labrador in 1978 yielded a number of well preserved oil casks, a close examination of which has revealed that Basque oil coopers had achieved a high level of technical skill by the 1560s.[3] Coopers were also employed on Basque pelagic or deep-sea whaling vessels where they were well paid and had the status of ships' officers.[4] Even after the Basques lost their dominance in the trade, Basque coopers continued to be highly regarded and their skills much in demand by the whaling fleets of other nations.[5]

The Basques seem to have adopted the *barrica* with an average capacity of about 211 litres as the standard size oil cask, and when the Dutch assumed whaling dominance in the seventeenth century they used a slightly larger cask called a *quardeelen*.[6] These early oil casks were relatively small, had little camber or pitch and were bound with wooden hoops, all of which made them weaker and more prone to leakage than later oil casks. This did not matter so much in northern whaling where the short whaling season and the viscous nature of the oil in the cold climate meant that leakage was not a major problem. More reliable iron-hooped casks came into general use at about the same time whaling spread into equatorial seas, and may have been a pre-condition for that development. Casks with iron hoops were not only stronger, more durable and less likely to leak, but they are said to have resulted in savings of cargo space of up to 15 per cent.[7] Iron-bound casks subsequently became an essential requirement for any whaling venture and one of the main fitting-out costs.[8]

Whale oil casks were also used in Japan where large scale commercial whaling began toward the end of the sixteenth century. The industry in Japan was a form of seasonal bay whaling and was conducted on a large scale with individual whaling stations employing up to a thousand people. The account book for one such enterprise survives for the year 1802 and it shows that the coopers (*okeya*) employed there were paid a relatively high wage, exceeded only by that received by the shipwrights who made the station's whaleboats.[9] This was in spite of the oil being only a by-product of Japanese whaling, the whale meat being the most valuable part of the 'fish' and fetching between four and eight times the value of the oil.

It would take more space than is available here to discuss the work done by coopers in the whaling trade in all eras and places, and for that reason the following account will concentrate on the situation in Britain and America between 1800 and 1850.

OIL COOPERS

A large British cooperage in the first part of the nineteenth century was typically located in a lofty brick shed that was open on one side to allow good ventilation for the fires within. Inside the building each man had his own berth equipped with a wooden block, a jointer and a bick-iron, all provided by his employer. Otherwise he was expected to provide his own tools, a set of which cost about £12 in 1850.[10] The British journeyman cooper was his own master to a large extent and could come and go as he pleased as he was generally employed on piece-work rates which meant he was paid for the work he produced rather than the hours he kept. However, because most piece-work coopers were laid off during the quiet winter months, they had to work hard during the busy season to earn enough to see them through the slack period.[11]

Traditionally, each cooper worked on his own cask, doing everything from dressing the staves to fitting the heads. However some co-operative effort was necessary for large casks as it took two or three men working together to drive the hoops onto a big cask. When he was finished, the cooper would make his mark on the head and roll the finished product into an adjacent yard to be tested. This involved quarter-filling the cask with boiling water and rolling it around - this would create a powerful steam that would find its way through any fault in the workmanship or flaw in the wood. After the final inspection had taken place, the house-mark was branded on the heads. Each stave was then individually numbered (to help with reassembly) and the cask was taken apart and made into an oil pack or shook.

The wood generally used for 'wet' or 'tight' cooperage was, and still is, oak. Flexible, strong and close-grained, it is impervious to liquid, hard-wearing and will not usually crack when heated. English oak is particularly durable but has been in short supply from Elizabethan times and most stave timber used in the United Kingdom since then has been imported. By 1850 British coopers could choose from at least five different types of oak, each with slightly different properties.[12] In America locally grown white oak seems to have been preferred for tight cooperage.

Good quality stave timber has always been expensive and in short supply. Oak grows slowly, and because of the way staves are cut from the billet, only about a quarter of the log's volume is capable of being used. In the case of oil work, the amount of usable wood was further diminished as the staves were usually split from the log rather than being sawn.[13] Dividing the wood in this way makes the stave more pliable and less likely to crack during the bending process as well as making the finished product stronger and less prone to leakage. But it also increased the amount of work involved, timber wastage and the sale price of the finished item. Freshly split staves were graded by size and class and left to season for between one and five years.

Most whale oil casks were fairly large which meant the staves were bigger, more numerous and the cask correspondingly more difficult to assemble. 'A cooper at large work is an old man ... at forty ... his physical energies then are nearly all exhausted', said one experienced cooper in 1850.[14] The years they spent stooping over their work in the heat, smoke and clamour of the workshops also meant that coopers as a group tended to look older than their actual years. The demanding nature of the occupation and long seven-year apprenticeship they had to serve also probably contributed to the vigorous way in which the journeymen coopers in Britain embraced the trade union movement after the repeal of the Combination Acts in 1824.[15] British coopers were quick to organise into trade associations and this willingness to combine together gave them an unusual degree of industrial strength in dealing with their employers.

Coopers in America, on the other hand, failed to develop the strong trade associations found in Britain.[16] Apprenticeships there were briefer and less formal as shown by the following agreement between a New Bedford cooper and his apprentice.[17]

New Bedford July 26th 1847

Amos Bosworth Received John Henry Paun for three years
to learn him the coopers trade and Sed. Bosworth Agrees to
Pay Sed. Paun one hundred & twenty dollars in the following
Payments

1st year	25		But if JH Paun staid But 2 years he is to
2nd year	35		Receive fifty
3rd year	60		1st 25
	....		2nd 25
	$120		......
			$50 for 2 years

The flourishing state of American whaling in the first half of the nineteenth century supported a large number of coopers catering exclusively to the whaling interest.[18] One such tradesman was Isaac Bly who had a workshop at Beetle's Yard in New Bedford in the 1840s. One of Bly's day books survives and it shows that he charged his customers an amount based on the total capacity of the casks supplied (measured in barrels), multiplied by the price for that grade of cask.[19] He sold new and used casks - fully assembled or in shooks - plus bundles of flagging, spare hoops and cask head boards (**Fig. 1**).

In Britain the most expensive casks of all were those made for the South Sea whaling trade. In London these sold for about 70 shillings a ton in the 1830s.[20] The main part of their manufactured cost was the wood and iron hoops used, the labour costs being a relatively small component, especially for the larger casks.[21]

ASSEMBLY AND STOWAGE

The oil casks for a whaling voyage were usually assembled on or near the docks by a team of journeymen coopers working under the direction of a foreman or master cooper.[22] The largest and strongest casks were selected for the ground-tier as they were

Fig. 1. A New Bedford cooper at work – note the piece of cloth or canvas placed over the bung hole before the bung was driven home. (*Old Dartmouth Historical Society, New Bedford Whaling Museum*)

not usually moved during the voyage and had to bear the weight of the riding casks placed on top of them (**Fig. 2**).

Once assembled, the casks were lowered into the hold and rolled to their stowed position where they were nested on their side in a bed of sand, gravel or slate ballast on the bottom of the vessel. They were always placed on their sides 'fore and aft' or lengthwise, with the bung-holes uppermost.[23] Stowage took place under the supervision of a ship's officer and started amidships so the centre of the hold could be well filled, with the stowing then proceeding outward toward the wings. As they approached the sloping walls of the hull, the ground-tier casks had to be progressively smaller in order

FITTING OUT

Fig. 2. 'Fitting Out' by Clifford Ashley, from William John Hopkins, *She blows! and sparm at that!* (Boston & New York, 1922). (*State Library of Tasmania*)

to create a level surface on which the upper-tier casks could be stowed (**Fig. 3**). Pieces of timber dunnage were placed between the casks to prevent them rubbing against each other or the sides of the hull, and extra dunnage was used around pillars and internal beams or where there was any break in the regularity of the stowing scheme. The ground-tier casks were then filled with water to preserve the wood and help ballast the vessel. An identifying number was painted on the head and as the voyage proceeded the contents of each cask were carefully recorded in a notebook kept by the first mate so that the weight was evenly distributed and the vessel did not get out of trim.[24] After the ground tier was in place, a landing platform was placed under the square of the hatch and the next layer of casks were lowered into the hold and rolled over boards to their stowed positions. The riding casks were stowed on top of the ground-tier casks either 'bilge to cantline', where the upper casks were stowed half their length further along so that their weight was supported by the four casks beneath, or 'square-tier' so that each was square to those below. Not all of the upper-tier casks were assembled and stowed in port - many were put aboard as shooks in order to save space. Most whaling vessels carried their oil casks in two tiers, although some larger vessels could stow three tiers.[25]

Most of the whaling equipment and provisions for the voyage were also stored in casks. These were stowed in the upper-tier or the forehold in order to be more accessible, but also so their contents could not be affected by seepage from the oil casks.

The cooper who was to accompany the vessel was often involved in the assembly and stowage work. If not, he would at least be expected to examine the casks before sailing, as once at sea they were his responsibility and by then it was too late to complain that they had been badly coopered or poorly stowed.

WHALING COOPERS

The principal duty of the whaling cooper was to assemble, maintain and repair the casks on board and to carry out any other duties as directed by the ships officers.[26] He was also expected to do any 'white' coopering work that was required. This might include making or repairing wooden buckets, line tubs, boat piggins, mincing tubs, the cook's steep casks, bread bins, wash tubs and even troughs for the ship's pigs. Another of his duties, at least on American vessels, was to keep the blubber spades sharp. The long-handled spades quickly lost their edge during the cutting-in process and this kept the cooper busy at the grindstone. He would also be expected to help out the ship's carpenter and take over that tradesman's work if he became unavailable for duty. If for any reason the vessel was shorthanded, he might even be called on to take an oar in a whaleboat, although this was unusual.[27] A cooper's mate or apprentice was often employed to assist the cooper, but this was not always the case, particularly if the owner was trying to cut costs as they often were in difficult times. On small whaling vessels it was not uncommon for the cooper also to be the ship's carpenter.[28]

It was important the cooper was a competent man as the success of a voyage could hinge upon his skill. His importance was reflected in the senior position he had in the hierarchy of the ship and in certain privileges he enjoyed, such as better food and accommodation and exemption from some routine duties, like having to stand watch. He usually stayed behind when the whale boats went out, sometimes acting as ship-keeper in their absence. But perhaps the main indication of the whaling cooper's

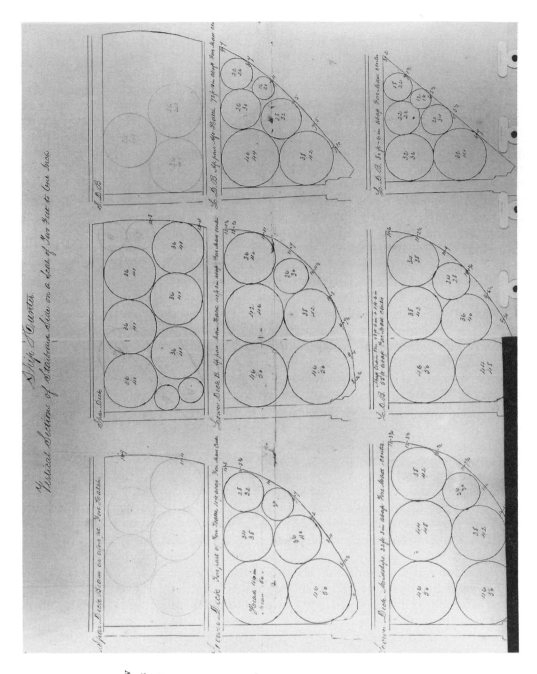

Fig. 3. Cask-plan cross-section for the starboard side of the New Bedford whaling ship *Hunter*, c. 1850, showing how various sized casks were used to make best use of the space available. (*Old Dartmouth Historical Society, New Bedford Whaling Museum*)

importance was the relatively large 'lay' or share of the profits he would expect to receive at the end of the voyage.

The main work of the voyage began when the first whale was taken. After the blubber was removed, it was cut into small pieces and heated in two large cauldrons set over a brick furnace located amidships. As the oil separated from the blubber it was drawn off into large metal tanks to cool. After the initial heat was gone from the oil it was drained into well seasoned oil casks lashed to the bulwarks for the second stage of the cooling process, which in warm weather could take several days. When the oil was ready to be stowed away, a wooden tub with a hole drilled in the bottom was brought out and placed over a similar sized opening in the deck from which a long flexible pipe fed down through the hold and into one of the ground-tier casks that had been pumped empty of its sea water ballast.[29] A plank was then placed against the lip of the tub and one by one the casks containing the now cool oil were rolled up the plank, nested over the tub and the bung removed. When all the casks assembled in port were full, some shooks would be brought up from the hold and made into casks by the cooper. These new casks usually received their oil on deck, directly from the metal cooler, the lukewarm oil helping to season the staves. As they were filled, the cooper would check for leaks and drive the hoops a little tighter onto the belly of the cask to take up the slack due to stave shrinkage caused by the tepid oil.[30] It was important the oil was filtered before it was casked as too much 'foot' or sediment in the oil could reduce its value.[31]

Oil leakage was always a problem on whaling voyages.[32] The qualities that made sperm whale oil such a valuable industrial lubricant also caused it to seep from the casks, especially during warm weather. To help minimise this, it was a standard procedure to open the hatches at regular intervals and hose down the oil casks with sea water in order to help keep the casks cool, clean, moist and tight.[33] While the first mate was generally responsible for the cargo, a competent cooper would be expected to keep an eye on the casks and carry out regular inspections himself. In fact, under the 'lay' or share system of payment it was in the interest of the entire crew to keep a close watch on the cargo on which their income ultimately depended. Yet while every effort was made to keep leakage to a minimum, this became an increasingly difficult as the voyage went on, and after the riding casks were in place about the only way the ground-tier casks could be checked was to regularly examine the pumped-up bilge water for excessive traces of oil. The cooper was therefore not fully answerable for the ground-tier casks, especially late in the cruise.

Although wooden casks are hardy containers, able to stand rough handling when both full and empty, they are not immune to hard usage. The weakest part of any cask is the chime, the groove into which the cask head fits, and it was there that most damage occurred. For that reason the stave wood was thickest where the chime was cut and a wide strong chime hoop was fitted for added strength. The pitch or centre of the cask was also susceptible to damage, especially on ground-tier casks where the weight and wear from riding casks could cause staves to crack across the bilge. To counter this, the ground-tier casks were carefully selected for strength, and extra hooped. The bung stave was particularly vulnerable as it had a large hole drilled in the centre and was stressed every time the bung was driven home. The cask heads, on the other hand, being recessed, were seldom damaged and usually outlasted the rest of the cask.

Another problem was that the iron hoops would often work loose during the course of a long voyage and cause the cask to leak, although this could usually be remedied by driving the hoops a little tighter onto the bilge of the cask. If a leak persisted, the hoops might have to be loosened and the leaky join caulked with a length of flagg. If oil was seeping from a knot or worm hole in the wood, the cavity was first enlarged with a punch and then a wooden spile was hammered into the hole and the protruding end sawn off level with the outside of the cask. Another routine task was to replace the iron hoops that would rust through quickly in the salty sea air.

Working with full oil casks in the cargo hold could be dirty and difficult work. In the dark lower reaches of the hold, the organic nature of the oil slowly seeping from the casks caused a slime to grow on their lower outer surface. Their continually moist surface also attracted any airborne particles of dust or hoop-rust, making them both dirty and slippery to handle. If that was not enough, the oil, and the large quantity of desiccated whale blubber that was kept aboard to fuel the try-works fires, supported a large population of rats and other vermin that often took up residence in the crevices between the casks.

When a cask had to be brought on deck, it was usually hauled out with a set of can-hooks that gripped the cask along the chime and had a bearing edge wide enough to span at least two staves; this was a safer method than using slings at sea. Most leaks occurred in the ground-tier casks and while they could be broken out during a voyage it seems that on many vessels they seldom were because of the work involved. If a major leak was suspected in a ground-tier cask, the oil was often simply pumped from the suspect cask into one that was sound.[34]

The unique lay or share system of payment used in the trade served well enough during the heyday of the industry but less so as time went on. As catches declined and oil prices fell, so too did the seamen's average wage that was tied by the lay system to the size and value of the catch. Declining average wages made it difficult for owners to find competent crewmen, especially skilled tradesmen such as coopers, carpenters and blacksmiths. This in turn allowed these men to demand a monthly wage instead of, or in addition to, a 'short lay'.[35] This was not always a happy situation for the owner, for as time went on and catches continued to decline it became entirely possible for a cooper on a set wage to make more out of an unsuccessful whaling cruise than the master or owner of the vessel. That is, provided the wages agreement was honoured.

Whether or not the cooper was paid for his work often depended on the state of the casks at the end of the voyage. If an unusual amount of oil was lost through leakage, the master or owner might dock the cooper's wages or withhold them altogether. In such cases it would be the anxious hope of the cooper that the casks would be found to be in good order, or in the words of one survey report, 'carefully stowed, bung up and bilge free'.[36]

DOCK COOPERS

London dock company regulations required a certain number of coopers to be on hand when casks were to be landed from arriving vessels.[37] Casks sometimes arrive in poor condition in addition to which a good deal of damage could be done during the unloading process. The principal cooper on the dock where the casks were to be landed would first go aboard the vessel before bulk was broken so the hatches could be opened in his presence and he could examine the cargo for any marks of violence or signs of working on the casks, such as would result from bad stowage, and decide if unloading could proceed.[38] Dock companies usually only employed a small number of coopers full-time, but these could be supplemented by any number of temporary men when a number of vessels arrived all at one time requiring their attention.[39] In London the owner of the vessel was billed for any work done by the dock company coopers and for this reason the masters of whaling vessels no doubt tried to have as much of this work as possible done by the ship's cooper.

After the casks were landed and made tight, their contents were measured by the gaugers who accompanied the customs officers.[40] When the customs men were finished, any deficiencies in the contents of individual casks was made good from other casks in the shipment. The casks were then loaded onto some sort of conveyance, again with the dock coopers on hand to effect any repairs needed due to mishandling.

If the oil was to be immediately taken from the docks, the casks would be deposited as near as possible to the cart areas. If, on the other hand, they were to be put into storage - bond or otherwise - they were conveyed to a place as near as possible to the warehouse or vault entrance, and from there they were run into storage by a gang of warehouse labourers. The person in charge of the storage premises would note their arrival and keep an accurate record of their number, contents and location, together with the name and rotation number of the ship from which they had been landed. Where possible, the cargo of each vessel was kept together. The warehouseman or vault-keeper was often a cooper as storage premises usually included the services of a cooper to maintain the casks until they were required.[41]

In the dark underground storage chambers it was often difficult to tell if a cask was leaking or not, so at regular intervals the cooper would walk through the vault and strike each cask on the head with a wooden mallet to measure its contents - an experienced cooper could tell the contents of a cask to within a pint or so by the sound of his blow on the head.[42] All casks were sounded in this way at least once a week in a procedure that took half a day in the average sized vault. But apart from fitting the occasional hoop, little real coopering work was done in storage premises. It was mostly patrolling the storage areas and being on hand when casks were delivered or removed. The oil left the premises when the owner or his agent came to the entrance of the storage chamber with a receipt docket to take delivery. The casks would then be broken out by a gang of warehouse labourers and, if requested by the owner, their contents might be dipped and the result compared with the landing-gauge. It seems that oil casks in London were generally regarded as being on loan and, like brewery kegs, were supposed to be returned to the owner.[43]

Dock work was looked down on by other coopers because it paid less than block coopering, was mostly maintenance work and entailed close supervision by dock officers.[44] The latter involved having to be searched before leaving work each day and being subject to fines for lack of punctuality or disobedience. Dock coopers were also not allowed to accept any fees or gratuities nor to partake of any refreshment on board ship on pain of dismissal. Other irregularities such as drunkenness were punished by suspension, and if habitual, by dismissal.[45] Dock work was nevertheless a valued source of employment, especially for older or less skilled men who might otherwise have had difficulty in finding jobs. They particularly appreciated the undemanding nature of the work, the short hours (only eight hours a day) and the large amount of slack time. There was little hard physical work involved as they generally had at their disposal a team of labourers who would do any heavy lifting required. The temporary dock coopers were paid at piece-work rates, a practice which worked in favour of the younger men, although on at least one London dock there was an informal agreement among the coopers to limit their earnings to a certain amount in order to help out their older and slower fellows.[46] Nevertheless, casual dock work was irregular and this could mean a good wage one week and little or nothing the next. The most fortunate men were the small number of permanent dock coopers who received a regular weekly wage all the year round.[47]

OTHER COOPERS IN THE WHALING TRADE

Coopers employed on Arctic whalers seem to have had less to do than their counterparts on vessels in warmer seas. Northern whaling voyages were briefer and the blubber was not usually tried out on board but was instead cut into small pieces and stored in casks so it could be processed back in port.[48] Back on dry land the blubber was usually boiled in premises located close to the river, canal or dock where the casks were landed.[49] The process took place under the direction of the master boiler - often a cooper - who usually had a dwelling or a shed on the premises so he could oversee the process, which often continued day and night. In London, and at some of the larger concerns in Hull, the oil was stored in large tanks or cisterns and only drawn off into casks when sold.

Coopers were also employed at bay whaling stations, such as those that sprang up around the coast of Australia and New Zealand in the first half of the nineteenth century. Activities there involved using small whale boats to pursue right whales migrating along the coast at certain months of the year. The coopers employed on such stations in the 1830s and 1840s sometimes received a set wage rather than a lay, probably because of the difficulty of getting skilled men to work at remote locations for anything less than a fixed wage.[50] Failure to pay reasonable wages or obtain good casks at these stations could be disastrous, as the Weller brothers in New Zealand discovered in 1835 when a 90 ton shipment of oil was reduced by leakage to just 40 tons by the time it reached London.[51]

Other coopers in the whaling trade included a small number of experienced men based at the London oil exchange, who seem to have been available for hire as gaugers and valuers of 'parcels' of oil up for sale. The following account describes the scene there in the 1820s.

> On that little spot, west of the statue, we used to be stationed in the precise order of the solar system. The Regent was the sun and centre, diffusing light to all around. 'The Trade' were the planets revolving around him, and the brokers were the satellites revolving about them, with the coopers, like fixed stars on the verge of our horizon. Where are Deacon, Dix and Nichols? We want a few coopers of the canvas-jacket-school. I think our system is not complete without those knights of the searching-irons and oyster-shell.[52]

Coopers were also employed to keep oil retailer's casks in good order. This was sometimes a difficult task, as Australian storekeeper John White discovered in 1832 when he opened a lighting goods store in Sydney called The Blazing Star. Soon after he started in business, Mr White found his oil stocks had run low, an event he put down

Fig. 4. Oil casks on a dock at Vera Fabrikker, near Sandefjord, Norway, c. 1917-20. (*Sandefjord Whaling Museum*)

to a higher than expected demand for his lamp oil, however the real reason for the shortage soon became clear.

> ...J.W. did not calculate that Oil refuses to stop in casks in Summer time, coopered ever so well and often; found out this Secret by finding some Tuns of his Oil in a neighbours well, and has been compelled to an expense of several Hundred Pounds to buy Iron tanks, Tin tanks, Lead tanks, Paved his Store with Stones in Stucco; Dug Wells and lined floors with Lead.[53]

With so many coopers employed in the trade over such a long period, it was inevitable that some should find their way into the upper levels of the industry. The best known figure in this respect was probably Samuel Enderby who after starting out as a cooper went on to become a major owner of British South Sea whalers and the leading spokesman for the London trade.[54]

Coopers continued to be associated with the whaling industry as long as wooden casks were used to store whale oil. This began to change toward the end of the nineteenth century as metal tanks were introduced to take their place.[55] However the transition took longer to complete than might be expected (**Fig. 4**), and wooden oil casks were still being made in America for export to Norway in the late 1940s.[56]

Acknowledgements

I would like to thank Virginia Adams, A.A. Aspinall, Richard Barker, Tony Barrow, Klaus Barthelmess, Arthur Credland, Honore Forster, R. Gambell, J.H. Hamlin, John Harland, Sarah Hayes, A.G.E. Jones, Arne Kalland and Eileen Reid Marcil for kindly providing information for this paper. My particular thanks to Geoff Schahinger and Rhys Richards for their comments on an earlier draft.

References

1 Daniel Francis, *The Great Chase; a History of World Whaling* (Toronto, 1991), 9; Charles Boardman Hawes, *Whaling* (London, 1924), 16; Rev. Henry T. Cheever, *The Whale and his Captors* (New York, 1850), 21.

2 James A. Tuck and Robert Grenier, *Red Bay, Labrador: World Whaling Capital AD 1550-1600* (St Johns, 1989), 43-51; James A. Tuck, 'Unearthing Red Bay's whaling history', *National Geographic*, 168 (1), 52-3.

3 Lester A. Ross, *Sixteenth century Spanish Basque coopering technology; a report of the staved containers found in 1978-79 on the wreck of the whaling Galleon* San Juan, *sunk in Red Bay, Labrador, AD 1565,* Parks Canada, Manuscript Report No. 408, (Ottawa, 1980), 24-39.

4 Brad Loewen, 'Change and diversity within traditional cooperage technology', *Material History Review 36* (autumn, 1992).

5 William Scoresby, *An account of the Arctic regions with a history and description of the northern whale fishery; Vol. 2* (Edinburgh, 1820, rpt. London, 1969), 39.

6 Lester A. Ross, '16th-century Spanish Basque coopering', *Historical Archaeology,* 1985, 19 (1) 10; Ole Lindquist, 'Comments concerning old whaling statistics; the British whale oil measures gallons and *Tun,* the Dutch and German *Quardeelen* and the ratio between them', *42nd Report of the International Whaling Commission* (Cambridge, 1992), 476.

7 Richard Barker, 'Barrels at sea: water, stowage and guns on the Portuguese Ocean', Forthcoming, *I Simposia de Historia Martime,* Academia de Maruilu, 9. The shift from wooden to iron hooped casks was gradual with both types being used together for many years; Alexander Starbuck, *History of the American Whale Fishery* (Waltham, Mass., 1878, rpt. Secaucus, New Jersey, 1989), 111.

8 Elmo P. Hohman, *The American Whaleman* (New York, 1928), 325; *Sydney Morning Herald,* 14 Feb. 1845, p. 4.

9 Arne Kalland, 'Pre-modern whaling in northern Kyushu', *Bonner Zeitschrift fur Japanologie,* 8 (Bonn, 1986), 34.

10 Henry Mayhew, 'The London coopers; Letter LXIX', *The Morning Chronicle,* 12 Sept. 1850, p. 5.

11 For information on British cooperage see: Sir William Foster, A *Short History of the Worshipful Company of Coopers of London* (Cambridge, 1944); Kenneth Kilby, *The Cooper and his Trade* (London, 1971); Bob Gilding, *The Journeymen Coopers of East London* (Oxford, 1971); Pat Hudson and Lynette Hunter (eds), 'The autobiography of William Hart, cooper, 1776-1857; Part I', *London Journal,* 1981, 7 (2), 144-60.

12 The five types of oak staves available to British coopers by 1850 were Quebec, Virginia, Hambro, Dantzic and English, with the first two being preferred for oil work. Because English oak was hard and difficult to work, British piecework coopers charged employers 30% more to use it; Anon., *Coopers prices agreed to be paid from 17 July 1834* [a journeyman coopers piecework price list], (London?, 1834); Mayhew, 5; Anon., *The cooper: his work and how it is done* (London, 1843), 39; James U. Thompson, 'Coopering – an ancient craft', *Scotland's Magazine,* March 1969, p. 32.

13 Clifford W. Ashley, *The Yankee Whaler* (Boston, 1926; rpt. New York, 1991), 97.

14 Mayhew, 5.

15 George Pattison, 'The cooper's strike at the West India Dock, 1821', *M.M.,* 55 (2), 163-84; Mark Howard, 'The Admiralty and the 1834 cooper's strike', *M.M.,* 80 (4), 472-4. While coopers in London served a seven-year apprenticeship, shorter periods were known elsewhere in Britain. London coopers were the best paid in Britain, but they generally worked longer hours and were expected to produce a higher standard of work.

16 Loewen, 85. The standard work on American cooperage is Franklin E. Coyne, *The*

Development of the Cooperage Industry in the United States, 1620-1940 (Chicago, c. 1940).

17 Captain John H. Paun, 'Account book, New Bedford, c1826-1871', Old Dartmouth Historical Society Whaling Museum, MSS 917, MF 154.

18 The New Bedford district alone had 60 cooperages; Ashley, 97.

19 Isaac Bly (New Bedford cooper), 'Day and waste book, 1838-1846, 2 volumes', Old Dartmouth Historical Society Whaling Museum, MSS 56, Ser B-25, MF 919. The three types of cask Bly sold were, in descending order of price, ground tier, sap drawn and sap casks. Sap wood was the soft porous outer layer of wood just under the bark and it could be either chopped out (drawn) or seasoned hard.

20 British Parliamentary Papers, *Master Coopers: copies of correspondence between the master coopers and the Lords of the Admiralty*, 1834, Li (55), 6.

21 *Ibid.*

22 One cooper who assembled oil casks on the New Bedford docks in 1855 charged customers 22½ cents an hour for his labour; *Account book of unknown New Bedford oil cooper, 1855-1867*, Old Dartmouth Historical Society Whaling Museum, MSS 1023, MF 712.

23 James Templeman Brown, 'The whaleman, vessels, apparatus, and methods of the fishery' in George Brown Goode (ed.), *The Fisheries and Fishery Industries of the United States* (Washington, 1887), 238-9.

24 Erik A.R. Ronnberg Jnr, 'Design and construction aspects of ship *Hunter*', *Nautical Research Journal*, Sept. 1990, p. 127.

25 The 'barrels' of oil carried aboard returning whalers refers to the amount of oil aboard and not the number of full oil casks. The 'barrel' was the standard unit of measurement in the trade, thus the *Charles Phelps* returned to port in 1850 with 376 casks containing 1,766 barrels of oil; Stuart C. Sherman, *The Voice of the Whaleman* (Providence, 1965), 55.

26 Whaling coopers used up to 50 different kinds of tools on the voyage, all of which were provided by the owner of the vessel; New Bedford whaling ship chandler's order catalogues, Kendall Whaling Museum, No. A101, A107, A109, A113-A, A113-B; R.A. Salaman, *Dictionary of Tools used in the Woodworking and Allied Trades, c1700-1970* (New York, 1976), 155-64; F.C. Morgan, 'Some old tools in Hereford Museum', *The Engineer*, Vol. CLXXIV, July-Dec. 1942, pp. 477-8; Hohman, 332.

27 Edouard A. Stackpole, *The Sea-hunters* (New York, 1953), 157.

28 Susan Chamberlain, *The Hobart Whaling Industry 1830 to 1900*, Ph.D. thesis, La Trobe University, 1988, p. 91.

29 Francis Allyn Olmsted, *Incidents of a Whaling Voyage...* (New York, 1841, rpt. Rutland, 1969), 181; and Ben-Ezra Stiles Ely, *There She Blows: A Narrative of a Whaling Voyage* (Middletown, 1971), 64.

30 Some later purpose-built whalers had their oil cooling tanks located in the blubber room on the between-deck level; this helped clear the decks, reduced the chance of accidents and made it easier for the crew to work the vessel: Brown, *ibid.*

31 Whale oil expands during hot weather so an ullage space of 3 ins or so was left at the top of each cask so the oil had sufficient room to expand without overflowing; Frank Tod, *Whaling in Southern Waters* (Dunedin, 1982), 30.

32 The average British sperm whaler during this period lost 10% of its oil through leakage; calculated from figures in: A Member of Lloyds, *Address to the owners of ships engaged in the South Sea Fishery and to Capitalists generally on the decline of the fishery* (London, 1844), 10-11; see also Harry Morton, *The Whales Wake* (Dunedin, 1982), 60; Briton Cooper Busch, *Whaling will Never do For Me.* (Lexington, Kentucky, 1994), 11.

33 Herman Melville, *Moby Dick* (London, 1975), 409.

34 Log of the New Bedford whaling barque *Spartan*, The Whaling and Marine Manuscript Archive, Nantucket, Massachusetts, MSS 915, MF 154, entry for 9 Sept. 1866.

35 The whaling cooper's 'lay' was generally similar to that received by whaling carpenters, blacksmiths and boatsteerers; see Charles Reichman, 'The whaling cooper', *The Chronicle of the Early American Industries Association*, Dec. 1988, 41 (4), 75; W.J. Dakin, *Whalemen Adventurers* (Sydney, 1963), 268; C.R. Straubel, *The Whaling Journal of Captain W.B. Rhodes* (Christchurch, 1954), 114; Robert McNab, *The Old Whaling Days* (Auckland, 1975), 193 and 211; NSW Archives, Vice-Admiralty Court Records, Boulton v *Caroline*, No.137/1844-5, 4/7598.

36 NSW Archives, Vice-Admiralty Court records, *Governor Halkett* v Owen, No. 20 of 1842, 4/7603 and 4/6673-4. 'Bung up and bilge free' was when the bung stave was uppermost and the cask rested on wooden skids or ballast

beds so that the bilge or belly of the cask was free from contact with the hull or other casks; Peter Kemp (ed.), *The Oxford Companion to Ships and the Sea* (Oxford, 1988), 119.

37 Pattison, 163.

38 The Directors, 'Instructions to the principal cooper and foreman of the cooperage' in *Rules, orders, regulations, and instructions for the governing, regulating, and managing the business of the St Katherine Dock ... 1828* (London, 1828), 275-6.

39 Mayhew, 5; Pattison, *passim.*

40 The duties of American whale oil gaugers and inspectors of fish oil are described in Hawes, 120.

41 For a personal account of early nineteenth-century London dock coopering see Hudson and Hunter, 'The autobiography of William Hart ...Part II', *London Journal* 8 (1) 1982, pp. 66-75.

42 Gilding, 33.

43 Unscrupulous outfitters sometimes used old whale oil casks as water casks on immigrant vessels even though they knew it would taint the water; Helen I. Cowan, *British Emigration to British North America* (Toronto, 1979), 159-60.

44 There may have been a recognized career path for journeymen coopers in the whaling trade. When young and strong they may have worked at the block, making oil casks at piecework rates, moving on to whaling ships in middle age and ending with dock work in the years before retirement.

45 The Directors, 282-3.

46 Mayhew, 5.

47 The London Dock Company's permanent oil coopers received 33 shillings a week in 1812 compared with 18 shillings for the docks permanent 'dry' coopers; Pattison, 165.

48 Elking says an eighteenth-century arctic whaler of 300 tons would carry two coopers; Henry Elking, *A View of the Greenland Trade and Whale Fishery* (Whitby, reprinted 1980), 22.

49 The South Sea Company paid £550 per annum for blubber rendering facilities at London's Howland Dock in the 1730s; Col. R.B. Oram, 'Surrey commercial docks', *Port of London Authority Journal,* July 1970, p. 175.

50 Dakin, 268; Mcnab, 211; Mitchell Library, Imlay Brother's account book, 1837-40, MSS 3031, MF CY-265, frames 659-64.

51 D.E. Fifer, 'The Sydney merchants and seaborne trade 1821-1851', Ph.D. thesis, University of Sydney, 1991, p. 192.

52 Thomas Blyth, *The Oilman: No.1; a series of letters to a few friends, unveiling the defects and suggesting improvements in the London oil trade* (London, 1835), 40. Searching irons were the metal gauging rods used to measure the amount of oil in a cask; the oyster shell was probably the receptacle experienced oil coopers used to hold a sample of the oil which he would then examine by sight, touch, smell and taste in order to determine its type, quality and value.

53 *Sydney Morning Herald,* 25 Oct. 1832, p.3.

54 A.G.E. Jones, *Ships Employed in the South Seas Trade 1775-1861* (Canberra, 1986), 266.

55 J.N. Tonnessen and A.O. Johnsens, *The History of Modern Whaling* (Canberra, 1982), 267.

56 Information in a letter dated 1 Nov. 1993 from Mr J.H. Hamlen of Little Rock, Arkansas, who owned one of the last American cooperages to make whale oil casks. They held about 50 gallons, were made from oil-grade white or red oak and were shipped to Norway in shooks, with a matching set of heads, work finished, other than assembly.

Mark Howard works for a trade promotion consultancy in Melbourne, Australia.

GIBRALTAR DOCKYARD: PROBLEMS OF RECRUITMENT 1939-1945

By Philip MacDougall

During the months which immediately preceded the declaration of hostilities in September 1939 and throughout much of the war itself, the royal dockyard at Gibraltar was faced with a major crisis of manpower. It resulted from a combination of factors, not least of which was a severe scaling down in the size of the workforce following the cessation of hostilities in 1918. During that earlier conflict, the yard workforce had peaked at around 4,300, with this number cut by around 70 per cent over the following decade.

At the time, such a policy appeared to make a good deal of sense. Although the yard was strategically positioned, able to meet the needs of vessels operating both in the Mediterranean and Western Approaches, the facilities within the yard fell far short of actual requirements. The major problem was that of the dry docks. Planned during the late nineteenth century (although not completed until 1905), all three were of an insufficient size to accommodate those battleships retained for postwar service (**Fig. 1**). For this reason, any larger ship requiring a major refit or repair had always to be directed either to one of the home yards or to Malta, all of which were much better equipped than the increasingly neglected yard at Gibraltar.

With increasing awareness that a further European war might one day occur, the decision was finally taken to enlarge two of the docks. The more extensive work was to be upon the No. 1 Dock, the width of which was to be increased from 95 ft to 118 ft. Additional internal alterations would be required, with this dock originally designed as a double dock which had required a centrally positioned caisson that allowed for the reception of a second small vessel. Less extensive were alterations to the No. 2 Dock which only had to be widened. Work on these two docks was staggered, with that on No. 2 Dock due to be completed towards the beginning of 1939 when work on the No. 1 Dock would begin (**Fig. 2**).

From the point of view of labour recruitment, the adopted time table for work upon these docks turned a relatively simple problem into a nightmare. With both docks, at differing times, placed out of temporary use, the number of skilled workers had been allowed to fall beyond previous minimum levels. As a result, and irrespective of the rapidly changing international situation, Gibraltar would have needed a substantial increase in all classes of workers. Furthermore, given the unfortunate completion date of late-1940 for the No. 1 Dock, this inevitably meant some sort of increase in numbers of building workers employed, so ensuring that this dock would be available earlier than originally planned.

To augment numbers skilled in ship repair work, it was the usual practice to recruit from the home yards. Shipwrights and other tradesmen would be offered a two-year posting that included their standard dockyard wage (untaxed) together with an

Fig. 1. A more detailed view of the No. 2 Dock at Gibraltar as it appeared shortly after completion. All three dry docks at Gibraltar had been planned and built in a pre-Dreadnought age, with none of these docks of a size sufficient to accommodate the capital ships of a subsequent decade. For this reason it was necessary to carry out a major enlargement programme on the eve of the Second World War.

additional foreign service allowance. Yet, the combination of ordinary yard needs together with the required expansion in numbers due to both the completion of the dry docks and the threat of a European war, meant that numbers required would be well beyond that which the home yards could afford to release. In giving attention to the matter in February 1939, the Superintendent of Gibraltar Dockyard, Rear-Admiral A.E. Evans, had indicated that should fighting take place in the Mediterranean, then an additional 1,000 workers would be required, with a further increase upon completion of work on the No. 1 Dock.[1]

Of equal importance was the urgent need to complete the No. 1 Dock in as short a time as possible. In theory, the recruitment of additional workers should have been considerably easier. Yet, once again, a serious problem was encountered. At other times, such an increase in numbers of building workers could have been met (if only partially) from within the local Gibraltarian community. However, this was no longer possible, several calls having already been made upon the pool available. In this respect, so it might be added, the dockyard was competing with itself, recruitment already in hand to fill needs connected with the repair and overhaul of the increased number of warships likely to be making use of the dockyard. In addition to this, building workers were generally in great demand, employed in the construction of a vast number of new air raid shelters, various military improvements and the laying down of an emergency airstrip on the North Front.

In such circumstances a resort to the use of Spanish labour was normally a viable option. At the time when Gibraltar's three dry docks were under construction, huge numbers of labourers had made a daily journey from Algerciras and La Linea with additional quarries having also been opened in Spain. In fact, it is estimated that somewhere in the region of 4,000 Spanish labourers were employed at this time. Once again, however, the situation during the early part of 1939 was very different. The newly installed Nationalist government appeared to have little desire to meet such British requirements, placing considerable restrictions upon the recruitment of such labour. In February 1939 the Governor of Gibraltar, General Sir Edmund Ironside, in a despatch to the Secretary of State for the Colonies, explained the immediate cause of the problem:

> We lately had an incident in connection with a reception given by a Nationalist Agent in Gibraltar to celebrate the capture of Barcelona; despite repeated warnings to the British inhabitants of Gibraltar and in particular, British employees of Government Departments, a number participated in this reception, and disciplinary action had to be taken against several men in the Dockyard and a Senior Operator in the Military Telephone Exchange, a man who has been previously warned as regards participation in political activity. This is now being used by the Nationalist Agent as a pretext for stopping labour which he argues must consist of men with Nationalist sympathies as it comes from Nationalist Spain.[2]

To overcome this particular restriction, some thought was given to the possibility of recruiting labour from Portugal. Again, according to the Governor's report:

Fig. 2. A contemporary view of Gibraltar dockyard. Clearly visible are the three dry docks, the upper two of which were enlarged at the start of the Second World War.

The Portuguese are reported to be good workmen, and would undoubtedly fit in with local conditions better than any other imported labour. It appears that there would be no difficulty about getting a supply from that source and I consider that we should take immediate steps in this connection.[3]

In his report General Ironside did, however, note that the accommodation of such workers would be a problem. Whereas Spanish workers would have continued living in Algerciras or La Linea, this would not be the case with Portuguese labour:

When this suggestion was first mooted, a few weeks ago, it was ascertained officially that the Spanish authorities would raise objection to Portuguese labour being housed in La Linea in view of recent developments, I am not in favour of this proposal as I consider that once again we would be too much in the hands of the Spanish Nationalists whilst there would inevitably be endless trouble over the changing of money.[4]

Instead, so he considered, there was one other possible option:

The alternative which presents itself is to house Portuguese labour upon hulks in the Harbour. These hulks or vessels would have to be obtained and adapted at the cost of the employer.[5]

On this occasion, the difficulty with Spain was quickly resolved, the Nationalist government choosing not to implement those particular restrictions. As a result no further thought was given either to the recruitment of Portuguese labour or where they might be accommodated.

The problem of accommodation was not a matter simply restricted to the recruitment of building workers. In general, there was a great shortage of housing on the Rock, resulting in large numbers of native born Gibraltarians choosing to live in Spain. Many of them, indeed, continued to work in Gibraltar, joining Spanish workers on their daily journey across the border. As for the provision of accommodation for a sudden influx of skilled workers from England, this also had no readily available solution. Indeed, it was to remain a major problem for the next six years, placing an artificial block upon the numbers that could actually be sent out from England.

As it stood, dockyard workers sent out from England on a two year agreement were housed in either New Mole House or the Cumberland Building. The former was reserved for single men, while the latter was used by married men who had come out with their families. Neither of these buildings had sufficient capacity for the accommodation of the much larger numbers now deemed necessary to meet the needs of a re-expanding dockyard. Instead, alternative options had to be sought out. The Superintendent of the Dockyard had pinned his initial hopes on getting them housed 'in a block of tenement flats which [had] recently been completed as part of a local slum clearance' scheme.[6] However, the Governor failed to give his approval and thoughts had to be directed elsewhere. In the event, the adopted solution was to make use of land that was then in the process of being reclaimed. The particular pocket of land stood to the east of the harbour and immediately in front of naval recreation facilities. Unfortunately, the reclamation project would not be completed until February of the following year, at which time work could begin on construction of a number of two storey hutments. These, in turn, would not be ready until October of that same year. However, as a temporary measure, it was agreed that an initial batch of workers could be housed in the South Barracks.

With the increasing likelihood of war with Germany, one more problem loomed. This concerned the position of Spain, with General Franco possibly choosing to adopt the stance of either a hostile neutral or actual combatant. If either of these eventualities occurred, then not only would the dockyard (together with other government facilities) be stripped of a large number of workers but it would also create a sudden boom in the size of the local population. This would come in the form of those Gibraltarians who had sought accommodation in the less crowded communities of Algerciras and La Linea.

> All the British subjects resident in La Linea, including Admiralty workmen with their families, would undoubtedly retreat to the Rock at the first sign of trouble and the Colonial Authorities would be hard put to find room for them.[7]

Again, thought turned to the possibility of using hulks:

> ...it is considered that the Admiralty should, in its own interests, take whatever steps are possible to assist the Colonial Government in solving the housing problem in an emergency, e.g. by lending obsolete vessels to provide additional accommodation.[8]

Because of the problem of accommodation, the Superintendent of the Dockyard was strictly informed by Vice-Admiral Sir Cecil Talbot, Director of Dockyards, that he should only request workmen from England in numbers that he knew could be satisfactorily accommodated.[9] For this reason, Gibraltar was in the peculiar situation of being restricted not by the facilities it possessed but by that of available housing. As a result, the number of skilled workmen eventually recruited fell far short of those that could have been made available from home. Admittedly, it would seem highly unlikely that the Admiralty would have agreed to releasing as many as a thousand workers (this being the number originally thought to be necessary to meet a war time situation), but the eventual arrival of 120 workers does seem unusually parsimonious. These particular workers of course, upon their eventual arrival in September, found themselves directed to the rather meagre accommodation of South Barracks. A small trickle of additional tradesmen arrived in the months that followed, many of these designated as reliefs for men previously posted to Gibraltar on a normal two year agreement. Only with the completion of huts on Reclamation Land was thought given to the possibility of a larger number being sent to Gibraltar.

One of the largest single postings occurred during the Summer of 1941, when the troopship *Pasteur,* a converted French liner, off-loaded about a hundred tradesmen who had been recruited from the various home yards. Although they, themselves, had a fairly uneventful voyage, spoilt only by the burial at sea of one of their number, a Devonport man who suffered severe illness on board, the tools of many of them never arrived. These had been loaded onto a separate ship which it was later learnt had been torpedoed.[10] Among those tradesmen was forty-year-old Cyril Cate, an electrician from the yard at Chatham. While it is interesting to speculate that many of those enlisting for service at Gibraltar were influenced by tax free wages, the additional foreign service allowance and the chance of seeing a wider world, these were certainly not among Cate's reasons. In a series of personal diaries that Cyril Cate kept during his time at Gibraltar, he clearly states his reason for volunteering. As a member of the Plymouth Brethren in his home town of Gillingham, he had learnt that the Brethren Chapel on the Rock was soon to be without any one in charge. The then current leader of the chapel, a two-year agreement worker who also emanated from the Medway Towns and was about to return to England, had written to the various Brethren chapels that were close to Chatham dockyard, asking for someone to replace him. Cate wrote of this in his diary, adding that 'God had His eye on this business and I say it reverently that He said, What about Cyril Cate?'[11]

With the new hutments now complete, Cyril Cate and those others who arrived in July 1941 were given immediate and permanent housing in the appropriately named 'Reclamation Buildings'. Each tradesman had his own single room that consisted of little more than a bed and small writing table. Of his home for the next thirty months, Cyril Cate's diary entry briefly noted, 'mine was D Block, No. 22'. However, over the weeks and months a more detailed description emerges of a very plain and simple room that possessed little more in the way of furnishing than a bed and bed side locker. Despite a small window, the room was rather ill-ventilated and unbearably hot at night. This, in fact, may explain why all of this block of rooms were frequently infested with bugs, Cate and his fellow workers often employed in dusting them down. On another occasion however, a full programme of fumigation had to be implemented. As for communal arrangements, in particular messing, these were centred on nearby New Mole House, the original home of unmarried 'agreement men'.[12]

Elsewhere in his diaries, Cyril Cate gives a valuable insight into the sometimes rather lonely life of an English yard worker on the Rock. Many were away from their families for the first time and lived for the regular letter from a wife or loved one. Cyril Cate, for his part, had been separated from his family since the beginning of the war, with his wife and two young children having been evacuated to Wales. Nevertheless, they were much in his thoughts, Cate suffering a clear tinge of sadness when an arriving convoy failed to bring the expected letter. Helping him overcome such difficulties was his religious commitment and the work that he started to undertake at the Brethren chapel that lay just outside the dockyard main gate (**Fig. 3**). When however, he was neither at the dockyard or in the chapel, Cate might be found shopping in Main Street or spending the warm evenings watching the returning Spanish workers as they stood in the lengthy queue that snaked towards the border gate. This, so it appears, was an activity shared by a good many other dockyard 'mateys'. As an alternative to such activities Cate, at other times, might be found at either the Toc H or Welcome Institute, both offering a range of non-alcoholic beverages. Other yard workers were not so constrained in their choice of evening activity, with unusually high numbers of yard workers consuming more alcohol than might be considered to have been good for them.

The diary also serves as a reminder as to why excessive use of Spanish labour was not advisable. Throughout the war, those of Spanish nationality, although employed on a large scale, were kept away from more sensitive areas of activity, it being known that German agents were engaged in recruiting their services. On the evening of 18 January 1942, Royal Navy trawlers *Haijo* and *Erin* both blew up while moored alongside the dockyard. In his diary, Cate noted,

> Went to [Brethren] meeting at 6.20pm & just on entering hall a terrific explosion occurred. A corvette [sic] alongside wall in yard blew up. I saw the debris in the air & much thick smoke. Great damage done to workshops & 3 or 4 men killed.[13]

Evidence would seem to point to this having been as a result of sabotage. Most certainly, in June of that same year, a Spanish maintenance worker, Luis Lopez Cordon-Cuenca, was arrested (and subsequently executed) for smuggling explosives into the yard. At

Fig. 3. Among those recruited to Gibraltar during the Second World War was Cyril Cate (front row seventh from left) and seen here with fellow members of the Plymouth Brethren's Gospel Hall. Unlike many who came to Gibraltar, Cyril Cate felt that he was called to administer to the spiritual needs of those stationed on 'The Rock'. (*Mrs Sylvia Field*)

about the same time a second Spaniard, Jose Martinez Munoz, was also arrested, having been accused of placing a bomb in the fuelling area of the yard.[14]

According to Cate, who always carefully entered such matters into his diary, no further yard workers arrived from England until December 1941 when the troop transporter *Rangitate* brought another 30 men, with a further 21 following later that same month. In turn however, further time expired agreement men were allowed passage to England. Overall, the numbers employed at Gibraltar remained fairly static until the latter part of 1942. Whereas those employed in the dockyard had managed to keep pace with the demands of both H-Force and various damaged Malta-bound merchant ships, it was not conceived possible that the workforce would be adequate to meet the needs of Operation Torch. It was planned that Gibraltar would serve as an assembly point for the invasion of North Africa, with any damaged ships initially sent to the dockyard for emergency repairs.

Accommodation, in itself, was still proving the major problem. If anything, the problem was getting worse, with the 'fighting services' having poured 'additional personnel into the Fortress until, in spite of the evacuation of a large proportion of the civil population, the whole place is grossly overcrowded'.[15] As was clearly recognised, it was not possible to acquire any additional accommodation, whether on a short or long term basis, from any other source. Instead, something would have to be done with that which was already available. Attention now turned to the Cumberland Building where thought was given to making better use of these particular facilities. Because of its use, in pre-war days, as housing for married workers, the facilities here were on a much grander scale than either the Reclamation Building or New Mole House. Furthermore, it was now possible to completely evacuate this building, most of its original occupants having returned to England.

It was the Cumberland Building that was to solve the immediate problem, providing space for 356 short-stay workers brought out from England. These were members of the Dockyard Mobilization Squad, a special force that had been formed from men of the home yards for the meeting of particular emergencies. Ready to travel anywhere in the world after only a few days notice, they were paid at a higher rate than the normal foreign service allowance. Because of their lack of permanence in any situation, those who formed the Dockyard Mobile Squad had also to accept a lower standard of accommodation than might normally be expected. For this reason, with their planned arrival in Gibraltar, it became possible to make more extensive use of the Cumberland Building, members of the Squad sleeping five or six to a room. As for their allotted cooking and eating space, this was shared with the military, so ensuring that no pressure was placed on existing messing facilities as used by the agreement workers.[16]

Yet not all was plain sailing. Among the agreement men there was a good deal of resentment when they learnt of the higher wages paid to members of the Squad. In particular, they were most unhappy to learn of the reason for this higher payment, it being made for what was termed 'special effort asked for and given'.[17] As the Commodore Superintendent pointed out, this was an 'unfortunate' choice of wording, for the agreement men themselves frequently 'put forward such effort with no special augmentation'.[18] Matters were made no better by the fact that many of the 'Squad were radically inferior and less experienced' than those already employed in the yard.[19] Apart from this, the skills possessed by members of the Dockyard Mobile Squad did not entirely match the actual skill needs of the Gibraltar yard, there being too many representatives of some trades and not enough of others.[20]

The Mobile Squad remained in Gibraltar only until the end of April 1943. At that time, with no other calls having been placed on their services, they returned to the United Kingdom for re-integration into the home yards.[21] Before their actual departure from the Rock, some thought was given to a possible retention of their services. However, bearing in mind the discontentment that had already been fostered among agreement men, it was decided to veto the idea without too much discussion. Besides which, as was also recognised, the Mobile Squad might well be required elsewhere. Nevertheless, some form of permanent increase to the dockyard workforce was certainly required. Furthermore, matters had become decidedly worse as a result of mobilization in Spain, the dockyard suddenly losing approximately 150 Spanish labourers during December 1942.[22]

Accommodation, of course, was the first stumbling block. While conditions of service for the Dockyard Mobile Squad might have allowed them to share several to a room, this would not be permitted for a new influx of agreement men. With no land available for the erection of new huts, it was decided to make further use of the Cumberland Building. Following the departure of the Mobile Squad, work was put in hand upon the conversion of rooms into smaller cubicles. In less than four weeks acceptable living space had been created for approximately 300 additional workers. If a problem still existed, it was with regard to messes. The mess areas in the Cumberland Building had also been converted into smaller rooms, forcing the latest recruits to Gibraltar to share the mess areas in New Mole House and the Reclamation Building. Those workers already present and making use of this space could not have been particularly happy about the new arrangement. Cyril Cate, unfortunately, has little to say on the matter, although he does indicate that a number of emergency meetings were held over the re-arranging of messing facilities.[23]

Prior to the departure of the Dockyard Mobile Squad, the Commodore Superintendent was asked by the Labour Division of the Admiralty to indicate the precise needs of the dockyard. In all, the Superintendent indicated that a total of 374 men would be required, the vast majority being skilled ship repair workers. However, in view of the recent loss of a considerable number of Spanish workers, a small number of labourers were also included.[24] To meet these requirements, the Director of Dockyards in London, together with members of his department, gave thought to the possibility of the entire Gibraltar requirement being met from the home yards. This had been the practice when such demands had been made previously. However, on this occasion, especially in view of the large numbers involved, it was decided to recruit from outside. The Ministry of Labour was approached and agreed to make known Admiralty requirements while permitting use of their own buildings for the carrying out of interviews. The particular inducements held out for those agreeing to go to Gibraltar (although the exact destination of this workforce was not at this time revealed) was exactly the same as that offered to agreement men together with the additional promise of employment in the Home Yards for the duration of the war should it be found possible to release them from overseas service before the conclusion of hostilities.[25]

Within a month of the Dockyard Mobile Squad having left Gibraltar, and providing only sufficient time for the conversion of Cumberland Buildings, the new work force arrived. The initial batch consisted of over a hundred men brought out on board the battleship *King George V*. From then on, smaller batches of specially recruited workers began arriving on a fairly routine basis, this also allowing for the return of time expired agreement workers. Cyril Cate, himself, eventually returned to Chatham in December 1944.

In April 1944 a hitherto untapped source of workers suddenly became available to the authorities at Gibraltar. This came in the form of returning Gibraltarians who had originally been evacuated to England in May 1940. At that time, some 15,000 Gibraltarians had been evacuated not only to the UK but also Jamaica and the Madeira Islands. Retained on the Rock however, were all males who, at that time, had been aged between 18 and 41 or otherwise employed in essential naval or military work (such as the naval dockyard). Those returning in 1944, of which there were approximately 1,400, consisted primarily of women and young children. However, with the passing of four years, it was realised that a number of younger evacuated males had not only reached maturity but had since gained skills of their own.[26] In the event, returning evacuees provided the dockyard with approximately fifty new workers, some of them skilled with others holding down unskilled posts. As for accommodation, which might formerly have been a problem, those returning families were allowed either to live in

Spain or given barrack room accommodation, the Gibraltar garrison having now been reduced in size.[27]

References

1 P.R.O. Adm. 1/10515, 5 Feb. 1939. *Extract from a secret despatch from the Governor of Gibraltar to the Secretary of State for the Colonies.*

2 *Ibid.*

3 *Ibid.*

4 *Ibid.*

5 *Ibid.*

6 P.R.O. Adm. 1/10515, 11 Aug. 1939.

7 *Ibid.*

8 *Ibid.*

9 P.R.O. Adm. 1/14621, 22 Jan. 1943. This, however, is a reference to earlier correspondence between the Commodore Superintendent of Gibraltar Dockyard and the Admiralty in London.

10 This is strangely reminiscent of the situation in Malta at the time when the yard at that port received its first English artisans in 1804. They also arrived without tools as a result of a fire on board their ship. See P. MacDougall, *The Formative Years, Malta Dockyard 1800-1815* in *M.M.*, vol. 76 no. 3, 209.

11 Diaries of Cyril Cate, unpublished. Undated entry, July 1941.

12 *Ibid.*, various entries.

13 *Diaries*, entry for 18 Jan. 1942.

14 T. Benadt, *The Royal Navy at Gibraltar* (1993), 177.

15 P.R.O. Adm. 1/14621, 22 Jan. 1943. Commodore Superintendent to Secretary of Admiralty.

16 *Ibid.* It is possible that the Dockyard Mobile Squad had its origins in certain events that took place in 1916. Following the Battle of Jutland the battlecruiser *Inflexible,* having received extensive damage, was brought to Gibraltar for repair. In order to ensure that this task could be performed both rapidly and efficiently some 600 tradesmen were brought out from the home yards and returned once the task had been completed. To provide accommodation a broken down French liner was towed into the harbour.

17 *Ibid.*

18 *Ibid.*

19 *Ibid.*

20 *Ibid.* It was also noted that members of the Dockyard Mobile Squad were, themselves, discontented upon first arrival in Gibraltar. Unaware of the proposed landing in North Africa, many of them felt that they had only been brought there to help solve Gibraltar's long-term labour shortage. Possibly, so it could be surmised, rumours began to abound suggesting that there would be no immediate return to the United Kingdom and that they were to live in the spartan conditions until the end of hostilities.

21 The success of the North Africa landings resulted in the Dockyard Mobile Squad being considerably under-utilised. To make some use of their available skills, the heavily damaged liberty ship, *Winooski,* was diverted to the yard at Gibraltar, the subsequent repairs carried out by members of the Squad allowing her to return to the U.S.A. under her own steam.

22 *Ibid.*

23 Cate, *Diaries*, 24 Feb. 1943.

24 P.R.O. Adm. 1/14621, Jan. 1943. Of the tradesmen, the largest single requirement was for shipwrights (with 60 requested). Other trades included shipfitters (12), smiths (4), joiners (12), caulkers (16), drillers, riveters, welders and burners (44), electrical fitters (37) and torpedo fitters (3).

25 P.R.O. Adm. 1/14621, 16 March 1943.

26 P.R.O. Adm. 1/16710, 30 Oct., 16 Nov., 22 Nov. 1943. The Admiralty, in particular, sanctioned the return of the evacuees realising that it would not only allow existing dockyard workers to once again live with their families but would also allow recruitment of young males with suitable skills. Other factors that led to the return of Gibraltarians living in England was that many of these families were living in parts of London that were then coming under attack from V1s.

27 *Ibid.*, 30 Oct. 1943. 'There has however been another development within the last day or so with regard to a possible reduction in the garrison of the Rock. The Governor is being asked for his views on the possible repatriation of some of the evacuees as a result of this garrison reduction if it comes about.' Director of Dockyards to Board of Admiralty.

Philip MacDougall has been a frequent contributor to *M.M.* on topics of dockyard history. He is the author of *The Chatham Dockyard Story* (1981) and *Royal Dockyards* (1982).

NOTES

RICHARD SWANLEY (c. 1592-1650), ADMIRAL OF THE FLEET ON THE IRISH COAST

This note augments in several important respects an article on Richard Swanley by M.L. Baumber.[1] It is based on further research in the Public Record Office, in particular in Chancery Court papers, and in the British Library, which has yielded the comprehensive and private instructions issued to Swanley, as Admiral of the Fleet on the Irish Coast, in 1643 by the Earl of Warwick. It distinguishes the Swanleys referred to in the article and not only indicates that its subject was the Richard Swanley, master's mate on the *Swan*, taken prisoner by the Dutch in 1617, but also confirms the view that he became Admiral of the Irish Seas. Some further personal details are given.

According to his Chancery depositions this Swanley was born c. 1592,[2] was related to the shipmaster of the same name who was killed in 1625,[3] and like the latter had a brother William.[4] Given that the family came from Gloucestershire, it is probable that he was Richard, son of George Swanley, baptised at Awre on 10 December 1592. His brother William was baptised there on 21 September 1595.[5]

Both Richards lived in Stepney, but fortunately both the parish register and their Chancery depositions distinguish them by reference to the part of the parish in which they lived. In addition, their wives had different forenames. Moreover the register most helpfully provides evidence on the fathers' whereabouts at vital times, by giving the ages of children at baptism. Thus the subject of the article can be identified as Richard Swanley of Limehouse, whose wife was Elizabeth; and the shipmaster as Richard of Ratcliffe, born c. 1585, whose wife was Margaret.

It is not easy to conjure from the archives the early history of the Swanleys, but it becomes clearer from 1616. In that year both Richards made Chancery depositions; and the East India Company fleet commanded by Captain Benjamin Joseph, including the *Charles* (900 tons), the *Unicorn* (700 tons), the *Globe* (500 tons) and the *Swan* (400 tons), sailed for Surat. It appears from the depositions that they had both been members of the crew of the *Elizabeth*

Consort, later rebuilt and renamed the *Swan*.[6] The deposition of Richard of Limehouse was dated 12 January; and a journal of the voyage to Surat records that the fleet sailed on 3 March 1616.[7] The deposition of Richard of Ratcliffe in the same case, however, was made on 28 May, i.e. after the *Swan* had sailed, ruling him out as a member of the crew on that occasion.

The journal also records that en route the *Swan* was dispatched to Bantam, from which she went on to Pulo Run and her capture on 2 February 1617. Petitions by his wife Elizabeth confirm that the master's mate, Richard Swanley, was one of those then taken prisoner.[8] The birth of a son Jeremy to Richard of Ratcliffe and his wife Margaret in May 1618 also rules him out as the mate on the *Swan*, who was a prisoner at the time of the child's conception. In addition, the master of the *Swan* was John Davies of Limehouse. It is hard to avoid the conclusion that it was Richard of Limehouse who was captured.

A William Swanley also sailed in Captain Joseph's fleet, initially as master of the *Unicorn*.[9] Joseph was killed in August 1616; and was succeeded as fleet commander by Henry Pepwell who died at the Cape in 1618, being succeeded in turn by William Swanley. In his will made on 2 February 1618,[10] Pepwell included a bequest to William Swanley, then master of the *Charles*; and in January 1619 William made a deposition in Chancery about the will.[11] This William was clearly the brother of Richard of Ratcliffe, not of Richard of Limehouse.

Given that Richard of Limehouse was the captured mate, the question remains whether it was he who was killed on the *Lion* in the fight with the Portuguese in 1625. In March 1620 a Richard Swanley sailed for the East Indies from Gravesend as mate on the *Exchange* and on the death of Captain Fitzherbert became master. His voyage extended over a period of four years four months, ending in June 1624,[12] and during this time Richard of Limehouse was serving with Captain Weddell in the *Jonas*.[13] A son Richard was born to Richard of Ratcliffe and Margaret in July 1620 and no other child of these two was baptised until Margaret, aged nine days, was baptised on 22 May 1625. It appears from this evidence that Richard of Ratcliffe was the master of the *Exchange*.

It is evident that Richard of Ratcliffe then became master of the *Lion*, part of an East India Company fleet from England which on arrival off the Indian coast in October 1625 was attacked by Portuguese galleons. The master was killed, and his widow unsuccessfully petitioned for relief in January 1627.[14] Margaret Swanley, widow of Ratcliffe, then married James Chapman in Stepney in February 1628. Richard of Limehouse was serving in Weddell's fleet at the time of the attack on the *Lion*,[15] and it is clear that it was Richard of Ratcliffe who was killed.

There remains to be clarified the mystifying record in the East India Company court minutes that on 24 January 1620 a Richard Swanley was appointed commander of the *Anne*, the ship which grounded off Gravesend en route for the East. However, on examination of the original, it appears that the record is a marginal note in a different hand from the minutes and is clearly incorrect. The minutes themselves, which refer merely to Mr Swanley, are concerned with William Swanley. Unlike the experienced William, neither Richard of Limehouse nor Richard of Ratcliffe would have qualified at that time for such an appointment, and no other Richard emerges from the records of the time.

The naval career of Richard Swanley, which is mentioned by Baumber in two articles[16] and by D.E. Kennedy in a third,[17] is extensively covered elsewhere.[18] Baumber found no direct evidence that the East India Company captain is the Richard who commanded the *Charles* in 1642 in the Parliamentary fleet, and who was subsequently appointed Admiral of the Irish Fleet. However the distinctive signature in his threatening letters to Captain William Minors,[19] to which Baumber alludes, corresponds with that of the naval commander on a certificate about supplies which as Admiral he had ordered Captain Thomas Beale to deliver to Duncannon Fort in 1644.[20] It also corresponds with that on the will Swanley made on 28 May 1649.[21]

Admiral Swanley is notorious on account of a report published in 1644 in the *Kingdom's Weekly Intelligencer* that he threw Irish prisoners into the sea. Newspaper reports during the Civil War were of questionable value, and it is noteworthy that no objection to this reported action seems to have been made.[22] If it occurred the action was presumably in tune with prevailing attitudes. In any case, the private instructions

issued to Swanley, as Admiral on the Irish Coast, in May 1643 required him not to 'suffer any of the Irish... to come over hither' and 'to punish such offenders by death'.[23] It must also be noted that on 4 June 1644 Parliament thanked him for his services and awarded him a gold chain and medal.

It appears that Swanley married twice. His first wife Elizabeth was buried in Stepney on 17 September 1623, and on 30 December 1623 he married Elizabeth Clarke in Whitechapel. George Swanley, who followed him into the Navy and the East India Company, may have been a son of the first marriage. Richard was survived by his second wife, together with their sons, Richard and John, and daughter Mary who married Captain Thomas Harwood RN. Margaret's will[24] was the subject of a Chancery complaint by Richard jnr (later Captain RN) against his sister Mary and her husband in 1663.[25]

References

1 M.L. Baumber, 'An East India Captain', *M.M.*, 53 (1967), 265-79.

2 P.R.O., C24/610 (Lorde v Clement, 1636) etc.

3 P.R.O., C24/659 (Swanley v Heath, 1641).

4 P.R.O., C2/Chas I/B9/57 (Boothby v Swanley, 1631).

5 *International Genealogical Index* (1992), Gloucestershire.

6 P.R.O., C24/427 (Appleby v Swanley, 1616).

7 BL, Egerton MS 2121, fo. 81.

8 *CSP Colonial, East Indies, 1617-21*, 5 Feb. and 4 June 1619.

9 *Letters received by the East India Company*, V, 1617, (London, 1901), 39.

10 P.R.O., PROB 11/132, 87.

11 P.R.O., C24/459 (Handson v Gifford, 1619).

12 BL, L/MAR/A/xxxi.

13 BL, L/MAR/A/xxxiv.

14 *CSP Colonial, East Indies, 1625-29*, 26 Jan. 1627.

15 BL, L/MAR/A/xl.

16 M.L. Baumber, 'The Navy and the Civil War in Ireland', *M.M.*, 57 (1971), 385-97, and 75 (1989), 255-68.

17 D.E. Kennedy, 'Naval Captains at the Outbreak of the English Civil War', *M.M.*, 46 (1960), 181-98.

18 J.R. Powell and E.K. Timings, eds, *Documents relating to the Civil War, 1642-48* (Navy Records Society, 1963).

19 BL, Egerton NS 2086, fos 135, 137.

20 P.R.O., SP 16/301/25.

21 P.R.O., PROB 10/722.

22 S.R. Gardiner, *History of the Great Civil War*, I (London, 1893), 296.

23 BL, Add. MS 4106/71.

24 P.R.O., PROB 11/312, 122.

25 P.R.O., C10/67/116 (Swanley v Harwood, 1663).

E.W.L. KEYMER
London

AN IMPRESSIVE NAVAL MEMORIAL

The first naval officer to die in a war generally attracts some notice but few can have had so magnificent and enduring a monument or such an impressive funeral as did John Western, the Third Lieutenant of the frigate *Syren* (32), killed on 21 March 1793, and whose unhappy priority is supported by both Brenton and James. The large tablet on the wall of the Groote Kerk in Dordrecht (Dort) records that he:

> After distinguishing himself by his Conduct and Intrepidity with which he assisted THE GARRISON OF WILLIAMSTADT at that Time besieged by the French FELL EARLY IN THE CAREER OF GLORY having unfortunately been killed by the Enemy off the Moordych...

The inscription goes on to record that the funeral was attended by the Duke of York, who had ordered the monument to be erected, and by the Officers and Seamen of the Royal Navy – 'the Companions of his MERITORIOUS EXERTIONS' – as well as by the Brigade of Foot Guards in garrison there. The monument is a reminder of one of the first operations afloat against the French although it was of short duration.

The demand for British assistance had come from the Dutch authorities in November 1792 following the successes of Doumouriez against the Prussians and Austrians. By then the French had occupied part of the Austrian Netherlands, declared the Scheldt navigation free to all and were said to be building up a naval flotilla at Antwerp. Since by treaties of 1788 and 1790 Britain had guaranteed the southern Netherlands to Austria and limited the Scheldt navigation to the Dutch the request for help had to be met. In January 1793 and before the French declaration of war on 1 February, a 50-gun ship and several frigates and sloops were sent to Flushing to prevent the French passing ships up to Antwerp but when in early February the Dutch were able to provide an adequate force of their own it was reduced to the *Syren*, Captain John Manley, and a handful of smaller vessels.

The Dutch main line of defence was along the River Waal running roughly from Steenbergen in the west to Nijmwegen in the east. An enemy seeking the most direct route to Rotterdam and the Hague would need to take the fortress town of Breda and then the smaller fortified places lying south of the Hollands Diep from Willemstad to Gertruidenberg. Once across this wide water obstacle Dordrecht was the only important town in the way and the rivers beyond it were narrower and could be bridged by a field army. Rear Admiral Pieter Melvill of the Admiralty of the Maas at Rotterdam was in charge of the water defences of this vital sector which was to be strengthened by fresh British help. It took two forms. The first was to place Captain V.C. Berkeley under the orders of the Ambassador at the Hague, Lord Auckland, with the task of furnishing a force of gunboats at British expense but with the Dutch providing the armament and Britain the crews. The second was the despatch of a brigade of three battalions of foot guards under the command of the Duke of York. These reached Hellevoetsluis on 1 March with orders to remain within twenty-four hours' move of that port, a not surprising proviso since they comprised most of the trained troops at the governments' disposal.

The provision of the gunboats, both those ordered by Captain Berkeley and the much larger number on Dutch account, was achieved very quickly but the problem of finding crews for the British craft, 16 of which were reported to be ready on 1 March, was not so easily solved. Some officers and men could be lent temporarily from Captain Manley's squadron but the rest, according to an Admiralty preoccupied with Fleet mobilisation, would have to be found from the crews of the transports that had brought over the guards. On 27 February Lord Auckland asked

Captain Manley to raise 100 good men from that source at about 30s. a month with the prospect of £5 for good conduct at the end of 'this service of short duration'. By then the need was urgent. Breda had fallen without serious resistance on 26 February. The French shortly afterwards reached the Hollands Diep and Gertuidenberg was taken. The small garrison of Klundert fought their way over to Willemstad which, stoutly defended by Colonel Boetzelaer, remained the only fortified town still held on the south side of the Diep. For the next three weeks its support became a main naval objective.

Lord Auckland was convinced that only a resolute and well co-ordinated defence could save the Dutch Republic. It was a time when 'diffidence and dejection are gaining ground in the Province and the temper of men's minds such that a small addition of alarm may throw the whole into despair and disorder'. Leadership was not coming from the Stadhouder, constitutionally incapable of making up his mind, and an overall commander was essential. On 1 March Lord Auckland arranged a meeting with the Stadhouder, the Hereditary Prince, officials and senior officers from which orders were issued that the Hereditary Prince should command the troops, with the British exercising local command in the Dordrecht area, and that he should co-operate with the new overall commander of the water defences, Admiral Jan Hendrik van Kinsbergen. Van Kinsbergen was a professional officer of considerable distinction who accepted the command with some hesitation partly because he felt it unfair to Admiral Melvill. Once appointed he acted with great energy. All craft likely to be of value to the enemy were removed or destroyed and inlets closed with obstacles, that of the vital Dort Kil with a chain. His policy was to attack French controlled vessels afloat or in harbour. In informing Captain Manley of his appointment Lord Auckland enjoined him to 'concert unreservedly and cordially' with him adding that 'he will second anything useful that you may suggest'.

During the next two to three weeks Manley sent cutters and once a sloop as far as Dordrecht island, the town itself now occupied by the guards and with its fortifications being rapidly repaired. Manning the British gunboats was a continuous problem with frequent appeals from Auckland for more men. Several officers came

from the *Syren* and the Admiralty finally relented and on 16 March the sloop *Childers* arrived with a draft. In spite of these difficulties the first five gunboats reached Dort on 5 March, another on 8 March, three more the following day and by 12 March ten were operational. These were concentrated to the west of the city, covering the north shore of the Hollands Diep. On 9 March the report of victories by Coburg had led the Ambassador to suggest that Dumouriez might make a final desperate effort to cross the Diep using the craft he had assembled. Four days later van Kinsbergen told Berkeley that the French were now expected to attempt a landing on 16 or 17 March and that his force should take them in the flank. This did not happen.

The French had mounted batteries on the Moordych to the east of Willemstad to annoy shipping going to and from Dort – they had an exchange of fire with British gunboats on the 18th – but their main effort was directed to the siege of Willemstad with their batteries firing red hot shot into the town. One was formed within 200 yards of the harbour itself but did not prevent supplies getting in. On 15 March the garrison made a sortie with 45 men, spiked its three 18-pounders and killed or captured 29 French without loss to themselves. The British gunboats no doubt helped in the convoy operations but James' implication that Lieutenant Western was responsible for driving the French from their batteries that night cannot be confirmed, Captain Berkeley's report merely stating that at the request of the Governor he had that evening anchored 300 yards from the French guns without receiving damage.

There does seem to have been some difficulty over the status of the British force. Captain Berkeley was technically under the orders of van Kinsbergen but he appears to have regarded himself primarily as commander of an independent British naval force. There is a reference in Dutch official papers to the desirability of reminding him of his formal position. He was also to some extent professional adviser to the Duke of York. We do not know how he got on with the Dutch officers of his own rank but he did suffer the indignity of being arrested with his boat's crew by a party of Dutch dragoons. The incident was settled amicably.

By 17 March it was evident that the French were withdrawing and had raised the siege of

Willemstad. It was accordingly decided to reinforce that garrison so that it could harass their rearguards. On 21 March 700 men were sent to the town in 22 transports under a convoy which included 8 British gunboats. On the way in fire was opened on French battery positions on the Noordschaans, which lay between Willemstad and the Moordych. The Dutch said that there was no reply. Berkeley claimed that a few shots had been fired but that the guns had soon been silenced. After the troops had been landed the British force went off on its own, turning east towards the Moordych where, according to Manley, 'an attack was meditated on a second battery, the object of which was to destroy the said battery and some craft in a creek'. (The first, unnamed battery was probably that engaged on the way in to Willemstad.) There is some uncertainty as to where the attack actually took place. While both the Moordych itself and the mouth of the Klundert Canal a little to the south-west were likely to have harboured small craft and to have been defended, the latter does seem the more likely. Lieutenant Kolff, the commander of a Dutch vessel lying off the Noordschaans, reported that at half past midnight on the morning of 22 March he detected movement in the harbour of the Noordschaans followed by gunfire. He made the danger signal and then closed to find that the British gunboats were making an unsuccessful attack in the face of intense musket fire. He thought that they were lucky to have suffered only three casualties: Lieutenant Western killed by a musket ball in the head while laying his boat's 12-pounder and Midshipman Marshall and one seaman drowned. The two latter were brought on board his ship.

Reporting to van Kinsbergen later that day Captain Berkeley said that after leaving the convoy at Willemstad he had gone on to reconnoitre the area in question and that some of his boats had got into the harbour mouth where they met with a heavy and sustained musket fire. He had replied with his own guns and muskets, concluded that a landing was impossible and had withdrawn after the enemy's fire was silenced. Van Kinsbergen was furious. He reported that Berkeley had described it to him as a reconnaissance. He had never ordered one and would have considered it a quite inappropriate operation. That afternoon Lieutenant Kolff reported that the French had withdrawn after throwing their guns into the water. They had also left Klundert and the immediate threat to the Netherlands was over.

Some hours after the return of the gunboats to Dort, Lord Auckland went to Willemstad with his family and Dutch officials, a visit which symbolised the end of the operation. On 25 March, the day after Lieutenant Western's funeral, he ordered Berkeley to take the gunboats to Rotterdam except for two which were to be left at Dort. On 28 March the latter reported that he had handed over the balance of the 15 purchased on British account to the Admiralty of the Maas. In thanking Lord Auckland for his support he said that he thought it had been very valuable to be able to show the British flag in these waters. However, not everyone was to be appreciative of the British contribution.

On 3 April the Ambassador reported that the States General had resolved to award

> the same gold chain as is given to Ministers of the 2nd Order at the close of their mission together with a gold medal to Captain Berkeley and a small chain and gold medal to each of the Lieutenants and to the family of Lt. Western.

This was too much for van Kinsbergen. No Dutch officer had been decorated although they had done their duty just as well as the English – and they had obeyed orders. He expressed his views in moderate language to the States General and with greater frankness to the Stadhouder. In his letter to the latter, which was later published, he said that he wished the States General had given Berkeley a hundred thousand guilders instead of these decorations. This would have given no grounds for complaint to the Dutch officers employed on the same service and in the same vessels as the British. His protest got no awards for his own people.

References

a) British

Adm. 1/2127, John Manley.

Adm. 1/4157, Letters from Secretaries of State. fo. 37, 45 and 46.

W. James, *Naval History*, Vol. I (1859 edition), p.98.

Fairly full reports of the engagement in various newspapers. For example, that under Foreign Intelligence in the *Exeter Gazette* of 27 March 1793 blamed the Dutch pilots!

b) Netherlands

Algemeen Rijksarchief Den Haag, Archieven van de Admiraliteits – Colleges 1, 01, 47, 10, 39 and 40.

Geschiedenis van het Ne. Zeewesen (1862). Vol. V., J.C. De Jonge (Haarlem, 1862).

R.B. Prud'homme van Reine, *Jan Hendrik van Kinsbergen 1735-1819* (Amsterdam, 1990). Includes illustrations of small craft involved.

ADRIAN REED
Uffculme
Devon

ADMIRAL STIRLING AT RIO DE JANEIRO, 1806

Rear Admiral Charles Stirling, in command of a convoy of warships, transports, and victuallers, sailed from Cawsand Bay on 28 August 1806 with supplies for British forces at Buenos Aires, captured earlier that year. Apart from delivering supplies, he was ordered to take over command of the squadron in the River Plate. His fleet consisted of *Sampson* (64), *Staunch* gun brig, *Prevoyante* storeship, two Indiamen, four victuallers, and two whalers going to the southern whale fishery. The voyage had the usual problems – wind and weather, ships parting and rejoining, storm damage – but gradually the problem of sickness in the *Sampson* comes to dominate the admiral's journal.

Within a fortnight *Sampson* had 64 men 'under the surgeon for ulcers', 15 of them unfit for duty. The first death occurred on 27 September, and by the middle of October three men had died and three more had legs amputated. 'Most scratches', Stirling notes on 15 October, 'turn to ulcers'. By the beginning of November 'bilious complaints' were 'getting worse'. On 10 November the surgeon decided that the problem was the condition of the water, which 'in the bottom tier is very bad'. One might think the surgeon was remarkably slow to reach this conclusion, but Stirling, normally ready enough to comment in stringent terms, makes no remark on his competence.

The source for all this is Admiral Stirling's journal, an unusually detailed and literate example. Stirling clearly wrote it up himself, more or less daily, in a small, neat, legible hand. It is composed carefully, in clear English, with scarcely any alterations: it betokens a clear mind.

It is a superb source of information on all aspects of the voyage, and on events at the River Plate in 1806-07.

The convoy was sailing along the Brazilian coast when the sickness was finally blamed on the water. Stirling was supposed to head for Buenos Aires with all speed to deliver his supplies, but on 5 November a Portuguese brig told him that Buenos Aires had been retaken by the Spaniards. This removed the urgency and Stirling changed his priorities: now he could put his men's needs first. He also needed more news about the situation to the south before reaching the Plate, if he could get it. He went into Rio de Janeiro on 13 November, still with 'men falling sick'.

The Portuguese Viceroy of Brazil, the Conde dos Arcos, was rendered understandably nervous by this unexpected visitation. He was newly appointed, Brazil was restless, and his homeland of Portugal was poised most uncomfortably between the imperious policies of the victorious armies of Napoleonic France and the victorious navy of Great Britain. He quickly invited Stirling ashore for a meeting. The admiral took with him General Grey, who was going out to govern the Cape, and his captains and lieutenants. They attended a soiree at the Viceregal Palace, and there the Viceroy and the admiral conducted a conversation full of barbed diplomacy and point-scoring. The Viceroy confirmed the news of the recapture of Buenos Aires by the Spaniards, and complained that the tightness of the British blockade at the Plate prevented news from getting out. Stirling records this with a trace of grim satisfaction since it meant that active hostilities were still in progress, and his voyage had a purpose after all.

Stirling wanted supplies, above all of clean, fresh water, and even before the visit to the Viceroy, a local merchant, John Peter Meyer, had introduced himself as the authorised agent for supplying foreign ships. Stirling had stalled him, and asked the Viceroy to recommend another merchant, hoping for some price-lowering competition. The Viceroy refused to interfere, remarking that 'Mr Meyer had been recommended by the Prince of Brasil at the instance of Lord St Vincent'. Stirling's attempts at bargaining were thus neatly blocked.

Worse, they backfired. When he contacted Meyer again he 'was told that every thing was dear and difficult to be got'. Stirling goes into great detail on this, with anxious calculations. He then discovered that there was only one source of water, a 'fountain' fed by an aqueduct, and that he had to hire a 'tank' to supply his fleet. 'As I had declared intentions to sail the moment the ships were complete, I perceived a strong disposition to throw every obstacle in my way by persons interested to keep the ships in port.' Paranoia threatened. He even detected a plot to make the water supply 'by some means to run very slow from the Fountain'.

The Viceroy mentioned that port regulations stated that all ships should provide certain information, to which Stirling objected. The Viceroy countered by sending the Chief Judge, no less, to make the enquiries. 'After a good deal of Conversation his questions were reduced to three, viz. whence the ship came? where bound? and what brought us here?' The uselessness of these enquiries rendered the conversation farcical. Stirling refused to answer personally, but ordered *Sampson*'s captain, William Cuming, 'to give in writing that the ship under his command came from England; that he did not know where she was bound, as he acted only by my orders; and that he supposed we came here for refreshments, altho he did not know from me that such was my motive'.

Stirling heard that a rumour was circulating in the town that he had insulted the Viceroy by not replying to the fort's salute of guns one-for-one when he arrived. He hastened to repeat the salute fully next day, so the early afternoon of Sunday reverberated to the sound of 40 guns being fired. The Viceroy was asked to deliver up any Englishmen in the town – the presumption being that any Englishman in Rio must have got there by deserting from a ship of the Royal Navy – and promised in return to put ashore any slaves who escaped to his ships. The life of a slave must have been harsh indeed for Royal Navy ships, riddled with sickness, to be preferable. Sure enough, he put the fugitives ashore as he left on 19 November, but *Sampson* lost five men by desertion, and *Staunch* four, who were not returned. One up to the Viceroy.

Stirling investigated everything. He noted down exhaustive details of the products of the land: imports of salt, wines, flour, and slaves, and exports of rum, tobacco, sugar, gold, and precious stones. 'There was no manufactures', he

commented, and 'there is not much attention paid to cultivation'. The Portuguese he judged to be 'lazy and indolent', and he got the idea that 'there is great plenty of everything, as the fruit and vegetables grow without culture, and many of them spontaneously'.

This inquisitiveness was not merely personal to the admiral; British interest in Brazil was long-standing. Much of Britain's gold supply came out of Brazilian mines, and Brazil was a good market for British manufactures, and all the more important as outlets to Europe failed – Napoleon's Continental System was initiated even as Stirling lay in Rio harbour, with the Berlin decrees of 21 November. Further, the Brazilian coast lay alongside the route to India. In 1792 John Barrow thought that Rio might be a naval base 'sufficient to command the Southern Atlantic', and Barrow was Second Secretary at the Admiralty in London from 1804 to 1806. He published his comments in the very year Stirling called at Rio. Two years before, the British former admiral of the Portuguese navy, Donald Campbell, wrote to the Cabinet emphasising the 'importance of preventing the French from possessing the Brazils'. In the last few years there had been conspiracies and plots and risings in Brazil inspired by French revolutionary ideas.

Stirling investigated the city with some care. The scenic beauty of the town's setting was 'extremely romantic' – his strongest term of praise – and the Sugar Loaf 'cannot possibly be mistaken'. The Viceregal Palace attracts a certain grudging approval, and the houses of the city are 'good and commodious'. He noted the Viceroy's establishment of a public garden and commended him for 'showing some taste in laying it out.' He remarked on the monasteries and nunneries, and that there were, 'of course', many churches. The theatre was 'tolerably good' and the opera performance to which he was bidden by the Viceroy on Saturday – laid on at short notice as a special honour – was 'above mediocrity'.

Much of his inquisitiveness had a military aspect. One day he was rowed about the harbour, noting the numerous islands, but was not able to define its navigable limits. He rode out into the surrounding country, noting the potentialities of the salt lakes south of the city. He thought the Rio Grande was navigable almost to the mines in Minas Gerais. Mules he judged to be excellent, but the roads were only sandy tracks outside the town. He organised a little spying. The royal dockyard inevitably attracted his interest, and he sent one of his passengers, a man called Clarke who was going out to be the Master Shipwright at the Cape, to investigate. Prices of wood, masts, sailcloth, blocks, the presence of 'a good many shipwrights to be hired', and the absence of docks, all are noted. In the context of the time this piece of minor espionage is suggestive.

Stirling looked, as he said, 'at Rio Janeiro with a military eye'. He calculated the Viceroy's forces, measured the strength and condition of the fortifications, and mentally planned out an attack aimed at capturing the city. He thought '5,000 men would easily capture the whole', despite his calculation of the total defensive forces at 4,000 regular soldiers 'badly off and much dissatisfied', and 20,000 militia who 'look well under arms'. He decided that the fort of Santa Cruz and the aqueduct were the vital points, whose capture would cause the fall of the city. He was soon to learn, at Montevideo and at Buenos Aires, just how difficult it was for even 15,000 British troops to capture a sternly defended South American city. It is curious, for instance, that he judges the Portuguese troops to be of poor quality because 'most of them are impressed, and their pay' was low. He was sailing, after all, in a ship full of pressed seamen, who saw pay only at the end of a voyage, if then. But he is also very clear that, if the inhabitants remained hostile, '30,000 men would not be able to keep possession' of the city.

The problem of money came back to plague him as the fleet was edging out of the harbour. The agent of transports, *Sampson*'s purser, the masters of the transports in the convoy, and the surgeon of the *Sampson* all presented bills, and he also found he had to pay the pilots. Most of these men had clearly waited for the moment when the ships were leaving, hoping that he would allow the bills to be paid in London. Stirling foiled them by breaking open one of the kegs of Spanish dollars he carried for the pay of the British troops at Buenos Aires. They had been captured, so Stirling logically reasoned that

he might as well use the dollars himself, especially if he could thus save money. Before plenty of witnesses he paid out a total of 765 dollars. In his journal he claimed that he had saved a fair sum by this means, but he refrained from going into too much detail – presumably in case he was wrong. His anxious concern not to spend money is particularly interesting in that he was eventually dismissed the service for corruption when commanding in the West Indies.

The problem which sent him into Rio, the sickness of *Sampson*'s crew, slowly subsided. Numbers of sick continued to rise, to a peak of 150 sick four days after the ship sailed – out of 460 sailors and marines on board – but thereafter the numbers declined. A week later the journal ceases to record sickness, presumably because it was no longer a problem.

Stirling's journal reflects the man's inquisitive mind, but there were to be no practical results for his enquiries. He went on to command the Cape station until 1810, and from there he no doubt watched with interest as the situation in Brazil changed drastically. In late 1807 the French invaded Portugal, and a British fleet under Sir Sidney Smith whisked the Portuguese royal family out of Lisbon and deposited them at Rio. Stirling's aggressive plan was not required, perhaps fortunately. The French had pushed Brazil into the British alliance: Rio became a friendly port.

References

Stirling's journal: P.R.O., Adm. 50/50.

Muster books of *Sampson* and *Staunch*: P.R.O., Adm. 36/16934 and 17261 respectively.

Sir John Barrow, *A Voyage to Cochinchina in the Years 1792 and 1793* (London, 1806).

Donald Campbell's reports to the Cabinet: P.R.O., FO 63/42 and the Chatham Papers PRO30/8/342.

Brazilian background: K.R. Maxwell, *Conflicts and Conspiracies: Portugal and Brazil, 1750-1808* (Cambridge, 1973).

J.D. GRAINGER
Institute of Advanced Studies in the Humanities
University of Birmingham

THE LOSS OF THE *REYNARD*

Midshipman Philip Colomb had been in the navy for three years, when in 1849 he joined his third ship the *Reynard* at Hong Kong. The two years he was to spend on her saw *Reynard* cruising the Chinese coast helping to suppress piracy. The ship was a screw sloop, and as such was an object of mysterious dread to the local population, who were unable to account for her movement through the water.

The *Reynard* was at Hong Kong preparing for home in May 1851, when there arrived an open boat crewed by some survivors of a wrecked English brig. The ship had come to grief on the Prata Shoal, a coral reef 150 miles to the south. The remainder of the crew had found a precarious refuge on the small, inhospitable, Prata Island. The *Reynard*, under the command of Captain Peter Cracroft, left Hong Kong on 28 May, in company with the *Pilot*, and headed for the shoal. At 4.15 on the morning of 31 May the *Reynard* was cruising at 3 knots, when she struck the reef herself.

The engine was put to full astern, sails hove back, boats lowered and anchors carried out. This was, alas, all in vain. The sea got up, the cable on the small anchor parted, the second anchor fell away into 400 feet of water and the ship was soon carried broadside on to the reef. Whilst the ship's company were having breakfast, the *Reynard* fell over on to her starboard side and began taking water. The *Pilot* was nowhere in sight by now, contact having been lost during the night. Despite their own plight, the shipwrecked mariners were not forgotten. The *Reynard*'s pinnance was loaded with provisions and sent to Prata Island, which could be seen 8 miles away.

Breakfast over, the hands were divided into two parties. One group remained on board, under the command of the first Lieutenant, whilst the second, under the command of the master, went into the ship's boats. The masts were still standing at this time, a feat Colomb attributed to the use of wire rather than rope for the rigging. Those on board proceeded to pass down to the boats under the lee of the ship, spars and gratings to make a raft. Philip Colomb was among the party who stayed on board. The work was strenuous for all concerned, and at one point he collapsed exhausted on the deck.

The raft was completed by nightfall and secured alongside. Despite the rain the ship's company spent the night on deck, as it was not thought safe to sleep below.

The morning of 1 June was spent loading the raft with provisions. This done it was towed inside the reef, a distance of some 400 yards from the *Reynard*. The pinnance then landed water and provisions on Prata Island. Tents were taken over ready for the ship's company. Colomb went below at this point, as he hoped to save his sketches and some clothes. He found the water up to the beams of his berth and his chest reduced to splinters.

Captain Cracroft still had not given up hope of saving his ship, and ordered the masts to be cut down. The starboard guns were hove overboard in the hope that the ship would right herself. This done the next large wave put the ship onto an even keel, whereupon she heeled over onto her port side due to the weight of the remaining guns. The sea now swept over her taking away everything not secured. Despite all this the ship's company were in good spirits, primarily because they could now see the masts of the *Pilot*.

With the approach of darkness Captain Cracroft determined to abandon the *Reynard*. Colomb took a last look below. He found the partitions washed away with the cabin, gunroom and steerage all as one. Not one item in the mass of debris that surged to and fro exceeded 12 inches.

Only the smallest boat was left to transport over a hundred men to the raft, which by this time was aground the far side of the reef. The officers were the last to leave, and having done so hauled their boat across the reef and secured it to the raft. Two boats were sent to Prata Island, leaving 80 men on the raft.

Captain Cracroft remained on the raft, where he addressed the men and led them in prayer. The ship's company responded with three cheers for their captain. Most of the provisions having been landed on Prata, supper consisted of pork and rum. The raft was awash due to one corner of it being caught on the reef. Those on board spent a miserable night, at times up to their waists in water. Colomb himself managed an hour's sleep, only by getting on to one of the three boats secured to the raft.

The morning of 2 June found the *Reynard* still apparently intact, and one of the ship's boats tried to reach her. This, however, could not get through the surf and the attempt was abandoned.

Captain Cracroft now turned his back on the ship and concentrated on getting his men to the island. Three hours later all were safely landed on Prata. This proved to be a low island in the shape of a horseshoe, with a clear bay between the arms.

Here everyone rested, received a cooked meal of boobies eggs with rice, and were then divided up into working parties. Tents were erected on the right-hand arm of the island and wells dug, although the only water found was brackish. The *Pilot* was in the offing, but could not close the island due to the reefs. Not long after the *Reynard*'s company had turned in early, the *Pilot*'s jolly boat came ashore with a letter from their captain, urging Captain Cracroft to leave.

The next morning, 3 June, the *Reynard*'s crew made their way in the ship's boats across the reefs and were safely embarked by the *Pilot*. She returned to Hong Kong, where the survivors were accommodated on the store ship *Minden*. Everybody was reduced to the clothes in which they stood, and had lost the keepsakes they had accumulated over nearly three years. Colomb himself was reduced to a flannel shirt, a pair of trousers, a straw hat and half a blanket. He considered his greatest loss to be some 80 sketches he had made of the China coast. The British community in the colony were so moved by the plight of the *Reynard*'s crew that a public subscription was organised to help them.

Philip Colomb went on to have a distinguished career in the navy, becoming a vice-admiral. He received the India General Service Medal with bar Pegu (*Serpent*), the Arctic Medal (*Phoenix*) and the Baltic Medal (*Hastings*). Amongst his inventions was a system of flashing light signals used by both the navy and the army. He became a prolific writer on naval matters, his ideas being published in books, pamphlets, magazine articles and numerous letters to the *Times*. He retired in 1886 and died at his home in Botley, Hampshire, in 1899.

Sources

Letter from Philip Colomb to his mother of 18 June 1851, written on *Minden* at Hong Kong.

Biographical notes prepared by Philip Colomb in June 1897.

Biographical notes made by his daughter Ellen in 1931 at Bath.

JOHN C. WELCH
Coulsdon, Surrey

THE OTTOMANS AND THE SEA[1]

This Conference was held at Newnham College, Cambridge, at the end of March 1996, one of a series organised by the Skilliter Centre for Ottoman Studies. Experts from 11 countries gathered to focus their skills on some 600 years of history of the Ottomans and the sea – the period covered was c. 1300-1900.

The main theme implied in the variety of topics chosen was that the Ottoman Empire was indeed a maritime one in its growth, maintenance, management and decline – and not merely a military/agricultural one.[2] As the Turkish Naval Attaché reminded the Conference at its close, 'history is the memory of a nation'. It became clear that the Turks have a long memory of the sea and sea lore, a fact not always associated with the Ottomans.

The Turks had been living on or near the Aegean littoral for several centuries before they erupted out to sea during the thirteenth century, with the decline of Byzantine sea power. 'A struggle then began between Latins and Turks for the control of the Aegean', as Elizabeth Zachariadou (Crete)[3] told the Conference. The Turks sailed at first as 'sea-lords' of local principalities, and mainly as pirate raiders.

The westward expansion of the Turks into the Aegean in the thirteenth to fifteenth centuries brought them into conflict with Venice, Genoa and Rhodes, all of whom sought to dominate the inter-island trade routes, and penetrate into the Black Sea. Kate Fleet (Cambridge) noted the continuation of Turkish raids into the early fifteenth century, when piracy remained 'an ever present danger to both Greeks and Latins resident in the islands, as to Byzantine and Latin shipping'.

The coastal princes already disposed of sizeable fleets of their own before any regular, imperial fleet came into existence. The Emir of Bergama mustered 250 vessels in one summer campaign, and landed 20,000 soldiers from boats in another. Dr Fleet asked, when was there an Ottoman navy as such, which was not merely a muster of pirate ships from coastal principalities? The Ottoman princes, with their complex diplomatic relations on both sides of the Straits, needed to cross from one section of their state to the other, accompanied by soldiery and horses. By early in the fifteenth century, at any rate, there was a base at Gallipoli, considered to be 'key to the east and west, to the Aegean and Black Seas'.

By 1410, 40 galleys were kept ready at Gallipoli, and this was probably the 'reserve' of the regular navy at this date. Not long before, the Venetians had sent out 60 war galleys to hunt for the Turks, and on another occasion 27 triremes had been captured from the Turks, suggesting that both galley and trireme, traditional Mediterranean ship types, were the nucleus of the Ottoman force at this date.

Catherine Otten (Strasbourg) explained that by the reign of Bayezid I (1389-1402) the Christians were facing 'attacks which had much more the aspect of a war'. By the fifteenth century, then, a regular fleet existed, even though it was usually supplemented by co-opted pirate vessels, corsairs, and hired ships of other nations.

Rhoads Murphey (Birmingham) offered an interesting insight into the maintenance and management of the Ottoman Navy in the pre-print era:

> Skilled craftsmen and naval (or military) practitioners serving under Ottoman colours are regarded by today's ethical standards as defectors, renegades and traitors but their service in the pay of a succession of different paymasters was perfectly normal by contemporary standards.

Builders, site foremen, ship designers, gunsmiths – these were the 'factotums' who operated across state boundaries and made practical, on the spot decisions, and who, in a number of cases, became commanders of the Sultan's fleet. (It became clear in the nineteenth and twentieth centuries that this state of affairs could not sustain an effective naval force when technology had become far more complex.)[4]

Palmira Brummett (Tennessee) reflected on the importance of the context in which Ottoman sea power was discussed. Assessing the impact of Ottoman sea power is a matter of assigning place in the competition for world power, with evaluation of military and cultural ethos, and with assessment of the prevailing Ottoman and European economic systems. The Ottoman state over the next two centuries became concerned with dominating and controlling trade entrepots and commercial networks across three zones: an island zone (Aegean and Adriatic), a caravan and inland sea zone (Syria, Aleppo, Persian Gulf),

and the zone of Egypt, the Red Sea and Indian Ocean.[5]

After the capture of Constantinople (1453) the Ottomans strengthened their presence in the Black Sea areas, and took over the trade there (1453-75). Alexander Halenko (Kiev) made the useful point that in the 1960s several publications based on Ottoman and Venetian sources testified that western nations were not entirely expelled from the Black Sea after the Ottoman conquest. Further, western nations became more dependent on the grain exports from the Ukraine during the sixteenth century:

> The Ottomans favoured the idea of a Black Sea economic commonwealth in which political ties were to play a restricted role, an idea that proved to be unrealistic...

The idea was certainly an enlightened one for the time. It was based, of course, on 'the exclusive Ottoman interest in tax revenue for the Sultan as absolute ruler', i.e. on customs duties and concessions.

The idea was unrealistic because it required regular maritime policing, which was not part of the Empire's financial weaponry. Victor Ostapchuk (Kiev) told the story of the 'episodic disturbance' of the Cossacks, who meted out to the Turks much the same treatment as the Turks had dealt to the inhabitants of the Aegean. Arriving in *kafkhans* and *kaiques* by the thousand, they devastated ports and towns and seized shipping for ransom. In due course the Turkish authorities ordered all merchant and war galleys to be equipped with a *shandul*, a manoeuvrable 'ship's boat', though whether this was for use in escaping the looters or pursuing them was not specified.

Again, it was the interest in customs duties, and the fear of losing them to the Portuguese, which partly motivated Ottoman expansion southwards, through Egypt, conquered in 1517. John Alexander (Cambridge) outlined the Ottoman arrival in the Red Sea with a fleet of 30 ships, set out with materials and stores from Turkey, but built by Turks and Egyptians jointly. During the reign of Suleiman I, 'the Magnificent' (1520-66), it was believed that 'with this fleet (or its successors) it was possible to seize all the Portuguese forts and fortresses on the coasts of the Indian Ocean'.[6]

Excavations at Ibrim and Suakin indicate Ottoman occupation and conversion into garrison-cities. Dr Alexander showed slides of them, and maps indicating the Ottoman involvement with the Ethiopians ashore, who were fighting on the side of the Portuguese. By the mid sixteenth century the Ottoman aim had been vitiated by the presence of Portuguese carracks mounted with heavy artillery. The Ottomans had to be content with the defensive success of keeping the Portuguese out of the Red Sea and out of Arabia, having pushed their southern boundary as far as the third Nile cataract, where it remained until 1853.

Gàbor Àgoston (Budapest) drew attention to the longer term, internal disadvantages from which the Ottoman Empire was suffering, with reference to the prohibited market in war materials. The retreat from the contest in the Indian Ocean was a symptom of the fact that

> the Ottoman war industry was no longer able to compete with its European rivals, not only in the fields of war industry, technology and know-how, but in infra-structure and state patronage.

The Turks had been using firearms since the close of the fourteenth century, and had adapted European weaponry and artillery. However, there were difficulties in production levels and stock piling, and these were of Turkish origin, not, as some have suggested, the result of a fall in European exports of war materials, such as gunpowder.

Here and there, the management of decline notched up successes, as in Crete, where, as Molly Greene (Princeton) explained, the Ottomans were more successful than the Venetians in performing anti-piracy duties and expanding agricultural output. Instead of forcing Cretans to the galleys, as the Venetians had done, the Ottomans in the seventeenth century allowed the peasants to get on with their farming and took their seamen from the Cyclades. They also encouraged the French, whose King held privileged status at the Porte, to take over naval policing duties in the eastern Mediterranean.

Alexander de Groot (Leiden) commented on the remarkable maritime Christian-Muslim culture that had grown up by the seventeenth century in the western Mediterranean, with the slave trade as its base. A mixed population of the two religions, many of whom were ex-heretics and Spanish Jews, kept maritime intercourse alive between Algiers, Tunis and Tripoli, as well as providing a skilled manpower transfer to Istanbul. Professor de Groot noted the Dutch captaincy and control of Barbery vessels, and their free entry, during the seventeenth and eighteenth centuries, into the three cities.

While several papers dealt with eighteenth-century trade, 'the sea road towards modernisation', as Professor de Groot called it, was taken more directly by William Blair (Princeton) who introduced 'the Development of the Ottoman Steam Navy in the 19th century'.[7] From the crowds' first welcome, in 1828, to the steamboat *Swift* to the extraordinary efforts to expand shipping engineering skills of the 1890s, there is the impression that neither client (Turkey) nor supplier (Britain) had the experience or will needed for success. New warships rolled so much that their guns were awash; by 1914 two-thirds of naval tonnage was still of sailing ships.

The desire to maintain the regime's prestige was the starting point for further difficulties with the submarine deterrent, which 'would render the Straits impregnable against attack by the most formidable iron clad fleet in the world'. A little incongruously, perhaps, an English clergyman, the Rev. George W. Garrett, was in charge of the trials of the two submarines, one named after the reigning Sultan, Abdulhamid II (1876-1908). Konstantin Zhukov (St Petersburg) told the Conference, 'their crews deserted as fast as they were recruited. At last the boats were left to rust away at Constantinople'.

Kaori Komatsu (Tsukuba) discussed the reign of Abdulhamid II, the so-called 'Dark Age of the Ottoman Navy', from the financial standpoint. At the close of the nineteenth century the government was heavily in debt; this was not so much owing to the inability of the Sultan to pay the costs of his own navy as that

> the technological innovation of this era made the Navy such an expensive force; the rebuilding of the Navy was closely related to the economic power of the nation.

Economic power, growing in some sectors, did not furnish the State with resources enough to maintain a modern sea power. The crisis of Ottoman power showed up in the reduction of its war budget by five-sixths between 1885 and 1895; of this, the naval share was one quarter.

In discussion, Eugene Rogan (Oxford) asked a question which was fundamental: did the Ottomans need a navy at all? The Conference offered no direct answer, but perhaps the implied thinking was that certainly a merchant navy was needed, but an iron-clad war fleet was a risky luxury. History might have suggested hiring, leasing, or reliance on one or more of the industrialised powers.

In closing the Conference, Geoffrey Lewis (Oxford) thanked the Director of the Skilliter Centre for Ottoman Studies for convening it; fascinating new areas of study for maritime research had been revealed, and new directions suggested for work on the Ottomans and the sea.

References

1 It is hoped to publish the proceedings of the Conference in due course.
2 Palmira Brummett, *Ottoman Seapower and Levantine Diplomacy in the Age of Discovery* (New York, 1994), 17.
3 Place of speaker's institute or university in brackets.
4 This writer's interpolation; see concluding paragraphs.
5 Brummett, 13.
6 Halal Inalcik with Donald Quataert (eds), *An Economic and Social History of the Ottoman Empire* (Cambridge, 1994), 323.
7 See the review of *The Ottoman Steam Navy* in *M.M.*, 81 (1995), p.497.

C.D. LEE
Oxford

SIXTH ANGLO-FRENCH CONFERENCE OF NAVAL HISTORIANS, JULY 1996

The spectacular campus of the University of Exeter was the venue for the sixth Anglo-French Conference of Naval Historians which assembled on 2 July 1996. From France came 25 delegates, from the United Kingdom 30, two from the U.S.A. and one from Canada. The theme of the Conference in this biennial series was 'Anglo-French Naval Co-operation through the Ages', a theme which (perhaps surprisingly) provided subjects for the presentation of 27 papers, 13 from France and 14 from Britain. The texts of some of the papers by French delegates were not available by the time this article went to press (and I was not commissioned to write this account until some days after the Conference).

Comment on them will not therefore be included but the subjects and their authors are listed at the end.

We began in the year 1204 with Susan Rose's paper 'Bayonne and the King's Ships 1204-1420' reminding us that in that year what is now southwestern France came under direct English rule on the death of Eleanor of Aquitaine. The use of Bayonne-built and -manned ships against the Welsh and the Scots would certainly come within the strict terminology of Anglo-French co-operation, but we were also told that these ships formed part of the English fleet which defeated the French at Sluys in 1340. Somewhat closer co-operation came during the Wars of Religion in the 1560s when what Nicholas Rodger described as 'a combined Calvinist fleet' of English and French Huguenot ships operated out of Plymouth and La Rochelle against Catholic, and especially Spanish, ships. Even so, the English participation was informal and Queen Elizabeth's support discreet.

A hundred years later, as David Davies told us, French and English ships fought together as a combined fleet against the Dutch (initially under the overall command of the future King James II), and the French fleet made use of the store houses and repair yards at Chatham but had to pay for them. However, despite careful planning to ensure the tactical compatibility of the two fleets, the battles of Solebay (1672) and Texel (1673) were not a success for the allies.

It was of no surprise that the period 1688 to 1815 was passed over in all but silence, though we were treated to an interesting paper by Patricia Crimmin on the relatively humane treatment of French prisoners-of-war in Britain during the Napoleonic wars; and H.J.K. Jenkins spoke on the somewhat limited British assistance to French Royalists in the Caribbean in the early years of the French Revolution.

The theme of the Conference then moved to the period following the defeat of Napoleon. Only four years after Waterloo there was a surprising act of co-operation which received only a passing reference. In 1819, at the behest of the Congress of the Great Powers at Aix-la-Chapelle, the French and British Commanders-in-Chief in the Mediterranean, escorted by their squadrons, joined forces to deliver representations to the rulers of Algiers, Tunis and Tripoli urging them yet again to suppress their corsairs from committing piracy. They met with little success.

On a larger and more effective scale was the Franco-British liberation of Montevideo from the Argentine dictator, General Rosas, in 1845, described to us by Professeur Avenal. The battle of Obligado that year contributed largely to 'the revival of the tarnished reputation of the French Navy after its defeats under Napoleon I', as the professor put it; but this time the British were their allies.

The Crimean War of 1854-6 was perhaps the first major war in history in which France and Britain were allies, and the omens were good when early in the war, as Michelle Battisti told us, the French named a new steam-powered floating battery the *Congreve* after the English inventor in the Baltic of the rocket. Bomarsund in the Baltic was soon captured by 10,000 French soldiers conveyed in British transports, and supported by a predominantly British bombarding fleet. In the Black Sea the long siege of Sevastopol produced some difficulties between the allies but success was eventually achieved.

Giving us a break from war Andrew Lambert sketched the career of Sir John Knox Laughton, 'the pioneer of naval history, strategy and doctrine', whose studies of French naval history were critical to his work and played 'a major part in the intellectual renaissance of the Royal Navy in the 1890s'. These studies included biographical essays on such heroes of the French Navy as Jean Bart, Duguay-Trouin, Suffren and Surcouf.

Martín Motte followed with a vivid survey of Franco-British naval relations in the second half of the nineteenth century, drawn from the unpublished memoirs of Vice-Amiral Édouard Barrera. As a young officer he served in both the Baltic and the Black Sea during the Crimean War and made friends with the British when calling on his way to China at Ascension Island, Simonstown, Singapore and Hong Kong. In China he took part in the Anglo-French occupation of Canton in 1857 which followed the Chinese seizure of a British trading ship. In the next year he was in the combined fleet which captured the forts of Tientsin. For this operation the French and British admirals flew their flags together in a British gun-boat. Forty years later during a particularly low period of relationships between our two countries, Vice-Amiral Barrera was C-in-C at Brest when the British liner *Drum-*

mond Castle was wrecked off Ushant in June 1896 with the loss of 245 passengers and crew. For his services in organising the search for survivors (there were only three) and his help to bereaved British families he was made a KCVO by Queen Victoria.

This first day of the Conference concluded with two short papers, one English by Mary Cross and one French by Jean-Philippe Dumas, on the cordial arrangements for the formation in 1888 of the Anglo-French Naval Commission charged with the joint government of the New Hebrides in the eastern Pacific. In 1906 the islands became the Anglo-French Condominium of the New Hebrides, and in 1980 the Republic of Vanuatu.

Delegates reassembled later in the evening for the Conference Dinner in the elegant surroundings of the University Refectory, with the Flag Officer Sea Training, Rear-Admiral Peter Franklyn, as our guest of honour.

Wednesday morning opened with three papers on Scientific co-operation. Rear-Admiral Roger Morris's paper on 'Co-operation in Exploration and Cartography to the end of the 18th century' began with a reference to the first book in English on hydrography which was written for Henry VIII in 1542 by a Frenchman from Dieppe, Jean Rotz. Such co-operation as there was during the rest of the century was with French Huguenots off Spanish America. The latter half of the seventeenth century saw the exchange of scientific papers between the Academie des Sciences and the Royal Society, collaboration in efforts to solve the problem of determining longitude, and in observing the transit of Venus across the sun. In the eighteenth century, despite the wars in Europe, explorers in the Pacific and Australia exchanged information and freely aided each other. This was specially so between Nicolas-Thomas Baudin and Matthew Flinders, though the latter's obstinacy subsequently led to his six years under arrest on the Île de France, now called Mauritius.

Ingénieur Général Pasquay, in a masterly survey of the co-operation between the Hydrographic Departments of the two countries since the Napoleonic wars, was able to say that at a local level co-operation began in the Mediterranean between Captains Smyth and Gauttier-Duparc as early as 1816. In subsequent decades ships of the two navies exchanged hydrographic information on the coasts of Africa, South America, the Caribbean, the Arctic, indeed wherever the ships met. Relationships between the Hydrographic Offices in Paris and London became equally close. Inevitably this cooled off during the tensions between the two countries towards the end of the century, but were restored with the onset of the 1914-18 war. In 1919 France and Britain were together instrumental in the formation of the International Hydrographic Bureau. Moving to the post-1945 period Pasquay reviewed in detail the increasing co-operation of the two Hydrographic Services in the age of sonars and satellites.

Jean-Pierre Descendres then told the moving story of a young French naval officer, Joseph-René Bellot, whose interest in arctic exploration was such that he persuaded Lady Franklin to support his application to join a British expedition in search of Sir John Franklin and his comrades. In 1851 he sailed as second-in-command of the British schooner *Prince Albert*, but after enduring the long arctic winter and many privations the ship returned to Scotland without success. In 1853 Bellot sailed again on another British expedition but lost his life when crossing a crevasse, aged twenty-seven.

Technological Interchange was the theme of the next two papers. The co-operation between the years 1670 and 1820 on which Davd Roberts spoke was, at best, covert, and certainly 'involuntary' on the part of the English. The period saw about a dozen missions by French spies sent to England to discover how her ships were built. Surprisingly, despite the great quantity of detail – plans, models, tools, drawings, measurements etc. – which the spies brought safely back to France, their efforts had only a very minor influence on French shipbuilding design or practice. Even so, by the end of the Napoleonic wars the French believed their ships to be inferior to the British, a view which was not held by the latter.

David Brown of the Royal Corps of Naval Instructors (which itself was based on the Corps du Génie Maritime) described the close co-operation of the two navies in ship design during the nineteenth century, even during the later years when France and Britain were potential enemies. Joint sailing trials were held in 1832 and visits were subsequently exchanged between naval architects of the two nations when much confidential information was disclosed. A par-

ticularly close friendship grew up between William White and de Bussy in the 1870s which influenced some aspects of the designs of British ships built in the following decade.

The theme of the Conference then moved to the period when the two countries were allies in two world wars. Sadly, the paper by Professor Paul Halpern (speaking with the detachment of an American scholar) on 'Anglo-French Co-operation in the Mediterranean Anti-Submarine Campaign, 1914-1918' showed that the one thing which was lacking throughout the war in that theatre was *real* co-operation, particularly at Admiral level. Nevertheless, as Halpern said, 'it worked within limitations, and one must always re-iterate that on the whole it was closer and less acrimonious than Franco-Italian co-operation'. In contrast, as is so often the case, co-operation between individual ships and flotillas was better.

A happier example of Anglo-French co-operation during this war, albeit on a small scale, was described by Jock Gardner in his paper 'Protection of the Channel Coal Trade, 1917-1918' – coal from British pits to French factories. In these two years over 32 million tons of coal were conveyed in escorted convoys to France with a loss of only 54 colliers out of 39,000 channel crossings. The initiative for this operation came primarily from France, its execution primarily from Britain.

He was followed by David Brown of the Naval Historical Branch on Naval Staff planning and co-operation in 1939 and early 1940; to some extent this was confounded by the much tighter centralisation in the French navy which allowed little or no discretion to Commanders-in-Chief. He then described the attempts by the British War Cabinet in June 1940 to persuade Marshal Pétain not to allow the French fleet to fall into the hands of the Germans.

No text is available of Georges Lesourd's paper 'La coopération navale franco-britannique entre le 17 Juin 1940 et le 7 Mai 1945'. Some of these years were bedevilled by tragedies and misunderstandings; but for my part I can personally testify to the very close co-operation between a large French force and two RN ships (in one of which I had the honour to be serving) which culminated in the liberation of the great naval port of Toulon in August 1944.

There are also no texts for the two French papers on the period 1945 to 1956; and the final paper of the Conference – 'Naval Collaboration in Procurement, 1950 to the present' by Peter Hore – is marked 'Not for publication'.

However, this does not mean that I can yet put down my pen. Those who could stay on for Thursday had a great treat in store for them, of which we had a foretaste after dinner on Wednesday. Although it was the fifteenth lecture of the day, not an eyelid dropped during Michael Duffy's enthralling talk on the history of Devonport Dockyard from its foundation in 1690. The tour the next day, with Dr Duffy as our enthusiastic guide, began at the former Royal Naval Hospital, Stonehouse, built in the 1760s and hardly altered externally apart from bomb damage. In the South Yard, now mostly an open-air museum, the tour included a building-slip of 1776 with its roof added in 1814, the eighteenth-century ropewalk, and the remains of the original officers' terrace of the seventeenth century. After lunch in the Wardroom of H.M.S. *Drake* we visited the nineteenth-century North Yard (the Royal Navy's first purpose-built steam yard) containing the late twentieth-century covered frigate refit complex and the docks where Britain's Trident submarines will be refitted in the twenty-first century. It was an absorbing day, so much so that it was not until supper-time that the two American professors in the group remembered that the date was the Fourth of July.

The gratitude of all delegates must go to Dr Michael Duffy for the much admired way in which he conducted our affairs, to Iain Mackenzie for undertaking the administration so flawlessly, and to the University of Exeter for all those facilities necessary for a successful conference.

It is hoped that all the papers delivered at the Conference will be published by the University of Exeter Press within the next two years.

Appendix

Papers read at the Conference of which the texts were not available at the time this article went to press:

A. Kroell, 'La coopération franco-anglaise en Asie au XVIIème siècle'.

C. Beyeler, 'L'expédition navale franco-britannique aux Pays-Bas (1832)'.

J-P. Dumas, 'La coopération navale franco-britannique aux Nouvelles-Hébrides (1881-1906)'.

P. Masson, 'La coopération navale franco-britannique de la fin des années trente (1930s)'.

P-A. Comor, 'La coopération navale franco-britannique dans la campagne de Norvège (avril-juin 1940): le point de vue français'.

G. Lesourd, 'La coopération navale franco-britannique entre le 17 juin 1940 et le 7 mai 1945'.

C. Sanderson, 'La coopération navale franco-britannique de 1948 à 1951'.

P. Vial, 'La coopération franco-britannique à l'Ecole de Guerre navale (1945-1956)'.

CAPTAIN HUGH OWEN, RN
Chichester

QUERIES

15. (1996) AN UNKNOWN CANNON The Museum of History and Industry (MOHAI), in conjunction with Puget Sound Maritime Historical Society (PSMHS) of Seattle, Washington, U.S.A., desires information on a bronze cannon in the MOHAI collection. The gun bears, *in intaglio*, the legend DELAVERIA, the date ANO 1572; and aft of that, the markings XIQ/XIQ, which is followed by a peculiar scroll symbol for which a sketch has been provided (**Fig. 1**). The letters are 15mm. high in simple block form, almost sans serif. The gun is 2.44m. long overall, with the outer diameter of the tube 0.14m. at the muzzle, and 0.24m. at the breech. The bore appears to be 70-75mm., but was diffi-

Fig. 1. The mark from a rubbing.

cult to measure due to some damage. It is of plain design, with only simple, stepped reinforcing bands at the muzzle; at 1.235m. from the muzzle (where the OD is stepped 25mm. with the same taper for the remainder of the length); and at the breech. Aft of the breech, the gun curves in a classic bell shape to a ridged ball finial at the end. Hoisting eyes (the left is broken off) are in the form of a scroll, and terminate in fiddle scrolls where the ends meet short posts on the barrel. Trunions are 0.173m. in diameter at 1.31m. from the muzzle. Condition of the gun is good, with only a crackle of scarring no more than 1mm. deep on all surfaces, and it has a lustrous brown patina. The bore is clear for 2.07m.

MOHAI and PSMHS desire information on the origin of the gun; the vessel or class of vessel on which it could have been originally mounted; and informed speculation on how it could have journeyed from its origin to its final resting place in the Hudson River at New York, from which it was dredged in 1942. MOHAI curators would also be interested in recommendations for conservation of this artifact, and illustrations of a typical gun carriage of the period on which the gun could be mounted for exhibition. We also desire to know if the curious mark illustrated is a founder's mark or a proof mark. It does not appear to be accidental, for it has the same height, depth, and groove form as the lettering.

Researchers here believe the gun to have a weight of shot of 11 quintals; and that the piece may have been a 'pasavolante'.
CAROL D. GREENE
Puget Sound Maritime Historical Society
Seattle, U.S.A.

16. (1996) WHY TUMBLEHOME? The vast majority of sailing ships, at least from the medieval period to the mid nineteenth century, seem to have been built with a marked degree of tumblehome. Why was this?

I have heard a variety of reasons suggested: that it enabled shorter deck beams to be used (but there seems to have been no difficulty in getting longer ones for the lower decks); that the chains securing the shrouds might be inboard of the waterline and thus reduce the probabilities of damage when coming alongside (yet such ships, especially warships, usually lay at anchor and, in any case, the simplest of fenders would have prevented this); that projectiles would be deflected upwards (nonsense); and so on. I find all these suggestions to be profoundly unrealistic and implausible, yet experts I have consulted

seem never to have considered the question thoroughly.

My own belief – for which I have no evidence – is that it was based on an entirely fallacious idea of enhancing stability, taking parallels from buildings ashore. In an age when the concept of the metacentre was known only to theoreticians, and hardly at all to shipwrights (I speak of late eighteenth century onwards) this seems more likely. After all, we know now that it is flare rather than tumblehome that enhances stability, by enabling the immersed wedge of a cross-section to exceed the area of the emerging one. I doubt that they did.
RICHARD GOSS
MASTS
UWCC
Cardiff

17. (1996) RECORDING A SHIP'S LINES: the Gauss rule. Austin Farrar's fascinating article in the May issue (*M.M.*, 82, pp.216-22) reminds me of a story from my student days. In learning the rules for numerical integration, then a vital feature of naval architecture, we learnt of the Simpson rules with evenly spaced ordinates and unequal multipliers, of Tchebycheff with a constant multiplier but unevenly spaced ordinates, very convenient for mechanical integration, and Gauss with uneven ordinates and unequal multipliers. For any given degree of accuracy, the Gauss rule would define a curve with the smallest number of ordinates and, so we were taught, was used in taking off the lines of prize ships in dock. I have never seen this story referred to since and wonder if any reader can throw light upon it.

For example, a fifth order parabola could be defined by 5 Simpson or Tchebycheff ordinates but only 3 at Gauss spacing. These would be amidships and at 0.7746L either side of amidships.
DAVID K. BROWN, RCNC
Bath

18. (1996) CROSS-CHANNEL MAIL 1793-1815 Throughout the Revolutionary and Napoleonic Wars there was a continuous flow of non-diplomatic correspondence both ways. Broadly, this consisted of private letters, financial transfers and official mail. Much of the first category at the British end came from prisoners of war and so was subject to the approval of the Admiralty

Transport Board and its agents. In France there were additional to British prisoners a large number of tourists caught by the resumption of war in 1803. The potential volume of this two-way correspondence was substantial. Financial transfers seem to have been relatively easy. Two months was cited in 1806 as the time it took a bank in Avignon to remit money via its London correspondents to recipients in Tiverton in Devon. There is also the likelihood that British banks transmitted money to France on behalf of neutral clients. Direct dealings with subordinate enemy authorities were not unusual. The Transport Board itself enquired of the Maire of a French town if a privateer captain with an Irish name was a native of that town. The reply being satisfactory the officer was put on parole instead of on trial for treason.

It is generally assumed that mail was sent via smugglers, notably by the famous 'guinea galleys'. If so, and there is no obvious alternative, it must have been an organised service which delivered mail bags to the representatives of both Post Offices and which ran the whole year round. Since the French free ports for smugglers were available in war as well as peacetime they may have taken the lead by choosing certain vessels as carriers. Who was responsible at this end? Did the British smugglers get any formal or informal protection for their contraband cargo when carrying mail? In short, how was the whole thing run?

ADRIAN REED
Uffculme, Devon

19. (1996) S/Y *TOFTEVAAG* The photograph **below** was taken at the International Marina at Torrevieja, Alicante Province, in Spain. A few brief questions asked of the Marina's Operations Director produced the following scant but interesting intelligence.

S/Y *Toftevaag* was built in Norway in 1910 as a fishing vessel, and worked principally in the waters around the North Cape. From 1930 onwards she was used for trading between the Norwegian fiords, and she also traded into the Baltic. In 1940, after the German invasion of Norway, she was siezed by the Kriegsmarine and was used for the transport of pilots throughout the war, which she apparently survived undamaged. In 1979 S/Y *Toftevaag* was purchased by her present Norwegian owner, and was refitted and restored to reflect her original 1910 condition.

Clearly this vessel is an unusual survivor of the Second World War, though by no means unique of course. I would be very interested in any information on the small ship's wartime service (I do not know if she operated under her name, or was 'numbered' and 'classed'), her station and any armament she may have carried. It would be particularly important to discover if the

Toftevaag was one of the large fleet of coastal craft operated by Transportflotte Speer in the period between late 1941 and 1944, sailing between the ports of Bergen, Stavanger and Lubeck.

ROBERT MORGAN
Secretary, Welsh Maritime Association
Morriston, Swansea

ANSWERS

6. (1995) RN SHORE ESTABLISHMENTS IN SW IRELAND 1900-1938 I do not think that the establishments in the south-west of Ireland at the beginning of the century actually carried names – they would have used the base or depot ship at the port as a 'parent establishment'. A list of these may be found in Lt-Cdr Warlow's *Shore Establishments of the Royal Navy* (Liskeard, 1992). Dittmar and Colledge's standard work on First World War warships, *British Warships 1914-1919* (London, 1972) contains details of all ships, including harbour service craft in use during the period, and I would draw Mr Rathbone's attention to both of these works. No Royal Navy ships are listed as serving in Ireland after 1923.

The main ships which formed the Queenstown establishment were the *Emerald* (ex-*Black Prince*) and the *Colleen* (ex-*Royalist*), which served at that port from 1899 to 1923. The *Ambrose* and *Vulcan* that he believed were the 'Berehaven establishment' were acting as depot ships for the submarine flotillas based in Ireland at the end of the war. As for the other vessels he mentions as being associated with Queenstown, all were old sailing warships, hulked for use at the port during the nineteenth century – most for service as receiving ships, although the old *Surprise* served as a convict hulk. A list of the ships, extracted from Cdr Warlow's work, is reproduced below:

QUEENSTOWN

Base & depot ships:
Royalist from Feb. 1900, renamed *Colleen* 1913; transferred to the Irish government 1923 (screw corvette of 1883)
Medusa tender to Colleen 1915-1919 (2nd class cruiser of 1888)

Training ships:
Aeolus 1903-1905 (2nd class cruiser 1891)

Emerald 1890-1904 (ex-*Black Prince* armoured frigate 1861)

Guardships:
Black Prince 1866-1867 (armoured frigate 1861)
Mersey 1867-1872 (screw frigate 1858)
Revenge 1872-1890 (steam powered 2nd rate 1859)
Triumph 1890-1893 (armoured ship 1870)
Warspite 1893-1896 (armoured cruiser 1884)
Empress of India 1901-1902 (battleship 1891)
Aeolus 1902-1903 (cruiser 1891)
Hood 1910-1913 (battleship 1891)
Endymion 1913-1914 (cruiser 1891)

Coastguard depot ships:
Hawke 1857-1865 (screw blockship 1855)
Frederick William 1865-1866 (screw 1st rate 1860)
Devastation 1885-1890 (turret ship 1871)
Howe 1897-1901 (battleship 1885)

Other ships:
Wolf coaling hulk 1866-1878
Alarm coaling hulk 1880-1895
Saint Patrick tank vessel 1917-1923; transferred to Irish government 1923

CORK

Receiving and guardships:
Trent 1818-1823 (5th rate 1796)
Crocodile 1850-1861 (6th rate 1825)
Actaeon 1866-1889 (6th rate 1831)

Other ships:
Surprise convict hulk 1822-1837 (5th rate 1812; although ordered sold in 1837 apparently survived until 1845)

BANTRY

Coastguard depot ships:
Valiant 1868-1885 (armoured ship 1863)
Shannon 1885-1893 (iron frigate 1875)

Aurora 1893-1895 (armoured cruiser 1887)
Dreadnought 1895-1897 (battleship 1875)
Collingwood 1897-1903 (battleship 1882)
Devastation 1898 (turret ship 1871)

BEREHAVEN

Depot ships, both supported the local submarine flotilla:
Ambrose 1917-1918 (1903 merchant vessel purchased 1915)
Vulcan 1917-1919 (depot ship 1889)

DAVID HEPPER
Enfield
Middlesex

17. (1995) WHY 'ON', NOT 'IN'? I was interested to read this query in the August 1995 issue of *M.M.* As a former Merchant Service officer who was in H.M.S. *Conway* before joining The Union-Castle Mail S.S. Co. Ltd. in 1948, I always referred to one being *in* a ship, never *on*: I would however observe that some people did say *on* a ship, though I am of the opinion they tended to be those who went straight to sea.

Captain R.F. Chapman RN seems to have stirred up the question, which was raised in September 1913 and was reasonably answered by Mr Ernest Richards, in Vol. III No. 12 (December 1913) on p.377, wherein he stated 'a genuine merchant seaman *never* says "on" but "in" a ship: he always began a yarn by saying "I was in a ship..." or "in the old...".

L.A. HASLETT
Hotwells, Bristol

17. (1995) WHY 'ON', NOT 'IN'? As one of a number of Naval recruits in 1942, I was instructed that I would be serving *in* a ship in the sense of serving *in* a ship's company; just as a soldier would be serving *in* his regiment. It had nothing to do with location but embraced forthcoming loyalties and obligations. Perhaps the reason for Joseph Conrad's anger at the use of *on* a ship suggested to him ignorance of these senses of belonging to and duties towards others.

WILLIAM M. BALL
Torquay

9. (1996) THE DEVIL AND BRUSSELS GAZETTE A version of *Heart of Oak*, probably written by Garrick, appeared at the end of Tobias Smollett's play *The Reprisal* in 1757 and Garrick revived it

for his own play *Harlequin's Invasion*, a celebration of Hawke's success in 1759.

Certainly that year was much more of an 'annus mirabilis' than 1757 had been, when Smollett felt that he had to try to revive public morale after the loss of Minorca and the execution of Byng.[1] But 1756, 1759 and indeed 1803 each saw a situation where flat-bottomed invasion barges were being built and collected in various French Channel ports, resulting in a state of some trepidation in London with the usual jingoistic reactions.

Garrick's friend Hogarth provides us with examples of such a reaction in his two 'Invasion' engravings of 1756 which show the French seeking to impose their religion on the English, thus presumably assisting the work of the devil.[2] The captions were written by Garrick and we may note the reference to 'hands and hearts of Oak' as Liberty's best defence. The portrayal of Louis XV as a caricature figure also seems to anticipate Garrick's play in which the villain as a French clown is helped by devils.

A 'gazette' in mid eighteenth-century usage was a news-sheet but when the name of a capital city was appended to it the suggestion was that it represented the official view of a particular government or nation, hence the London Gazette, the Paris Gazette, etc.[3] The gazette from Brussels, the principal city of the Austrian Netherlands, was in 1757 the most immediate source of offical Austrian views: Britain's former ally having recently entered into an alliance with France, thus increasing the threat of invasion by raising the possibility of French troops moving into Austrian positions in the Netherlands.[4] The news of Frederick of Prussia's defeat at Kolin and the raising of the siege of Prague would also provide the Austrians with welcome news for their gazette in 1757. Even in 1759 the Brussels 'Gazette' was still trying to sound confident, announcing on 18 November the imminent invasion of England.[5]

For your correspondent Captain Moore's purposes, I should recommend *Quiberon Bay* by Geoffrey Marcus (1960), especially Chapter 20 which contains much useful information on Garrick's song.

References

1 C.N. Robinson, *The British Tar in Fact and Fiction* (1909), 229-30.

2 S. Shesgreen, ed., *Engravings by Hogarth* (1973), 90, 91.

3 *Oxford English Dictionary*.

4 J. Corbett, *England in the Seven Years War* Vol. 1 (1907), , 195.

5 G. Marcus, *Quiberon Bay* (1960), 169.

T.M. CONWAY
Rowlands Gill
Tyne & Wear

9. (1996) THE DEVIL AND BRUSSELS GAZETTE In response to Query No. 9 in *M.M.* 1996, I am sure that there are those who know a lot more about this than I do, but I feel I should contribute. In the book *Quiberon Bay* by Geoffrey Marcus (Hollis & Carter, London, 1960), at p.173 the four verses of *Heart of Oak* are quoted. It was the culmination of a stage piece entitled *The Harlequin's Invasion*, written for Christmas (1759) at Drury Lane. The pantomime included 'many a Devil in a flame colour'd Stocking' on the French side to assist in an invasion of England. This presumably accounts for the devil in the last verse. As for the newspaper, Marcus writes (p.171):

The dismay of the French at the defeat of the expedition on which all their hopes had been set was reflected in the intelligences which presently flowed in from the Continent. Even our inveterate opponent, the Brussels *Gazette*, appeared to have lost much of its aplomb.

From this I conclude that it was a contemporary newspaper noted for its slanted journalism.

Marcus cites as his references for the song the *Universal Magazine* of March 1760, pp.152-3, and other works which presumably refer to the life of Garrick.

COLIN JONES
Middle Park
Victoria, Australia

10. (1996) HOLYSTONING As a Port Line apprentice in the late 1950s and so representative of perhaps one of the last group of seafarers to be regularly engaged in holystoning, I can answer Frank Garie's query with some degree of authority.

Even in the late 1960s refrigerated cargo-passenger liners in the Australian trade were still widely fitted throughout with wood-sheathed decks, for both aesthetic and practical reasons, which included a measure of insulation over accommodation and cargo spaces.

It was my understanding that holystoning achieved all of the functions mentioned, by effectively taking off a thin layer of dead wood, which was discernible as a fibrous residue after the process was completed. After this, decks (if other than teak) were then sometimes treated with raw linseed oil, perhaps tinted with a little red lead powder.

Holystones (and small handstones for awkward corners) were used on decks wetted with fresh water and in conjunction with loose sand and a patent fluid such as 'Atlas' or 'Climax' or caustic solution, the stones being used with the grain of the wood. A similar but less effective process known as 'barkerising' consisted of wetting the decks, applying sand and 'Atlas' or 'Climax', then scrubbing the decks vigorously with stiff deck brooms. On occasions heavy steel-wire brooms known as 'bears' were used and these could shave off minor damage. I believe that in Indian-crew ships the sand-filled halves of the outer husks of coconuts were used in lieu of stones.

In response to Mr Garie's comment re brass polishing, I suggest most seamen do not consider this a useless chore, and the bell and ports in my ship are polished daily, 'reflecting' tradition and pride in the ship's appearance.

CAPTAIN JAS. W. MARTIN FNI
Master mv *European Pathway*
St Margarets Bay
Dover

10. (1996) HOLYSTONING In reply to Frank Garie's enquiry in May 1996, I can assure him that the holystoning of wooden decks was carried on at sea well into the 1970s, when scrubbing with heavy long-handled scrubbing brushes called bears, using detergents, took over – with electric rotary deck scrubbers coming into general use in passenger liners.

Even today sailors take a pride in their ships and the cleaning of decks – and polishing of brass – are certainly not considered 'useless chores'. A clean, well maintained ship has always been happier and more efficient than a scruffy one (provided the crew are, of course, also decently fed, led and cared for by captain, officers and senior hands).

A block of sandstone approximately 14 x 8 x 8 inches was so called, I believe, because a man using it knelt down to obtain maximum purchase and this position made him look as though he were at his prayers. I have holystoned a constricted area, a wheelhouse's deck for instance, in this way when I was a cadet, the deck being first sprinkled with sand. For open deck areas the long-handled version was used, consisting of a steel rectangular frame bolted round the stone, with a 7 foot steel handle. Procedure was: the bosun pre-wetted the deck by wielding the seawater hose, then walked ahead of the crowd (six or seven sailors) sprinkling sand from a bucket. The long-handled holystones swung into action along the planks then, often to what I suppose amounted to a modern chanty. Afterwards – and this was nearly always a pre-breakfast job – the sand was swept up for recycling and the decks hosed down, excess water being squeegeed off by the bosun.

Holystoning in this fashion was performed on a regular basis at sea, usually once weekly with a scrub or 'barbarise' on the other five mornings. In consequence the decks gleamed smooth and white, all whiskers and slivers of timber removed. Incidentally, the mate's large, comprehensive store book, submitted to the company's stores controller twice a year, included the item 'Sand, fine, for decks'. This was supplied in sacks though it was not unusual for the ship's motorboat to be sent round to a nearby beach in such ports as Fremantle or Port Adelaide to 'obtain' a few sacks. Good excuse for a swim.

Sand is still carried today, though in steel-decked vessels it is kept ready to use in cement boxes, those universal short-term remedies to a damaged pipe or other crack in the steelwork. I have seen a cement box applied to a place under the forecastle head when a crack appeared at the always-vulnerable point where hawspipe pierces shell plating and that same cement box was still in situ effectively sealing the crack when the ship was sold for further trading twenty years later.
CAPTAIN A.W. KINGHORN
Cullercoats
North Shields

10. (1996) HOLYSTONING Newly worked wood, when exposed to the sun, changes colour – teak going from light brown to silvery grey, other woods darkening down. Holystoning was similar to sand papering and kept the surface of the wood smooth and looking new by removing the 'dead' wood from the surface of the deck. It also removed any blemishes caused by working cargo, and in power-driven vessels holystoning was used to remove stains caused by funnel soots.

'Mufflestones' were also used for scrubbing decks. These were ordinary holystones with coir doormats tied to the bottom, bristles down. For badly marked decks 'bears' were used. A bear had a handle attached to an iron frame, weighing about 40 lbs, and into this frame could be slotted a brush of very stiff natural bristles or wire bristles.

Another method of cleaning wooden decks was to 'barbarise' them. To barbarise a deck it was first wetted down with a solution of caustic soda, or a branded chemical such as Atlas or Climax, sand was sprinkled on it and it was scrubbed vigorously with deck scrubbers. If the solution was too strong the deck could be 'burned' and become stained brown.

In the Merchant Service by the middle of this century it had become practice to call all shipside rails fitted with a wooden cap taffrails. In many companies taffrails were varnished, but in others it was preferred to keep them plain wood. To keep the unvarnished rails looking good they were 'sand and canvased'. The rail was wetted and then wet canvas sprinkled with sand was rubbed along the rail to remove 'dead' wood.

In the company in which I served my apprenticeship decks were holystoned to keep them looking good, but it was also an exercise that only seemed to be carried out by the apprentices. I cannot recollect having seen even a deck boy holystoning let alone an AB, and the apprentices only seemed to be turned to holystoning when we had incurred the Mate's displeasure.
SIMON WAITE
sv *Cutty Sark*
Greenwich, London

10. (1996) HOLYSTONING Years ago my colleagues, Dunkirk pilots, sent me to Bembridge (IOW) to fetch a 40 ft glass fibre pilot launch, designed by Peter Thornycroft. Our station was then the first in France to trust that new fabric. On arrival I found out that we would be delayed. Be it in France or in the United Kingdom, shipyards would always be shipyards and I would

never be back to my home port station in less than a week.

In the meantime Peter was driving me around, showing me points of interest which he knew so well. I remember his telling me that in the past, close to the shore, there stood an old, desecrated chapel made of whitish, chalky stones. Naval vessels used to anchor thereabouts, and boat-swains to send beach parties in pinnaces to load 'Holy' stones with which Jack Tar would scrub the deck planks and make them as white as ala-baster.

ETIENNE LE CAËR
Nice

CORRESPONDENCE

From Robin Ward:

'A Surviving Charter-Party of 1323' (*M.M.*, Vol. 81 No. 4, p.391)

Alec Tilley's observation (*M.M.*, Vol. 82, No. 2, p.225) that *vin(s) tint* may have meant simply 'red wine' could be perfectly valid. However it does raise the interesting question of what was the colour of imported Bordeaux wines. The charter-party paper was written, it must be ad-mitted, with the assumption that all the wine on the *Saint Mary* was red, or at least reddish, in colour. If the 1 tun 4 pipes, which were somehow different from the rest, had to be specified as 'red', rather than as a 'special red', then the bulk of the wine was white. But was white wine shipped from Bordeaux to England in the four-teenth century?

Margery James, strangely, does not discuss the colour in her definitive work on the Gascon wine trade;[1] the *Calendars of Close* and *of Patent Rolls,* other charter-parties and various refer-ences to Gascon wine in household accounts very rarely mention colour but when they do it is to specify white wine, giving the impression that red was the norm.[2] Hugh Johnson mentions both red and white grapes growing in the four-teenth-century Bordelais but suggests that red wine and *clairet*, a mixture of red and white wine, were better able to withstand the sea voyage and had the body and strength enjoyed by the Eng-lish.[3] Johnson's suggestion echoes a passage in the earlier work of André Simon who attributed the popularity of Gascon wines in England to their lower price, great strength and fine red colour and quotes a poem in which white wine is improved by the addition of red.[4] Perhaps in Giffard's cargo the bulk was *clairet* with 1t 4p of pure red?

N.A.M. Rodger's comments (*M.M.*, Vol. 82, No. 2, p.225) on the language and personnel are most interesting and useful. Foreign going ships' masters such as Walter Giffard must have been at least bi-lingual; those regularly engaged in the Bordeaux trade would perforce have a knowl-edge of Gascon French. Presumably Mauran, himself a Gascon, wrote the agreement in the vernacular which both parties understood? To translate *liberavit* as 'paid', however, does not appear to work too well; Polhowe is already shown as having paid (*de quibus solvuntur*) £46 10s. and the *liberavit* in the next paragraph refers to his acceptance of the 86 tuns of wine and 43 tuns of flour.

Apologies must be made for a mistake in the original paper; on p.393, 6 lines from the bottom, 'gallons' should of course be 'tons'.

References and notes

1 Margery K. James, *Studies in the Medieval Wine Trade* (Oxford, 1971).

2 Two interesting exceptions are the 1,000 tuns of wine, specified as *clairet*, ordered by Edward II for his wedding celebrations in 1307 (Hugh Johnson, *The Story of Wine* [London, 1989], 145) and a licence to Thomas White to re-export Gas-con wine *debilis coloris* which could not be sold in England (*Calendar of Patent Rolls, 1374*).

3 Johnson, *The Story of Wine*, 147, who fur-ther suggests that it was made with the ancestors of the Cabernets and the Merlot grapes in a process similar to the modern *vin d'une nuit* to give an effect perhaps similar to Beaujolais Nou-veau.

4 André L. Simon, *History of the Wine Trade in England* (London, 1906), 261-73, in which he quotes from *la Desputoison du vin et de l'iaue:*

> Les autres vins fet honnorer,//Quant de soi
> [Gascon wine] les veult coulourer;//Force
> donne, aide et confort,.//Et d'un vin foible
> fet un fort;//Il a de vin plaine sustance,//Il

nourrist sans faire grevance;//Aus testes est bons et au flane,//Et du rouge y a et du blanc.

32 Boileau Road
London W5 3AH

From Richard Barker:

The *Liao* and the displacement of ships in the Ming Navy: Defoe's view of Chinese claims, *c.* 1700

A passage in Daniel Defoe's *Farther Adventures of Robinson Crusoe* came to hand when reading André Sleeswyk's article on Chinese shipping (*M.M.*, Vol. 82, pp.3-13). It reveals that scepticism about Chinese claims is much older than supposed by recent discussion of treasure ships, presenting incidents occurring about 1700. One passage loosely concerning shipping is given here from the Dent edition, 1895. Other comments on matters such as the Great Wall and the condition of the Chinese people are even more pointed, albeit literature (even satire) rather than precise commentary (pp.253-5 and 266-8):

> They told me, in particular, of one workman that made a ship, with all its tackle, and masts, and sails, in earthenware, big enough to carry fifty men. If he had told me he launched it, and made a voyage to Japan in it, I might have said something to it indeed; but as it was I knew the whole of the story, which was, in short, asking pardon for the word, that the fellow lied; so I smiled, and said nothing to it.

24 Gordon Road
Borrowash
Derby DE72 3JX

From John F. Coates and David K. Brown:

The *Liao* and the displacement of ships in the Ming Navy

The analysis used by Mr Sleeswyk in the February *M.M.* to relate structural weight to dimensions goes back at least as far as William Froude's 1874 paper to the Institution of Naval Architects. The relationship between weight and length to the third power is valid only for structural members stressed to the acceptable limit by longitudinal bending. There are many structual components which are not involved in longitu-

dinal strength, e.g. transverse bulkheads, and many more which are not stressed to the limit by bending but whose scantlings are set by local strength to which this relationship does not apply.

Coates has shown ('Hogging and Breaking of Frame Built Wooden Ships', *M.M.*, Vol. 71, 1985) that the strength of frame built wooden ships was determined by shear force rather than bending and this is confirmed by Brown's statistical study of early nineteenth-century warships (*Before the Ironclad* [Conway, London, 1990]) where it is shown that structural weight varies as:

Length x Beam + Beam x Depth + Depth x Length

which confirms that loading was not dominated by bending.

D.K. Brown
9 Park Lane
Bath BA1 2XG

John F. Coates
Sabinal,
Luckland Road
Bath BA1 4AU

From Dr Julian de Zulueta:

Health problems of the Royal Navy in the eighteenth century

In the recently published *The Oxford Illustrated History of the Royal Navy* (reviewed in *M.M.*, Vol. 82, pp.376-7) some inaccurate statements are made relating to health problems of the Royal Navy in the eighteenth century, which are significant enough to alert maritime researchers against the danger of being misled.

On p.141, referring to the high mortality suffered by the squadrons of Neville and Hosier in the West Indies, it is stated that 'The cause in both cases was the virulent form of malaria known as "yellow fever"'. This is entirely wrong; in the eighteenth century it was known that they were two different diseases and since the beginning of this century we have known that malaria is produced by blood parasites of the genus *Plasmodium* and yellow fever by a filtrable virus. We also know that the two diseases are transmitted by two entirely different mosquitoes.

On the same page there is also reference to scurvy, and it is said that 'In the mid-1790s, scurvy was tamed by bottled lemon juice'. This is also inexact; lemon juice had been bottled before without solving the problem of scurvy. It was Sir Gilbert Blane who 'tamed' scurvy by adding 10 per cent of spirit of wine, thus preserving the vitamin in the lemon juice issued to the men on board ship with their daily issue of grog. This was first done in Lord Rodney's fleet in the West Indies and later, in 1795, throughout the Royal Navy.

It is surprising that such errors and omissions have appeared in a book so brilliantly presented by the Oxford University Press, and it is hoped that they may be corrected before the book is reprinted.

Casa de Mondragón
Apartado Postal 29
29400 Ronda
(Màlaga)

From Keith McBride:

Lord Fisher's ships and his Baltic Project

I much appreciated Ruddock Mackay's remarks in his Note in *M.M.*, Vol. 82, pp.211-13, but would like to add a few more points. I think that the Admiralty Constructive Department were encouraged to find a possible 'Baltic (or 'Digging the Germans out of their harbours') Roles' for any design where it was possible. The 'Flower' class sloops were intended to sweep for mines ahead of the Grand Fleet, and it was at first intended to armour them. Instead, they were

given a protected magazine aft, triple thickness bow plating, and coal bunkers all round the boiler rooms, which stood them in good stead against mine and torpedo attack. It was hoped that, if 'digging out' were attempted, they could fight the latest German destroyers with their two 3 in. guns; the latter were believed to have only 'two 15 pdrs and four machine guns' (a gross underestimate). I take it that 'digging out' and 'the Baltic project' were one and the same, and that both were largely an attempt to justify the building of ships needed for other purposes (the Monitors?).

In the action of 17 November 1917, quite apart from the question of handling, the four 15 in. apiece of the *Courageous & Glorious* were too few and slow-firing to be effective against light cruisers and destroyers dodging in and out of smoke-screens, while their 4 in. were too short-ranged. Also, being 786 ft long, they were good torpedo targets. Finally, early in the First World War, the idea got about that shallow draught was a good defence against underwater attack – this came out in the early *Hood* studies. I do not know if this was to allow torpedoes and mines to pass under, or to ease damage control if the ship was actually hit.

149 Boston Manor Road
Brentford
Middx
TW8 9LE

REVIEWS

FINANCING THE ATHENIAN FLEET: Public Taxation and Social Relations.
By VINCENT GABRIELSEN.
The John Hopkins University Press, Baltimore and London, 1994.
xvii + 306 *pages*. Price £37.00.
ISBN 0-8018-4692-7.

Vincent Gabrielsen says in his preface that his 'attempt to describe the system of fleet finance employed in classical Athens originated from a belief that a fresh and thorough treatment of the subject has long been needed'. After the first decade of the fifth century B.C. the fleet consisted of triereis until first tetrereis (330/329) and then pentereis (325/4) appeared in the naval inventories. These ships have recently become

more of a physical reality to students of Athenian history; but that has only emphasised the difficulty of understanding how the building, maintenance and manning of a fleet of such complexity and magnitude could have been organised and financed. Gabrielsen's achievement is therefore timely, and certainly a fresh and thorough treatment of the often scanty and usually controversial evidence relevant to his concern, provided by the few passages of the Greek historians, inscriptions preserved incompletely in the naval inventories (440-323/2 B.C.) and the surviving speeches of the Attic orators of the fourth century. His concern is 'the classical Athenian trierarchy and naval finance'. The reader acquainted only with modern navies will be surprised to find how the trierarchos, commander of an Athenian warship (trieres, tetreres or penteres), was responsible for financing the manning, equipment and maintenance as well as the service of his ship.

In Part I Gabrielsen accepts that in the archaic period Athens had a fleet of pentecontors and triacontors, but scorning 'explanations based on etymology' rejects the usual conclusion that the naukrariai, local subdivisions of Attica on the advent of democracy replaced by Kleisthenes with demes, were responsible for it. The appearance of Kleinias at Artemision in 481/0, in a warship of his own with a crew of 200 (hence a trieres) recruited by him, is taken by Gabrielsen as an indication of aristocratic command and ownership of the archaic Athenian fleet. 'Whether they were called naukraroi or had anything to do with naukrariai is unknown.'

Gabrielsen's fresh account of the evolution of the trierarchy is sensible and attractive. He argues that the Athenian fleet of state-owned triereis expanded slowly and that the expansion 'was spurred in 483/2 by the sudden windfall of the silver mines'. He sees the development of the trierarchy as a liturgy (a financial burden imposed by the democracy on the wealthier citizens) happening in the 480s in tune with the liturgies of the dithyramb, tragedy and comedy (502/1, 487/6). The trierarchy was in fact a means of financing the expensive new ships, rather than of finding commanders for them. The trierarchs would have been in the same socio-economic class as the Kleiniases (and the naukraroi?).

Part II discusses the qualifications for the trierarchy and the method of appointment, the length of service and allocation of ships and finally the procedures of exemption, and the hiring out of trierarchies. Part III is concerned with the recruitment, pay and victualling of crews, the funding of the fleet and the cost of service, hulls and equipment. He concludes that the leniency with which the withholding and misappropriation of gear by trierarchs was treated resulted from the democratic government's realisation that liturgical contributions in a year came to more than half the national revenue and that those who qualified as liturgists must be treated gently.

Part IV describes the reforms introduced by Peisander and Demosthenes to lighten the burden on the wealthier class which had caused the

oligarchic movements of 411 and later. The controversial subject of the symmories in this part of the book is difficult reading; but here as throughout the book the reader must admire the author's scholarship, courage and tenacity in attacking a subject which since Boeckh has presented those interested in one of the great navies of history with aspects of great complexity.
JOHN MORRISON
Cambridge

MATERIALIEN ZUM SCHIFFBAU IM ALTEN AGYPEN.
By NORBERT DÜRRING.
Achet Verlag Köpenicker Straße 7 a, D-10997 Berlin, 1995.
218 pages,72 illustrations, 12 *plates*.
ISBN 3-9803730-0-2.

In the last decades there have been only a few studies exclusively on ancient Egyptian ships following Landström's *Ships of the Pharaohs* (1970) or Göttlicher/Werner's *Schiffsmodelle im Alten Aegypten* (1971): they are Lipke's *The Royal Ship of Cheops* (1984) and the fairly small and popular books by Steve Vinson, *Egyptian Boats and Ships* (1994) and by Dilwyn Jones, *Boats* (1995). The models in the British Museum have been published by Glanville in 1972, and those found in the tomb of Tut-Ankhamun by Jones in 1990, not to mention books by Boreux, Reisner, Winlock or numerous articles by other scholars of the past and present. No recent thesis on Egyptian shipbuilding is known to me except Dürring's, which was completed at the University of Berlin. He makes good use of all these former publications and discovers his own ways of discussing and presenting all the well and less known finds such as bas-reliefs and models and, of course, written sources, and he also analyses fragments of boats which can hardly be called wrecks. The model fragment ill.62 is fairly new among the Nile archaeonautica. The Dahshur boats and the funerary barque of Cheops (Lipke) are not considered in detail. Some 40 pages deal with the building of papyrus raft and boats which play such a big role in Egyptian navigation and iconology and which are part of their national identity.

Dürring writes about technical problems and gives a valuable list of words relating to papyrus craft. Six pages are devoted to skin boats which are of minor importance, while Chapter 3 con-

cerns wooden boats, their construction princi-
ples and their terminology. Chapters 4-6 focus
on the typology of boats and ships according to
the shape of bow and stern, and Dürring has
identified 19 types according to their function:
freighters, ferries, travelling boats, sea ships,
warships, Royal and official boats, smaller working craft (for fishing, hunting and pleasure), funeral boats and sacred barges. He discusses the
various means of propulsion. Part B will be new
and exciting for anyone who has ever studied
ancient ships. Dürring outlines the 'Berufsbild
des Schiffbauers', the shipwright's job description, the sources, the terminology, his training,
qualifications and social status and image. This
chapter should serve as an example for other
studies on shipwrights in Greece, in Rome, in the
Viking countries.

The two indices are about parts of ships and
about terms for all kind of watercraft. In addition
to 72 drawings the book has 12 plates, a valuable
means of verifying much of the evidence presented in the text. The bibliography of some 270
titles is up to date, reliable and comprehensive,
thus making the book a most welcome addition
to the maritime history of ancient Egypt.
ARVID GÖTTLICHER
Bremervörde, Germany

THE EVOLUTION OF THE SAILING SHIP 1250-
1580: Keynote Studies from *The Mariner's Mir-
ror*.
Selected by BASIL GREENHILL (Series Editor
DAVID J. STARKEY).
Conway Maritime Press, London, 1995.
264 pages, 214 illustrations. Price £20.00.
ISBN 0-85177-655-8.

This book contains a selection of 70 articles,
notes, queries and answers published in the first
six volumes of *The Mariner's Mirror* between
1911 and 1920 (publication was suspended during the Great War). This material was hitherto
difficult to get hold of, unless one possessed a
very good run of *M.M.* or had easy access to a
maritime library. This is the first of a series of
Keynote Studies from The Mariner's Mirror to be
published under the auspices of the SNR's Publications Committee, a series that is intended
both to show the scholarly value of the work
produced by the founders of the SNR, and to
make it easily available to modern scholars.

The studies selected are principally those concerned with iconographic evidence for the development of the ship between the mid-thirteenth
century and the beginning of the seventeenth
century. The source of each piece is given fully,
although in the book they have been assigned
numbers, for ease of reference, with each illustration numbered according to the section that it
is in. The items reflect the interest of the early
members of the SNR in the technological development of sailing ships, a topic discussed in the
interesting Introduction to the book by Dr
Greenhill.

Many of the illustrations are line drawings
(mostly well reproduced here), redrawn at the
time from the originals or from photographs, for
the costs of extensive photographic reproduction in the early part of this century would have
been prohibitive. They are a testament to the
artistic skills of the early contributors, particularly those of R. Morton Nance. The redrawing
of such material does add another layer of interpretation, but pending the day when vast numbers of medieval illustrations become available
on the Internet, this is the only easily accessible
publication that many of these images will receive, and serious researchers can always use it as
a catalogue guide to the original sources.

The selection of the items has been thoughtful,
and accompanying notes update any points
where new information or ideas have emerged.
All of the contributors displayed an awareness of
the fallibility of medieval and sixteenth-century
ship illustrations as direct evidence of the appearance of ships of the time, and attempted to obvi-
ate this by the systematic study of a range of
images. However, even they could get carried
away, and give more credence to aspects of the
material than was deserved, and the book rightly
reproduces a 1912 article by Gregory Robinson
is which he humorously takes his colleagues to
task on the matter, and takes a highly sceptical
view of technical value of the work of artists who
were not remotely ship-portraitists.

This book will be of considerable value to
anyone interested in the study of medieval and
sixteenth-century ships. Even if one does not
always agree with the methods or conclusions of
these pioneer scholars, their work has to be read
by those wishing to take the subject further. The
Series Editor, Dr Greenhill, and the SNR Publications Committee are to be congratulated for

bringing this material back into circulation: it retains an intellectual freshness, and a sense of humour and scholarly humility, that keeps it alive.
IAN FRIEL
Littlehampton Museum

PROVIDENCE ISLAND, 1630-1641: The Other Puritan Colony.
By KAREN ORDAHL KUPPERMAN.
Cambridge University Press, 1993.
xiii + 393 *pages*, 4 *maps.* Price £40.00.
ISBN 0-521-35205-3.

Most historians will be unfamiliar with the history of Providence Island, a small island located off the coast of Nicaragua which was developed by English puritans in 1629. The beginnings of the colony were much like those along Massachusetts Bay: the creation of a Godly society removed from England's political and religious climate. As interesting as this is for general historians, for readers of *M.M.* it is the mixture of Godly pursuits with plantations and privateering that is of particular interest. The colony was a throwback to the glories of the Elizabethan days when it was suggested that from a base in the West Indies, England could combine trade with attacks on the Spanish. It was a scheme worthy of the aspirations of Drake or Ralegh. The colony was begun just as the short wars of Charles I with Spain and France were ending. Among its supporters were Robert Rich, second earl of Warwick, who was a prominent supporter of, and participant in, privateering. The colony only lasted a few years and its failure was caused by the general ignorance in establishing colonies and in finding a successful formula for economic success. Examination of the individuals involved shows their participation in other colonization attempts throughout the Americas.

The author is best known for her work on Native Americans but this book should considerably raise her profile among maritime historians. Well written and researched, the book corrects a longstanding ignorance of the island's history and deserves examination by those interested in both privateering and colonization.
TODD GRAY
University of Exeter

GLASGOW: Volume I, Beginnings to 1830.
Edited by T. M. DEVINE and GORDON JACKSON.
Manchester University Press, Manchester and New York, 1995.
xii + 435 *pages*, 26 *illustrations*. Price £60.00.
ISBN 0-7190-3691-7.

Conceived within the History Department of Strathclyde University as the first instalment of a three-part history of Glasgow, this volume examines, through chapters by various contributors, the evolution of the west of Scotland's leading city and maritime centre from the Middle Ages to the eve of the Victorian period. As well as covering the main aspects of the city's maritime history, the book also provides discussions of the topographical development of the town, the government of the city, religious and intellectual life during the Enlightenment, and working-class radicalism. Carefully researched and nicely organised, this volume will become a standard reference work on Glasgow; it will be much thumbed by Scottish, urban and maritime historians.

Five of the eleven chapters include substantial material on maritime history. James McGrath, examining the medieval and early modern burgh, discusses Glasgow's trade with Argyll, the inner Western Isles and Ireland down to the end of the sixteenth century, and shows how east coast Scottish ports such as Aberdeen, Leith and Dundee had a strategic advantage, through geographical location, in trade with Europe. Covering the period 1660 to 1740, Gordon Jackson traces the growth of long-distance commerce that enabled Glasgow to emerge as a world class entrepôt rather than stay as a regional maritime centre. The establishment of two outports, Port Glasgow and Greenock, provided local facilities to cope with the growing volume and diversity of trade at a time when it was still not feasible to dredge the barely navigable River Clyde. 'Entrepôt trade', as Jackson notes, 'was the fastest way of creating mercantile wealth on a meagre economic base' (p.77).

The classic case of Glasgow as an entrepôt was, of course, the Anglo-Chesapeake tobacco trade of the eighteenth century, and it is appropriate that the dustjacket of the book should illustrate the tobacco fleet at anchor at Port Glasgow. In recounting an oft-told tale, T.M. Devine outlines the significance of large partnerships in this trade, the growth of the Scottish store system in the Chesapeake, and the importance of marketing large amounts of tobacco to the French Farmers-General. He also examines the contribution of tobacco to Glasgow's economic development. This is the least fresh part of the book, because Devine has written on these themes many times before. It is nevertheless a competent summary of the state of research on the topic except that, as in his previous publications, Devine curiously makes insufficient use of many relevant mercantile sources in the United States.

R.H. Campbell focuses on the making of the industrial city but his chapter also includes good material on commerce. He shows how Glasgow became the centre of a region in which there was extensive expansion of industrial activities throughout the eighteenth century; he emphasises the importance of good local supplies of coal, and hence steam power, for industrialisation; and he points out that Glasgow had no comparable urban rival in the west of Scotland. Overlapping the period covered by Campbell, Jackson provides an overview of changing horizons in trade for Glaswegians from 1780 to 1830. This chapter provides the freshest new perspectives on Glasgow's maritime history in the entire book, taking account of shipbuilding and shipowning, the construction of the Forth & Clyde Canal, the deepening and improved navigation of the River Clyde, and the growth of trade with diverse areas of the world after the collapse of the tobacco trade.

Throughout the book two importat points are stressed on Glasgow's commercial and industrial development. First, a partnership between trade and manufacturing was sustained at Glasgow from the late seventeenth century to the mid-nineteenth century, with sometimes trade gaining the ascendancy over industry and sometimes vice versa, but with both intertwining to promote the city's economic development and transition to industrialisation. Secondly, by 1830 Glasgow's urban economy was distinctive compared with other British ports. The two editors neatly encapsulate this in brief phrases. In Devine's words, 'Glasgow combined the functions of great ports such as Liverpool and leading industrial centres like Manchester in one urban entity' (p.14). Jackson comes to a similar conclusion: 'the new industrial development in cotton, iron, shipbuilding, chemicals, and even coalmining took place within the same urban space as the port. This produced the only city in Britain which was both a major port and a major industrial complex' (p.235).

KENNETH MORGAN
Brunel University

THE ANGLO-DUTCH WARS OF THE SEVENTEENTH CENTURY.
By J.R. JONES.
Longman, Harlow, 1996.
xi + 242 pages. Price £39.99.
ISBN 0-582-05630-6.

This is an effective and efficient study that is organised in two sections, the first thematic, the second narrative. Jones is an acknowledged expert on the subject and indeed used to stage wargames based on the conflicts. He has a fine feel for the practicalities of seventeenth-century warfare, and anchors his study on an assessment of the physical environment. Jones notes that the most distinctive feature of the main theatre of operations was the constant close proximity of the fleets and their bases to each other. The short distances within a compact theatre made possible a rhythm of intensive naval warfare, but the constraints of seventeenth-century naval warfare were such that combat could be inhibited by bad weather, outdated information and navigational uncertainties. The first was especially serious because the Little Ice Age ensured that the path of the high-altitude jet stream was considerably further south than in the twentieth century, and it was also stronger.

The wars did not produce any radically new technological developments – the Dutch project for a revolutionary mechanical ram and the English invention of an incendiary shell both failed – but the deployment of large, heavily gunned warships by the English in the First War put the Dutch at a considerable disadvantage. The English emphasis on superior gunnery made the Dutch fleet obsolete and the gap was only closed in the Third War. However, the Dutch had fewer problems than the English in manning their wartime fleet, while lack of money exacerbated every administrative and logistical problem faced by the English in 1665-7. For 1672-3 financial problems were less serious, but supply and manning deficiencies reduced English naval effectiveness. The weak state of naval logistics thwarted plans for prolonged blockades.

Although he concentrates on the North Sea and the Narrow Seas, Jones has a feel for the wider geographical contexts of conflict. For example, he points out that the final collapse of the Dutch West India Company's longstanding attempt to drive the Portuguese from Brazil was a consequence of the First War, because it prevented the despatch of crucial reinforcements and supplies.

The First War made all Dutch politicians realise that the geographic situation of the Dutch Republic left their mercantile economy vulnerable to the English. This ensured that the role of France became even more important in the Second and Third Wars as both sides sought French support. Jones emphasises the impact of the Medway raid in the Second War, although he also points out that the Dutch suffered from the absence of the network of subversion that William of Orange was to organize and use in 1673-4 and 1687-8.

The Third War illustrated the problems both of combined operations and of co-operation between allies. As so often in the period, both ensured the failure of plans for invasions, in this case of Anglo-French schemes for an invasion of the United Provinces. Thus, in 1673 Charles II ruled out attempting a landing both because the Dutch fleet had not been defeated and because the French army could not provide assistance.

Jones skilfully integrates the political and commercial dimensions in order to provide an account of what were far from being limited wars. He suggests that Dutch survival owed much to the limited nature of naval power in the period, more specifically to the inability of contemporary warships to keep the seas in conditions that their Napoleonic period successors could cope with. As a result, the Dutch economy could not be disrupted as successfully as was to be the case during the Fourth Anglo-Dutch war of 1780-4 and then again from 1795. Jones draws attention to the scale of the conflict. In global terms, it is an instructive example of the degree to which large-scale naval warfare did not entail capability gaps as great as much land warfare. Naval warfare, of course, has been defined in European terms largely because of the wars that did not occur: between Portugal (and later Portugal/ Spain) and China, Japan and Korea in the late sixteenth century or between the Dutch and the Chinese over Taiwan.

Jones is to be congratulated on producing the best available treatment of his topic. The only major disappointment is that he does not set his study within a wider context of seventeenth-century naval developments.

JEREMY BLACK
University of Exeter

LOOKING FOR LA PÉROUSE: D'Entrecasteaux in Australia and the South Pacific 1792-1793. By FRANK HORNER. The Miegunyah Press - Melbourne University Press, 1995. European distributor, Gazelle Book Services Limited, Falcon House, Queen Square, Lancaster LA1 1RN, U.K. xiv + 318 *pages*, 10 *illustrations*, 13 *maps* and *line drawings*. Price Aus$49.95; £28.50. ISBN 0-522-84-51-0.

On 7 February 1788 the French explorer Jean-François de La Pérouse wrote to the Minister of Marine in Paris from Botany Bay, giving details of his proposed route back to France, saying that he expected to return by mid-1789. On 10 March 1788 he proceeded to sea and his two ships, the *Boussole* and *Astrolabe*, were last seen making their way to the north before vanishing into the vastness of the Pacific. In due course the French Assembly ordered a rescue mission, but it was not until 28 September 1791 that Antoine-Raymond-Joseph Bruny d'Entrecasteaux sailed from Brest in the *Recherche* accompanied by the *Espérance* commanded by Jean-Michel Huon de Kermadec. Among the officers, who subsequently achieved fame, were Charles-François Beautemps-Beaupré, the expedition's surveyor, and Elizabeth-Paul-Édouard Rossel, its chief astronomer.

When the expedition reached Table Bay, d'Entrecasteaux was informed that Captain John Hunter, on his way home from Port Jackson in the hired Dutch snow *Waaksamheyd,* had seen some large canoes near the Admiralty Islands manned by natives wearing clothing of European origin. This report led d'Entrecasteaux to decide to make directly for the Admiralty Islands in order to forestall Captain William Bligh, whom he thought was also likely to visit these islands in the *Providence,* thus becoming the first person to establish the fate of La Pérouse.

D'Entrecasteaux first called at Amsterdam Island, discovered on 18 March 1522 by D'Elcano in Magellan's *Victoria* and not in 1696 by Vlamingh as stated by Horner, in order to verify its position. The weather and the poor sailing qualities of his two ships now forced d'Entrecasteaux to approach the Admiralty Islands by going south of Australia. He first made for Van Diemen's Land, where he intended to anchor in Adventure Bay, but due to a fortunate navigational error, discovered instead the magnificent D'Entrecasteaux Channel, which he proceeded to survey. The brief description of Beautemps-Beaupré's survey techniques is, however, difficult to follow (p.71). According to Horner the French had as their guide the chart drawn by Bligh when master of the *Resolution* during Cook's third voyage, quoting in his notes the manuscript chart by Bligh held in the United Kingdom Hydrographic Office. However, it seems much more likely that d'Entrecasteaux was guided by the similar chart engraved in the French account of Cook's third voyage, which differs from Bligh's chart in a number of ways.

D'Entrecasteaux next examined the south-western coast of New Caledonia, which had been left unsurveyed by Cook. Then, after finding no trace of La Pérouse in the Admiralty Islands, he called at Amboina to obtain fresh provisions and to rest his crew. From here he returned to the south coast of Australia, surveying it from Cape Leeuwin to the head of the Great Australian Bight, naming Esperance Bay and the Recherche Archipelago after his two ships. After further survey work in D'Entrecasteaux Channel, he then returned to the South Pacific where he discovered Raoul Island, named after the officer who first sighted it, calling the island group the Kermadec Islands after his second in command. D'Entrecasteaux then made short visits to Tongatapu and New Caledonia, before making for Santa Cruz Island. It was as he approached this island that he came nearest to discovering the fate of La Pérouse, when he sighted in the distance Vanikoro, on which it was learnt many years later that La Pérouse's two ships had been wrecked.

Symptoms of scurvy now appeared in both ships and on 20 July 1793 d'Entrecasteaux was the first to die. Discord now broke out between royalists and republicans on board the two ships as they made their painful way to Sourabaya. Here the Dutch, who were now at war with France, arrested the two ships. They also sided with the royalists with the result that when the ships' companies were finally allowed to return to Europe it was the royalist Rossel who took with him the nautical records of the expedition, but in the Atlantic Rossel was captured by the British and taken to London together with the records of the expedition.

At first Rossel was content to remain in London, working on the expedition's charts in the Admiralty Hydrographic Office, but with the signing of the Treaty of Amiens in 1802, he decided to return to Paris after passing the records of the expedition to the French minister in London. Meanwhile Jacques-Julien Houtou de Labillardière, the expedition's botanist and a republican, had published an account of the voyage in 1799, which was a great success and which was promptly translated into English. Nevertheless, Rossel was instructed to prepare an official account of the voyage, published in 1808, accompanied by a magnificent atlas of 39 finely engraved charts by Beautemps-Beaupré. Rossel's account did not achieve the same success as Labillardière's, and only an appendix by Beautemps-Beaupré on his hydrographic methods was translated into English.

This is a well researched and well written book on a most important voyage of exploration. It is a significant addition to the growing number of books relating to the exploration of Australia and the Pacific published by Melbourne University Press under their Miegunyah imprint.
ANDREW C. F. DAVID
Taunton, Somerset

SAINT-FAUST IN THE NORTH 1803-1804: Orkney and Shetland in Danger.
By R.P. FEREDAY.
Tempvs Reparatvm Monographs, 29 Beaumont Street, Oxford, OX1 2NP, 1995.
115 *pages*, 11 *illustrations* and *maps*. Price £15.99.
ISBN 1-87131405-4.

The subject of this well researched and clearly written book is a barely known episode during the Napoleonic Wars: the ill-fated expedition commanded by Jean Jacques de Saint-Faust. This well armed flotilla was fitted out by the Batavian Privateer Company to make a descent on the unprotected coastline of 'North Britain' as a diversion for Napoleon's planned invasion across the English Channel.

The author, an Orcadian, has a clear understanding of the North Sea terrain and the material available. With the latter he must be commended for his diligence in seeking out both British and Continental primary sources to piece together this interesting, albeit minor, episode in Napoleonic history. As a study it is self-contained and, in many ways, exemplary in its methods and should appeal to both the specialist and general reader of this period alike. The choice of contemporary illustrations is as good as can be expected for such a specialised topic. The maps contribute to the reader's understanding of the coastlines and anchorages involved, sea areas not usually examined closely by maritime historians.

This book makes a successful contribution to maritime history by reason of its detailed recounting of what was, in fact, a prime example of an attempted 'north-about' quasi-naval raid in Scottish waters. A tactic designed to play havoc with the Shetland fisheries and the merchant shipping that marshalled in Orkney during wartime. Indeed, the very threat was sufficient to persuade their Lordships of the Admiralty to divert disproportionate and scarce resources to defend the northern flank.

This strategy of taking the sea war back to the British by attacking 'North Britain' has a long pedigree. It was first used by the exponents of the 'guerre de course' in the previous century, Forbin and Duguay-Troiun, and later by Thurot, Paul Jones and Ryan. In this context the Saint-Faust episode was the first of the new century and the precursor to the cruise of U.S.S. *President* ten years later. Students of naval practices and maritime jurisdiction will find the sections on the Saint-Faust's use of Bergen (then under Danish sovereignty) as a privateering base well worth the read of this rather highly priced short book.

ERIC GRAHAM
Loughton, Essex

A SAILOR BOY'S EXPERIENCE ABOARD A SLAVE SHIP.
By SAMUEL ROBINSON.
Reprinted by G.C. Book Publishers Ltd, Wigtown, 1996.
137 *pages*. Price £12.95.
ISBN 1-872350-66-6.

This account of two voyages in the slave trade, made between 1800 and 1804, is a reprint of a volume originally published in 1869. On the face of it, Robinson was publishing letters he wrote as a teenager to a former school friend from the various ports of call he made on his voyages. In a short introduction, written when he must have been over eighty, he claims this is a 'plain, unvarnished record of simple facts'. Unfortunately it is no such thing. The letters do not read like the work of a fourteen-eighteen year old, despite the fact that four years in the slave trade would undoubtedly have given any youngster a wealth of experience beyond his physical years. Some of the basic facts relating to the ships and the voyages can be substantiated but others are questionable. His price for slaves of £9 a head is at variance with other evidence which suggests it was three times this amount at this period.

If the original letters did exist they have been expanded and embroidered to a point which makes them dubious as contemporary historical evidence of the slave trade. A description of a 'characteristic African' contains about every racial prejudice known and does not read like the words of a fourteen year old boy. In particular, reference to a phrenologist (p.34) is clearly a later addition – the *Oxford English Dictionary* gives the earliest use of phrenology as 1815. In another passage he claims never to have seen any cruelty: 'On the contrary, I never saw anything in their treatment but what was kind and merciful' (p.56). Later he compares life for the African in Africa where he was 'a very hapless animal' with the joys and luxuries of life in the Caribbean.

The volume is offered to us without any introduction, additional discussion or annotation. This is a pity given the problematic nature of the text. Whilst there is much detail that may be true, this volume should be regarded as the significantly prejudiced memoirs of an old man, an apologia for the slave trader, rather than the simple account of a teenage boy that it purports to be.

ANTHONY TIBBLES
Merseyside Maritime Museum

THE HULL WHALING TRADE: An Arctic Enterprise.
By ARTHUR G. CREDLAND.
Hutton Press Ltd, Beverley, Yorks, 1995.
155 *pages*, 112 *illustrations* (including 12 *colour plates*), 9 *appendices*. Price £10.95.
ISBN 1-872167-73-X (paperback).

Hull boasts a longer association with Arctic whaling enterprise than any other British port.

Hull master mariners like Thomas Marmaduke were amongst the first English captains to prosecute the Spitzbergen Fishery after 1610 and the last to persevere with the Davis Straits Fishery over 250 years later. At its peak in the first quarter of the nineteenth century Hull ships regularly comprised 40 per cent of the national whaling fleet and for a decade between 1812 and 1822, some 50 to 60 vessels sailed annually from the Humber to hunt the Greenland whale. It was an enormous financial enterprise by the standards of the day and employed thousands of men at sea as well as onshore.

Given the significance that the Northern Whale Fishery once had for the port and its communities it might seem surprising that it has taken so long for a modern study to emerge. T.S. Sheppard's short article, published in *M.M.*, Vol. 5 (1919), is amongst the oldest and Gordon Jackson's more recent contributions to the subject remain the most scholarly. Mr Credland's book, on the other hand, is likely to be the most popular and widely read. Liberally illustrated and plainly structured it provides a connected narrative of owners, masters, ships and practices. It is rooted in the superb collection of documents, whaling artefacts and marine paintings of the Town Docks Museum of which the author is Keeper. The book has limited aims and is clearly intended to serve a double purpose: as a general handbook which provides a context for visitors to the museum's collections and, more specifically, as a 'starter' volume for students, local historians and researchers, including family historians, interested in the history of Hull and its environs. It is likely to be successful in both roles. The content is factual rather than analytical and the approach vaguely antiquarian, but the information is accessible and generally coherent.

Although it may well be true that you cannot judge a book by looking at the cover, in this case the cover reveals both the strengths and weaknesses of this publication. There is a striking cover illustration which uses a painting by Thomas Binks of the ice-bound whalers *Jane, Viewforth* and *Middleton* beset in the Davis Strait during the winter of 1835-36. It establishes the flavour of the content at a glance. Alternatively, inside the front cover the reader will find a corrigenda which rather undermines the effect of the illustration. Closer scrutiny reveals that the corrigenda itself is incorrect and incomplete!

There seems to be no error on p.47, despite the entry, but there *are* further errors elsewhere: on p.72 and p.79, for example, to do with dates, though neither of them are included in the corrigenda. This is a pity and the author was probably as irritated by the errors as I was. Fortunately, they do not fundamentally undermine a useful book designed and written for a target audience.

TONY BARROW
Newcastle College

RITES & PASSAGES: The Experience of American Whaling, 1830-1870.
By MARGARET S. CREIGHTON.
Cambridge University Press, Cambridge, 1995.
xiv + 233 *pages*, 35 *illustrations*. Price £35 (hardback); £14.95 (paper).
ISBN 0-521-43336-3 (hardback); 0-521-48448-0 (paper).

As the title suggests, the purpose of this book is less to describe than to interpret certain aspects of American whaling history. Based for the most part on diaries and journals kept by young foremast hands, the author seeks 'to consider the ways that gender shaped the sailor's experience' and to discuss the 'transformative' events that marked the transition from landsman to seaman and from youth to manhood.

The book begins with a brief, largely familiar account of the 'Evolution of American Whaling, 1650-1900', then narrows the focus to four decades, 1830 to 1870, when the industry reached its largest size and began its slow decline. Subsequent chapters describe the recruitment of whalemen and their experience at sea, with emphasis on such matters as affected their social and psychological adjustment, including authority and discipline, shipboard duties, recreations and rituals, and relations with women – those left behind, those encountered at ports of call and those that trod the deck as captain's wives.

How fruitful the reader will find Dr Creighton's examination of 'gender issues' will depend to a large extent on his or her interests. There are, however, some problems of presentation and methodology that should be borne in mind, among them the adequacy of the source material. The primary evidence for the author's discussion is drawn from 172 whaling journals or logbooks, 38 similar accounts kept on merchant ships, and a smaller number of letters by or to whalemen. Given the fact that over 5,000 whaling voyages are recorded in logbooks and journals in public collections, the evidential base seems unnecessarily small. Even more restrictive – as the author readily admits – is the authorship of the consulted accounts, all of which were kept by literate, white Americans, primarily from coastal New England. To what degree they spoke for their illiterate crewmates, or for those of different colour, language or national origin is not evaluated, leaving the reader with what comes close to a one-dimensional image of the American whaleman.

A second problem, arising from the author's search for 'rites and passages', is a tendency to over-emphasize those that may qualify. In a chapter on 'Crossing the Line: Fraternity in the Forecastle' the author recounts the arrival of King Neptune on the whaleship *Hannibal* and describes the initiation ceremony as if it were a customary event on whaleships. It was not, and although one in four of the consulted journals and logbooks are said to make reference to it, some of these seem likely to come from accounts kept on merchantmen. Most whaling masters paid no heed to crossing the Line and discouraged or forbid recognition of the fact.

Two other examples of over-emphasis should be mentioned, the first because it applies an unusual designation – the 'Sailor's Pleasure' – to the rather mundane pursuit of overhauling sea chests on Sundays. Described here as a 'shipboard ritual that allowed seamen some limited landward focus', it is the phrase itself that tends to elevate the pastime into something more formalistic than it probably was. One source is cited for the usage, not that of a whaleman, and the phrase is otherwise unknown in the lexicon of American whaling.

The second example occurs in a chapter on 'Sailors, Sweethearts, and Wives: Gender and Sex in the Deepwater Workplace', in which the author notes that 'Captains' wives went to sea increasingly in the nineteenth century'. Her discussion of some of these women again leaves the reader with the impression that the practice was more common than it actually was. In the decade of the 1850s, when more wives accompanied their husbands than at any time before or after, they were present on 250 of the 2,100 voyages made during those years. Whatever influence they may have exerted on whaleship crews,

beneficial or otherwise, was clearly not widespread.

Despite these reservations, Dr Creighton deserves credit for improving our sense of the stresses and strains that befell many a crewman on his voyage to the whaling grounds and his passage to maturity. The gender interests she has brought to the task have yielded mixed results, but new questions have been raised and answers suggested. Readers may wish to measure the distance she has come, or has yet to go, by consulting Briton C. Busch's *'Whaling Will Never Do for Me': The American Whaleman in the Nineteenth Century*, reviewed in these pages in November 1994.

RICHARD C. KUGLER
Westport, Massachusetts

SHIPBUILDING ON PRINCE EDWARD ISLAND: ENTERPRISE IN A MARITIME SETTING 1787-1920. By NICOLAS J. DE JONG and MARVEN E. MOORE.
History Division Mercury Series Paper 46, Canadian Museum of Civilization, Hull, Quebec, 1994.
vi + 411 *pages, photographs, maps* and *tables*.
Price $34.95 (paper).
ISBN 0-660-14021-7.

Hard on the heels of Eileen Marcil's splendid study of shipbuilding in Quebec, *The Charley Man*, comes this equally admirable and detailed account of shipbuilding on Prince Edward Island. These works supplement and complement the studies undertaken by Professor Lewis Fischer and his colleagues at Memorial University of Newfoundland, and, taken together, they immeasurably expand our knowledge of an internationally important Canadian industry which was for some time inexplicably neglected in calculations of Canadian balance of trade.

This new study has two strengths: for the local and regional historian it details the location and output of the many shipyards on the Island, and furnishes us with much new information on the builders themselves. No less important is the international context, since this was a market driven sector of the economy, and the market was essentially Britain. The authors have been able to locate and exploit records of some of the shipyards in their links with British agents and shipowners, and these repay careful study for the insights that they give us into the changes and fluctuations in the British market for new tonnage. However, there is little attention given to the nature of British demand in an age of rapid technological change, so that few comparisons are made with the relative costs and quality of British-built tonnage with which Island shipbuilders were competing. Where the Island tonnage had an advantage was that most vessels were relatively cheap and, built on speculation, they furnished British shipowners with virtually 'instant' tonnage, permitting a quick response to the fluctuations in the freight market. Durability took second place to the prompt satisfaction of demand, and it would have been useful had the authors examined the extent to which Lloyd's Register of Shipping influenced the quality of production, or the extent to which Lloyd's modified their categories to accommodate Island shipbuilders: numbers of PEI-built vessels appear to have had their years in the A1 class uprated in a quite arbitrary manner. Another feature of PEI vessels was standardisation of much of the output with tonnage measurement carefully calculated to minimise costs: hence builders anticipated a feature of the modern 'paragraph' ship.

Reservations must be expressed over the author's attempt to rationalise tonnages by applying old tonnage laws to post-1836 vessels. This has unfortunate results in respect of many vessels for which the authors provide selling costs per ton: moreover, this approach invalidates some of the otherwise valuable tabular data. One must also query the assumption that vessels that maintained PEI registration were necessarily owned there. Selling agents in Britain, notably Sir James Malcolm of Liverpool, not only negotiated the sale of tonnage to British shipowners of modest means, but granted them mortgages too, and prudence might dictate that PEI registration was maintained until interest payments were secured. The now classic study by Basil Greenhill and Ann Giffard, *Westcountrymen in Prince Edward Island*, which this new study complements rather than supersedes, recognises that several of the vessels owned by the Yeo/Richards association maintained PEI registration; this was particularly the case in respect of the bigger barquentines built in the 1880s.

This is a well produced volume that deserves a place on the shelves of all maritime historians. The authors have found illustrations of PEI-built vessels that did not feature in their earlier book and which enhance the text. The index, however, is imperfect in that it lumps together different vessels which had the same name, and some personal names are misspelt.

ROBIN CRAIG
St Margaret's Bay, Kent

THE VOYAGES OF THE *MORNING*.
By GERALD S. DOORLY. Introduction by D.W.H. WALTON.
Bluntisham Books, East Street, Bluntisham, Huntingdon, and The Erskine Press, The Old Bakery, Banham, Norfolk, 1995.
xx + 225 *pages*, 24 *illustrations*. Price £24.95.
ISBN 1-85297-040-5.

This is a reprint, with modern introduction, of a rare Antarctic book published by Smith, Elder in 1916. The voyages it describes are those of the little auxiliary barque *Morning,* over a decade earlier, as relief ship to the National Antarctic (*Discovery*) Expedition, 1901-04, led by Captain R.F. Scott. The very able and resolute commander of the relief expeditions of 1902-03 and 1903-04 was Captain William Colbeck of the Wilson Line, Hull, to whom the presentation of a unique silver loving-cup was made by Sir Clements Markham at the time of Scott's lecture in the Royal Albert Hall, November 1904. Despite Scott's encouragement, Colbeck never wrote more than a brief report on the voyages. However, his letters home survived and were quoted by the present writer in her recent 'biography' of the *Discovery* (Virgin, 1992, 1994). It fell to Gerald Doorly, Third Officer of the *Morning*, whose papers are in the Mitchell Library, Sydney, to write the first published narrative – and a lively, humorous and descriptive one it is, shedding light not only on the voyages of the *Morning* and the *Terra Nova* (1903-04), but on aspects of life and work with the main expedition at the *Discovery*'s winter quarters, McMurdo Sound. Especially interesting is Doorly's account of the return of the Pole party, in February 1903. Shackleton and Wilson had been confined to their bunks after the pioneering journey, while all three were ravenous from near starvation:

'Shackles', I heard him [Scott] call, 'I say, Shackles, how would you fancy some sardines on toast?' In a little while the smell of toasting bread at the ward-room fire permeated the place. I heard Wilson thanking the captain for the luxury! This continued at intervals during the early hours, and struck me as being at once humorous and pathetic (p.110).

The modern introduction by D.W.H. Walton provides a short biography of Doorly and points out the musical interest of the voyages of the *Morning*, a piano having been presented by Sir Clements Markham, which had to be cut down to get it below deck then reassembled. Two of the songs are reproduced in music and verse. Such an introduction must be kept short to keep costs down, but one wishes that the blank page and a half could have been used to say more. The reprint is a welcome one.

ANN SAVOURS
Bridge, Canterbury

To The Sixth Continent: The Second German South Polar Expedition.
By WILHELM FILCHNER. Translated and edited by WILLIAM BARR.
Bluntisham Books, East Street, Bluntisham, Huntingdon, and The Erskine Press, The Old Bakery, Banham, Norfolk, 1994.
42 + viii + 253 *pages*, 95 *figures*. Price £49.95.
ISBN 1-85297-038-3.

A few years ago Bluntisham Books published a translation of the narrative of the First German South Polar Expedition in the *Gauss*; they have now brought out an English version of the account of the second, translated by William Barr. The Second German South Polar Expedition of 1911-12 in the *Deutschland* reached the southern extremity of the Weddell Sea and discovered the ice shelf since named after its leader, Wilhelm Filchner. The fortunes of the two expeditions had much in common. Both made important geographical discoveries and carried out extensive scientific programmes, but failed in their main objectives; both were beset in the ice, the *Gauss* drifting for nearly a year, and the *Deutschland* for eight months, but survived and returned home safely.

The *Deutschland* was apparently riven by some of the bitterest disagreements ever to have taken place on polar expeditions, always a fertile ground for personality clashes. Hardly a hint of this appears in Filchner's book, originally published in 1922. He had undertaken the expedition from patriotic motives and suppressed the internal dissensions for the same reason, until in old age he wrote an account of his own personal view of events, which was published after his death and is translated here with some supporting documents as an addendum to the volume.

Filchner was an army officer with a passion for exploration. He made a number of demanding journeys through Central Asia, undertaking geophysical observations, at a time when few Westerners had reached the area. However he had no previous experience of polar exploration when he undertook the organisation of the *Deutschland* expedition. At first he had no government help and the funds were raised through a lottery. These were not sufficient to allow two ships, as originally planned, and as other expeditions (including Scott's second) were heading for the Ross Sea, Filchner instead made his objective to try and reach the unknown southernmost point of the Weddell Sea. The object of the expedition was to see if a strait or ice barrier separated the land of East and West Antarctica into two at that point. In his later statement Filchner accused the *Deutschland*'s captain of sabotaging the expedition by leading them to attempt to set up their base camp on an iceberg, which was vulnerable if the coastal ice began to break up (as it did), instead of on the ice cap.

Barr's introduction sets the scene for this endeavour, outlining the history of Antarctic exploration up to that date. He also gives an account of Filchner's life, based on his autobiography. His competent translation is welcome, giving readers of English the chance to follow the expedition's course, culminating in the dramatic events surrounding the break-up of the ice barrier, and the long drift of the *Deutschland*. However, in the introduction events are seen very much from Filchner's viewpoint, and no editorial analysis is offered of the expedition, indeed there is not even a brief summary of its activities and results in the introduction. Little is said, for example, of the other members, or of their contribution, beyond their part in the strife between captain and leader. However reprehensible their actions, and however real Filchner's grievances (he tended, understandably, to see everything in a personal light, and blamed the campaign to undermine his authority, which continued after the expedition's return, on the jealousy of an assistant on one of his Asian journeys) underlying causes are only hinted at. No real attempt is made to analyse the stresses that fuelled the situation – the inter-service rivalry, academic jealousies, the effect of the captain's illness and, probably, fear of the elements. They are mentioned in the preface but not again and this seems to be a lack, as is the failure to describe the more positive results of the expedition. Filchner accuses the oceanographer Wihelm Brennecke of being one of those most active against him, but the fact remains that the scientific work Brennecke did on the voyage was excellent and influential so that at least in one section of the scientific community the expedition is not perhaps quite as forgotten as the translator claims! (For those interested in this topic, the problems of the Filchner expedition are described in a more recent publication: Cornelia Lüdecke's work on Drygalski, 'Die deutsche Polarforschung seit der Jahrhundertwende und der Einfluss Erich von Drygalskis', published by the Alfred-Wegener-Institut in its series of *Reports on Polar Research in 1995* [Vol. 158, pp.223-7].)

There are some mistakes and omissions in the text. The misspelling of Kling, one of the subsidiary authors, on the title page is unfortunate. The German publication of Filchner's statement by Kirschmer (1985) is mentioned in the text of the introduction but not in the bibliography. In the main, however, this is a handsomely produced volume, which gives English readers the chance to learn about an expedition which has certainly not received its due attention, and about the problems surrounding it. The introduction, apart from the omissions mentioned above, gives a good account of the circumstances in which the expedition took place, and adds information not given by Filchner himself, especially about the adventurous training trip undertaken in Spitsbergen before the expedition set out.
MARGARET DEACON
University of Southampton

THE OTHER WAY ROUND: Memoir of a Sea Journey Around the World.
By FRANK P. VERDON.
The Radcliffe Press, 45 Bloomsbury Square, London WC1A 2HY, 1996.
204 pages, 8 colour photographs, 19 black and white 'plates'. Price £24.50.
ISBN 1-86064-030-3.

This book describes some of the events which occurred during the easterly passage around the world by the U.K. government's oceanographic research vessel R.R.S. *Charles Darwin* between July 1986 and August 1989. The book's title is an allusion to the westerly circumnavigation of the world by H.M.S. *Beagle* under the command of Robert FitzRoy, accompanied by the scientist Charles Darwin, from the end of 1831 until the beginning of October 1836. The author, Frank Verdon, makes frequent comparisons between the two scientific expeditions, notably in terms of duration; the contrast in scientific instrumentation; and the continuity of the (very limited) scientific personnel of the nineteenth-century voyage versus the frequent changes in scientists, and to a lesser extent ship's crew, during the twentieth-century circumnavigation. Of equal importance is the change in emphasis both geographically and scientifically. H.M.S. *Beagle* spent 43 months out of 58 off the coast of South America, quite apart from the time in the Galapagos Islands; R.R.S. *Charles Darwin* had a similarly disproportionate period, 17 out of 38 months, in and around the Indian Ocean. The scientific emphasis of the nineteenth-century voyage was biological; the twentieth-century one pre-eminently geophysical with plate tectonics a constant theme. Both expeditions studied 'basic science', the twentieth century one almost exclusively, and at the present time there must be some debate as to whether this is an appropriate use of public funding.

The book provides items of interest, both amusing and technical, to virtually anyone with a maritime leaning. These range from the time when the much vaunted 'Gloria' – an acronym for Geological LOng Range Inclined Asdic – became stuck in an arch in Mombasa, while the subsequent diversion caused havoc to the town's infrastructure, to highly scientific descriptions (e.g. p.58). Some of the extracts from the individual scientists' cruise reports are quite opaque – (were my cruise reports ever this indigestible?) – but Verdon does his best to translate these into something meaningful, and usually succeeds. There is a helpful glossary of terms, although occasionally the units used in the text almost defy comprehension, e.g. $gCm^{-2}d^{-1}$. It was interesting to read of the way in which politics became directly or indirectly significant to the decisions made and how the objectives of the ship's officers and those of the research scientists did not always coincide. Nor does the book's author hide the darker side of events whether they be the series of disasters on Sinha's first cruise; other losses of equipment; or the storms encountered during the Antarctic summer. The saddest moment is undoubtedly that of the committal of the ashes of one of the ship's captains to the Atlantic Ocean near the end of the voyage.

Where *The Other Way Round* disappoints is in the length of time of its gestation – it is ten years since the circumnavigation began – and, more especially in the production standards. A larger format should have been chosen, but it is particularly in the quality of reproduction of some of the colour photographs and of the black and white figures that tend to militate against the whole. Figure (so-called 'plate') 13, and to a slightly lesser extent figure 17, are almost meaningless. Over-reduction is a frequent problem, while plots of the track of the vessel (e.g. figures 7, 8 and 18) are unrewarding to those not directly involved in the original research.

It may be rather churlish to end in this somewhat negative fashion. In fact, the reviewer thoroughly enjoyed reading *The Other Way Round*. It is just a pity that with a relatively small number of changes a good book could have been transformed into an excellent one.

ALAN CARR
Taunton

JUTLAND: The German Perspective.
By V.E. TARRANT.
Arms and Armour Press, London, 1995.
318 *pages*, 81 *line drawings* and *plans*. Price £20.00.
ISBN 1-85409-244-8.

Given its unique status as the only major fleet action of the Dreadnought era, and the inconclusive controversies concerning the conduct and outcome of the battle, it is likely that Jutland will always inspire interest among naval historians. As such, it has probably attracted more written analysis in the eighty years since it was fought than any other naval battle.

Although the better balanced of these accounts give due credence to the German version of events, the fact remains that no English translation of the German Official History, *Der Krieg zur See, 1914-1918,* has ever been published. Author V.E. Tarrant has gone some way towards rectifying this omission by drawing upon *Der Krieg zur See* as his primary source in constructing this lucid narrative account of the battle.

There are over one hundred substantive quotes from the Official History, written by a senior German officer who participated in the battle, and this material is supplemented by other German naval records such as war diaries and action reports. Of interest, for example, is the appendix setting out a comprehensive summary of German signal traffic relating to the battle.

The resulting perspective on Jutland provides some thought-provoking contrasts to the more traditional British accounts of the battle and will be of enduring value to English-speaking readers by availing them of the opportunity to gain a fuller appreciation of the German viewpoint. It should be said, however, that the book does not generally seek to go beyond presenting a chronological narrative account by subjecting the German version of events to any significant critical analysis. In this respect, the reader is often left to adjudge the extent to which the German Official History's interpretation of the key stages of the battle serviced to justify the claim that Jutland was a victory and a brilliant feat of arms for the High Seas Fleet.

It is unfortunate that the somewhat elementary line drawings of participating German warships and British Dreadnoughts and battlecruisers provide scant compensation for the complete lack of any photographs. Although no photographs were taken of the battle on the German side, the opportunity surely existed to reproduce German warship photographs that are otherwise rarely seen in English publications. In addition, Claus Bergen's paintings, commissioned by the German Admiralty to commemorate the battle, would have provided an excellent complement to the text.

This is, however, an aside on a well written work that is well worth its cover price and which can arguably take its place among the more comprehensive and useful studies of its subject.

IAN SKINNER
Jersey

THE FIRST SEA LORDS: From Fisher to Mountbatten.
Edited by MALCOLM H. MURFETT.
Praeger, 1995.
313 *pages*. Price £53.95.
ISBN 0-275-94231-7.

The First Sea Lord was for the whole period of this book the professional head of the Royal

Navy and its principal representative in that great department of state and operational headquarters, the Admiralty. For most of the period, the post included that of Chief of the Naval Staff, thus gathering all the principal sources of power.

The story of the 19 men who in turn assumed this responsibility is told by some 14 authors; the pattern is chronological and, broadly, biographical though personal detail is rightly kept in check. Professor Murfett states that he conceived the book as being analytically based, 'in which the question "why" is addressed more often than merely "when"'.

The function of strategic and operational oversight, and of administration, is to make things happen. To fulfil this function, for what was for most of the period the most powerful navy in the world, complex organisation was required, and perhaps one's only major criticism of this interesting book is that there is insufficient explanation of how that machinery evolved. The Editor's Introduction does indeed devote a page and a half to it, but much more is required to explain how the navy was served (or sometimes dis-served) by its Whitehall organisation. Composite books of this nature often need a strong thread to bind them together and this reviewer's judgement must be that a more tightly drawn Introduction would have helped.

That said, there is much of interest in every one of the contributions, and many new insights, particularly into personalities and their interactions. Churchill's extraordinary (and by no means always benign) influence on naval affairs for half a century, often to the fury of the professional head, stands out, but what is one to make of the damaging personality clashes between the admirals in the late 1920s and early 1930s? (It would have helped, by the way, if the Kelly brothers had been clearly differentiated.) It is all the more to the credit of Chatfield that he healed the wounds and in 1938 left, in his own words, a 'navy united'. Of all the officers in this volume he emerges as the most effective, the least flawed. The navy was lucky to have such a leader in those critical years.

It may seem perverse, but some of the most indicative elements of this book are the references. The early chapters' endnotes are overwhelmingly from personal papers and letters, or secondary sources. Later, and particularly after the Second World War, they are predominantly

from official documents: board minutes, staff papers. This in itself is a measure of the way the job changed: to extend Professor Murfett's interrogatives, it does give some idea 'how' things were made to happen.

Indeed one can carry further the value of this book if read between the lines. For example, there is no extended examination of the wisdom of the Admiralty's being an operational headquarters. This is a fascinating question and one at the heart of the First Sea Lord's wartime function. Yet, though there is no analysis of it as such, the accounts of both First and Second World Wars help the reader to form a judgement, or at least to formulate the right questions.

Thus, although it is to some extent lacking in the continuity provided by (for example) Jackson and Bramall's brilliant *The Chiefs*, this book can be recommended as a valuable addition to the literature.

RICHARD HILL
Southampton

GRAVE OF A DOZEN SCHEMES: British Naval Planning and the War Against Japan, 1943-1945. By H.P. WILLMOTT.
Naval Institute Press, Annapolis, Maryland, 1996.
xv + 316 *pages, maps*. Price not stated.
ISBN 1-55750-6.

This is a very odd book. If it were fiction one would describe it as a novelette. Less than half its 316 pages is in fact devoted to the narrative suggested by its title. The remainder is filled with a variety of appendices, beginning with the preface which includes a list of codenames for all the operations planned by the indefatigable planning staffs, an outline of the wartime defence planning organisation and a detailed *dramatis personae*, and concluding with a description of the Eastern and East Indies fleets, in what the author calls 'operational chronologies' which detail what those fleets were actually engaged in doing, complete orders of battle for both fleets as of VJ-Day, and an account of Operation 'Zipper', the naval reoccupation of Malaya in September 1945, after the Japanese surrender. All this makes *Grave of a Dozen Schemes* an invaluable work of reference.

What it does not make the book is particularly easy to read. It is in fact a narrow, non-stop account of all the orders and ratiocinations imposed on the unfortunate planning staffs by the overwhelming political need (and the accompanying pressure from on high, from Churchill downwards) to be seen to be doing something active and the obstacles put in the way of any action by geography and the lack of available resources. Geography complicated matters by interposing the Malayan-Indonesian barrier to entry into the Pacific from the west. It faced British planners with the inexorable choice between adding to the overwhelming U.S. Navy's armadas whatever combination of two pence worth of naval forces Britain could scrape together and supply in the Pacific or concentrating on the liberation of Britain's lost empire in Southeast Asia. The first of these alternatives meant that British forces would take part in the final invasion and subjugation of Japan, and what was more important, be seen by American public opinion so to take part. The second would avenge the loss of Malaya and Singapore and do a little to restore the image of British power in Southeast Asia.

The problem with both was the lack of any margin of British naval power, especially naval air power on the one hand and landing-craft on the other, not to mention a naval supply train adequate to mount either of these alternative operations on the necessary scale. German U-boat warfare had crippled British mercantile carrying capacity. The backwardness of both Royal Navy and Royal Air Force in the development of naval air power meant that it took about three of Britain's best carriers to sustain in the air the same number of aircraft as either the American or the Japanese navies could do with a single carrier. Political choice gave the Americans control over the production and availability of landing craft. Not only was Churchill's dream of a fleet-led amphibious assault on Malaya and Singapore not feasible; even an attack on the Andaman islands seemed beyond the available resources. Willmott's whole book is a study in the contrast between imaginative reach and practical grasp in strategy. It has to be said, however, that even in the greatest days of British naval supremacy, amphibious operations on such a scale would have been out of the question against a defended shore. Not that such thoughts made dealing with Churchill any easier for his besieged Chiefs of Staff.

Willmott tells his story well. I have only two criticisms. At least one of them may strike the author as otiose in view of all the information he has provided by way of his appendices. But properly to judge the scale of the British effort in Asia in August 1945, one does really need to know what the rest of the Royal Navy was doing and where they were. Britain, after all, entered the war with 19 capital ships. The East Indian and Eastern fleets in 1945 included only four.

The other is more serious. Britain's honour in the war against Japan was regained, if such a comment seems correct, by the defence of the Indian frontier against the Japanese offensive in 1944 and the clearance of Burma by Fourteenth Army. Their activities are not the subject of Dr Willmott's book. But it would have helped to set the activities of the unfortunate planning staffs and the pressures to which they were subject if some background account of the activities of British land forces could have been linked to his story. Much the same could be said about the Australian advances across New Guinea, and the recovery of the Solomons. Both Mountbatten and Macarthur presided over staffs and commands which, at least in name, were integrated, and fought campaigns which made demands on the available resources, especially in sea-carrying capacity, whether their forces were engaged on land, at sea or in island-hopping.

That being said, Dr Willmott's reputation, already well established, can only benefit from the publication of this, his doctoral thesis, idiosyncrasies and all.

D. CAMERON WATT
London School of Economics

A PICTORIAL HISTORY OF THE SEA WAR 1939-1945.
By PAUL KEMP.
Arms and Armour Press, London, 1995.
194 *pages*, 450 *black and white photographs*.
Price £20.00.
ISBN 1-85409-299-5.

This is a collection of photoraphs from various sources, but many from the Imperial War Museum collection, of the Second World War at sea. We get no colour, which is a pity – some colour diagrams or maps would have been welcome, for example – and some of the photographss are very fuzzy due to the printing rather than the photographer. For example, the National Archive photograph of U.S.S. *Franklin* sinking, on p.54, which is very dramatic, deserves more space and according to Edwin Hoyt in *Carrier Wars*, was hit by the *Kamikaze* on 10 March 1945 (not the 19th).

There is a good photograph of some of the damage to the *Admiral Graf Spee* on p.8, showing her burnt out aircraft. In fact, though Captain Langsdorf's ship was damaged in some very important ways – the fire-fighting equipment was mostly out of action, the auxiliary boiler for drinking water was useless, the galley, bakery and laundry were wrecked, there were nine holes on the outer plating and she had been hit by 15 shells on the starboard and 12 on the port side. She was short of 11-inch shells, but in spite of this the reason for Langsdorf's decision not to break out was that the lookout reckoned he had seen the *Ark Royal* (then near Rio) from the lookout position. Langsdorf saved his crew, many of whom returned to Germany by a civil airline to fight again, he prevented his ship from being captured and then finally he took his own life because he was a man of principle and a leader of the old school, not a Nazi member. This drama does not come out in this book.

Where the book does succeed, however, is in Section 8, 'The Commanders', in which Kemp gives us potted biographies of the naval leaders on both sides during the war. There is Admiral Donitz looking very young, who took over from Hitler at the end of the war as German leader. He lived until the 1980s, and one of our Somerset A-level students wrote to him for help with her essay on the U-boat war. She received a 12-page letter in neat handwriting by return of post and, with the help of the German department, used it all in her essay which deserved an A plus mark

So who exactly is this book for? It is not a veteran's book, not a historian's book, but it is useful for the young reader who wants to know what the war was like at sea. It would have been more useful with an index and a few maps and diagrams.

JOHN KINROSS
Bridgwater
Somerset

THE DESIGN AND CONSTRUCTION OF BRITISH WARSHIPS, 1939-1945: The Official Record. Major Surface Vessels.
Edited by D.K. BROWN.
Conway Maritime Press, London, 1995.
154 *pages, c.*150 *illustrations.* Price £25.00.
ISBN 0-85177-673-6.

Yet another significant work from the former Deputy Chief Naval Architect which will be of immense value to researchers, students of naval history and, one might add, naval people who will find much that they never previously knew about the ships they once served in. In this, the first volume of three projected to cover all types of warship, there are eight chapters separately dealing with battleships and battlecruisers, monitors, fleet carriers, light fleet carriers, escort carriers, cruisers, fast minelayers, and destroyers, of all classes laid down or built during the Second World War. Here for the first time is a more or less complete record compiled from official printed, typed or manuscript archives which were originally intended for publication after the war but which have hitherto had only a limited distribution or none at all.

The editor's introduction describes the responsibilities and organisation of the Naval Construction Department under its two wartime Directors, Sir Stanley Goodall and Sir Charles Lillicrap; provides a lucid account of the Washington and London Treaty limitations; and explains the influence of the prewar decline in national building capacity and the new sciences of the prewar years. There is a glossary and an explanation of the basics of hull stability and strength calculations.

The various chapters start with accounts of earlier classes, from 1914 onwards, units of which were still in commission in 1939 to show where experience and continuity of policy, or otherwise, contributed to new designs. They then cover in great detail how design and construction progressed from the staff requirements, and their many amendments. These had to take into account the many developments and wartime inventions in armaments, radar, protection, aviation and power plants, down to such items as air conditioning, action information (i.e. operations rooms), arcticising, replenishment at sea and central messing. Designs were adjusted in the light of experience of fighting and damage sustained, and the actual availability of equipment, especially guns. Ever under review were structural strength, manoeuvrability, seakindliness, and the choice of metals and techniques to be used in building. Innovative ideas were the subject of investigation and experiment. The book includes extensive tables of particulars and building programmes and the careers of the completed ships are briefly given. Over 300 ships were involved, though some, of course, like *Vanguard* and *Ark Royal,* were not active until after the war.

The editor has enhanced our perspective with his useful notes to each chapter, as well as hundreds of footnotes (which most readably appear in the margins) with corrections, generous cross-references to other writers, and other observations. The reader will learn much of the effort required of the Royal Corps of Naval Constructors and conclude, with the editor, that, although some mistakes were made, 'the performance of this vast fleet... does seem very creditable'.

Handsomely produced, and liberally illustrated throughout with arrangement drawings and well selected photographs, this volume is worth every penny.

B.H. WAINWRIGHT
Chalfont St Peter, Bucks

ALL THE WORLD'S FIGHTING SHIPS 1947-1995.
Edited by ROBERT GARDINER.
Conway Maritime Press, London, 1995.
783 *pages*, innumerable *illustrations.*
Price £75.00.
ISBN 0-85177-605-1.

In 1983 Conway published a two volume book dealing with the period 1947-1982. This single volume updates the earlier books and carries the end date to 1995 providing a complete review of the ships of the Cold War era. The Soviet section has been completely rewritten by Dr Norman Friedman and is the best short account of that navy and hence this review will concentrate on that section.

The section opens with an 11-page survey of the rise and fall of the Soviet Navy starting with Stalin's grandiose wish for sea power and changes at the whim of successive leaders. There could, perhaps, have been a little more on background problems such as alcoholism in the shipyards. These pages provide an excellent study of Soviet sea power and lead into 19 pages of detailed descriptions of Soviet weapon systems and

sensors which are invaluable in assessing the capability of the individual ship classes.

The ship section of 58 pages is particularly good in describing the designs which were never built, often as a result of policy changes at the top. Ship design within a big navy is much more evolutionary than it seems from the outside; apparently revolutionary jumps are often seen as evolutionary change when the missing links are found. At last, one can be reasonably certain how many ships were completed in each class and the usual data of builder, launch date etc. is given. At its height, the Soviet Navy was a truly formidable force, only slightly less so than some of the more alarmist estimates.

The other navies have been revised in detail, usually by the original authors. Dr Friedman is, again, the guide to the might of the U.S. Navy which also experienced several switches in role. There is nothing to match the power of the big carrier force though it is slightly surprising that a 12 carrier force can only muster two at the sharp end. Ninety pages for the U.S. Navy compares with 64 for the Royal Navy written by Anthony Preston. Both sections have comprehensive guides to weapons and sensors. Accuracy in a book of this sort is all important but very difficult to check. There do not seem to be any obvious errors.

A personal obsession is the number of ships which have required very visible strengthening, for instance, British Type 21 (commercial design) and 42 (Ministry design), the French *Tourvilles,* the Soviet *Sovremennyy,* the U.S. FFG7 etc. Politicians have tended to equate weight with cost, forcing undue attention to cutting scantlings. The design of a lightweight, flexible structure supported in most irregular fashion by the sea is not easy and requires both skill and experience, not helped by excessive staff cuts.

The numerous illustrations (typically two per page) are well chosen and well reproduced. The editor has wisely limited the contents to real fighting ships, omitting the service craft, customs launches etc. which inflate the size and cost of annuals such as *Jane's Fighting Ships.* If you do not have the earlier two volume edition or need a complete record of the Soviet navy you will find this book good value.

DAVID K. BROWN, RCNC
Bath

BATTLESHIP MISSOURI: An Illustrated History.
By PAUL STILLWELL.
United States Naval Institute Press, Annapolis,
Maryland, 1996.
450 pages, many *illustrations* and *diagrams*. Price
£25.00.
ISBN 1-55750-780-5.

U.S.S. *Missouri* was the last battleship in commission on this planet's seas, and it seems extremely unlikely that there will be another. In
1989 the United States Naval Institute published
a book – Robert F. Sumrall's *Iowa-Class Battleships; their Design, Weapons and Equipment* – on
her class's technical history. This is the human
and service side of one of them. Paul Stillwell, the
Naval Institute's Director of History, who
served in her sister, the *New Jersey*, traces her
story from laying down in 1941, through four
wars, much peacetime service and twenty-nine
years laid up, to 1995.

She never met an enemy battleship or cruiser
in surface combat, but served as an anti-aircraft
ship, monitor and finally as a missile platform –
a task undreamed of when she was designed. Her
combat experience included withstanding Kamikaze attack, as close and deadly as the 'boarding
and entering' of earlier days. She spent a lot of
time as a heavyweight diplomatic counter – a role
familiar to earlier generations of capital ships.
She covered vast distances and weathered many
storms.

Despite her vast size, she always needed a bigger crew than the planners had foreseen and
some men had to share bunks. Seaplanes, standard in 1941, had long since vanished by the middle of her career. Three generations of men
served in her; some traditions survived, others
arose over the years. The shipboard film show
was well established by 1941, but was replaced
by TV viewing on the many internal screens built
into her for other purposes. Among the many
'characters' associated with her were Commander Cooper, the gruff Executive Officer who
had much to do with her initial working up,
Margaret Truman, daughter of the then Senator
for Missouri, who performed the launching ceremony and kept in touch with the ship thereafter,
and Boatswain's Mate Warrick Woodard, who
won a million dollars in a lottery, but soldiered
(sailored? – why not?) on aboard the *Missouri*.

In many ways the ship stayed very much the
same, but the United States, the world and weap-

onry changed around her. She was designed to
fire shells at ships, but lived to deliver and receive
missile fire. Drugs were not a problem in 1944,
but grew mightily until ousted by drastic action
in the 1970s. 'Negroes' were menials only in the
Second World War, but provided many officers
by the 1990s. Her only serious mishap was a
grounding, due, like many others, to over-confi-
dence. She was a good seaboat though – again like
many others – she did not entirely like typhoons.
The men who maintained her, even during the
years when she was laid up, get due mention.

Her life was as long as that of many Wooden
Walls (the *Sovereign of the Seas*, the super battleship of her day, lasted fifty-nine years) and far
more active. There is much more of interest –
R.N. ships appeared dirty to the Americans, a
target island was completely missed in gunnery
practice, and the loss of a helicopter crew came
as a blow to the whole ship.

This book tells clearly the story of 'The men in
'em' in a ship whose active life stretched from one
age to another, and whose like will not be seen
again.
K.D. McBRIDE
Brentford, Middlesex

WAR IN THE INDIAN OCEAN.
By MIHIR K. ROY.
Lancer Publishers, New Delhi, 1995 (U.K. dis-
tributors: Spantech & Lancer, Langham Road,
South Godstone, Surrey RH9 8HB).
312 pages, 17 pages of *photographs*, 2 *maps*. Price
£17.95; US$27.50.
ISBN 1-897829-11-6.

This is an interesting book, but not an easy one
to read. *War in the Indian Ocean* combines a
survey of India's maritime strategic situation and
future with a history of the Indian Navy during
Vice-Admiral Mihir K. Roy's distinguished career in that service. It suffers from this combination the more so because of a clear lack of
editorial direction of a writer who has much to
say and the potential to say it well. Both topics
were worth Admiral Roy's attention as an
author, but neither subject is presented in a coherent fashion and much is only touched upon
that would bear development at greater length
particularly in view of the unique insights which
the Admiral can bring to his work.

That said, this book is valuable for the student
of the Indian Navy because of the new light

which it casts upon important events of the past thirty years in which the author was personally involved. Much attention is given to the naval elements of the 1971 Indo-Pakistan War. As a captain, Mihir Roy served as Director of Naval Intelligence and was instrumental in organising the highly effective waterborne guerrilla war in East Pakistan. Roy is perhaps ingenuous in the extent to which the direct involvement of the Indian Navy is minimised (see Commodore Ranjit Rai, *A Nation and its Navy at War* [Lancer, New Delhi, 1987], pp.77-78, for a more frank assessment) but he includes much detail not before available in the open press. Amongst other subjects, the loss of the Pakistani submarine *Ghazi* is at last clearly ascribed to her own mines and not depth charging by Indian units. Roy is, moreover, forthright in his admission of tensions between the Western Command C-in-C Admiral Kohli and the more aggressive CNS, Admiral Nanda, during the prewar period when plans were being made for operations against Pakistan. He is equally open in his criticism of the decision to hold back some of the Russian built missile craft from operations against Karachi, which might have been even more successful than was the case, as well as the erratic and less than aggressive employment of the major units of the Western Fleet.

Other tensions in the Indian Navy are evident in Roy's account of the lease of the nuclear powered submarine *Chakra* from the Soviets, a project which he pursued over the objections of at least one Chief of Naval Staff. The Admiral is clearly an enthusiast for nuclear power but, despite some interesting suggestions on financing in-country building in state owned shipyards, he effectively admits that sheer lack of resources remains an almost insuperable obstacle for many of the ambitions of the Indian Navy unless defence priorities are drastically reordered. Admiral Roy's accusation of 'sea blindness' amongst his countrymen has, in the circumstances, some justification, but his audience would beneflt from a more detailed delineation of the pressures, including the differing strategic outlooks of the three services, which prevent the Indian Navy receiving its due.

War in the Indian Ocean is a book to be mined for detail by specialists but is not one for the general reader's library. The publisher, Lancer, has done great work in bringing this and other books on the Indian Navy into general circulation but it is time that higher standards of editing and proofing were set. Despite its current difficulties, the Indian Navy is one of the most significant naval forces in Asia, both by reason of size and of situation. It deserves the attention of historians and contemporary analysts.

JAMES GOLDRICK
Gladesville, Australia

NAVIES AND GLOBAL DEFENSE: Theories and Strategy.
Edited by KEITH NEILSON and ELIZABETH JANE ERRINGTON.
Praeger, Westport, Connecticut, 1995.
246 pages. Price £49.50.
ISBN 0-275-94898-6.

These papers on the theme of naval strategic history were presented by ten well known naval historians at the Royal Military College of Canada's annual military history symposium. In 1994 the collection was dedicated to the memory of Barry Hunt, who had been a distinguished teacher at the college, and whose own work in the field of naval history has an enduring honesty and strength which will ensure its continued value. The title misleadingly suggests an analytic work directly concerned with assessment of the potential of naval force following the end of the Cold War, but all the contributions, even the last paper by Holger Herwig on 'the future', are strictly historical. The value of the four analytical papers and six chronologies lies in the summaries the authors have made of their studies. None of the papers is fundamentally new work, but they will be useful to students finding their way into the field.

The cast is impressive. Don Schurman, Geoffrey Till, Andrew Lambert, David French and Andrew Gordon contributed papers on the British use of naval power, and the American side is presented by John Hattendorf, Ken Hagan, Nathan Miller and Colin Gray. Herwig's paper provides a conclusion. Notably absent is any paper on the role of naval power in Canadian defence strategy, which is a curious oversight reflective of the operational and bureaucratic biases of Canadian naval historiography. More understandable in a book of this length is the decision not to attempt to include papers on the naval strategic history of non-anglophone states.

Geoffrey Till's paper on 'Sir Julian Corbett and the British Navy in Naval Warfare', and John Hattendorf's on 'Alfred Thayer Mahan and American Naval Theory' are admirable analytical summaries of the problem of applying naval force to the strategic needs of states. In most instances, even the narrative histories transcend their chronological procrustean beds and focus on the strategic instruments of sea power. David French's essay on 'The Royal Navy and the Defense of the British Empire, 1914-1918' is a fine summary of the work that has been done on the strategic utility of sea power in the First World War, and reflects my own findings on blockade and guerre de course. This conclusion is consistent with Andrew Lambert's assessment that naval bombardment of dockyards and coastal cities was the fundamental strategic rational for ship design and operations in the later nineteenth-century Royal Navy. Andrew Gordon's paper on British naval strategy between 1918 and 1945 does not address the question of what mechanism of power could be harnessed by the Royal Navy, for the understandable reason that essential postwar economies and arms limitation treaties reduced the strategic calculus by the end of the 1930s to the problem of surviving the onslaught of the German, Italian and Japanese navies combined. American sensitivity to British exercise of sea power in the First World War, especially the blockade of the Central Powers, lay behind the treaties which alienated Japan, and made British attempts at appeasement of Germany and Italy unavoidable. Mahan, anglophile in his later years, would have agreed that American policy was shortsighted, or simply aggressive. From the British point of view, however, more attention should be given to the fact that in the longer term it was the British policy of appeasing the United States which was to be decisive to the events of 1939-1945. If in 1921 the full implications of abrogation of the Anglo-Japanese alliance, and imposition of the 5:5:3 battleship ratio, could have been known, there would still have been only one appropriate course of action for the British government. Colin Gray's essay on the role of the United States Navy in the Cold War is a distinct change of gear. Only marginally chronological, this densely written paper seeks to show that the strategic utility of naval power in the modern epoch differs little from the historical models.

Occasionally, greater editorial intervention might have been useful. It is also unfortunate that the editors have not included a bibliography of Barry Hunt's contributions to the field, nor any attempt at an obituary.

NICHOLAS TRACY
University of New Brunswick

DOING NAVAL HISTORY: Essays Toward Improvement.
Edited by JOHN B. HATTENDORF.
Naval War College Press, Newport, Rhode Island, 1995.
vi + 160 *pages.* Price US$8.00.
ISBN 1-884733-06-9.

This book should come with a health warning; the contributors seek fundamental changes in the writing of naval history. As John Hattendorf remarks in his Introduction, naval history must achieve the standards of sophistication and innovation achieved in other branches of the discipline.

The conference from which this book springs aimed to 'suggest broad standards... listing critical ideas issues and themes for naval historians to examine' (p.2). It was the second Yale-Naval War College seminar, the first resulting in *Ubi Sumus?: The State of Naval and Maritime History* (ed. Hattendorf, Naval War College Press, Newport, R.I., 1994). Commander James Goldrick RAN, who must be unique in being both a serving officer and a notable historian, reminds us (p.23) in his 'The Problems of Modern Naval History' of our need for 'an appropriate level of technical understanding of the subject'. Volker Berghan's 'Navies and Domestic Factors' cautions us to be aware of 'the interaction of domestic and international factors' (p.66). Paul Halpern, fluent in several tongues, addressing 'Comparative Naval History', pleads (p.76) for a 'holistic naval history'. Political scientists commented on the historians' papers. Robert Jervis in 'Navies, Politics and Political Science' exhorts us to study the causes of naval policy – development patterns and policy influences. Robert Wood's 'Domestic Factors, Regime Characteristics and Naval Forces' points out (p.71) that 'geopolitical and domestic concerns intertwine', while William Thompson makes 'Some Mild and Radical Observations on Desiderata in Comparative Naval History', observing that naval history has been 'relegated to the margins because its interests often seem too narrow or obscure' (p.102).

The health-threatening contributions are those of John Sumida and David Rosenberg on 'Machines, Men, Manufacturing, Management and Money: The Study of Navies as Complex Organizations and the Transformation of Twentieth Century Naval History', and Nicholas Rodger's 'Considerations on Writing a General Naval History' setting new bench marks in methodology, required skills, breadth of vision and the systematic organisation of naval history. Sumida and Rosenberg divide naval history into 'core', 'ancillary' and 'cognate' categories. 'Core' deals with operations and policy, 'ancillary' with equipment, personnel, manufacturing and management, and 'cognate' naval history is written from essentially non-naval viewpoints, with the navy as an instrument of some general policy, and engaging 'the large questions' (p.28). Rodger (p.117) observes that 'perhaps the single most urgent task, is to reconnect' naval history 'to the main stream of historical scholarship'. As Dennis Showalter in 'Toward a New Naval History' notes (p.129), Rodger's agenda is 'no less legitimate for being intimidating'. Paul Kennedy remarks that we have neglected the study of navies as organisations and have hardly dealt with the politics of sea power. In 'Context and Approach in Naval History: Admiral Tirpitz and the Origins of Fascism', he emphasises the different levels at which we must operate – unit, fleet, inter-service, national strategy. Mark Shulman, 'Hitting the Target: Perspectives on Doing Naval History', appeals for a multi-disciplinary and multi-national approach. Naval history surely can never again be marginal, parochial, unsophisticated and unregarded. Naval historians have nothing to lose but their self-imposed chains; it is time to rejoin the mainstream.
MICHAEL SIMPSON
University of Wales, Swansea

Short Notices

SHIPS AND SEAMANSHIP IN THE ANCIENT WORLD.
By LIONEL CASSON.
The Johns Hopkins University Press, Baltimore and London, 1996.
xxviii + 470 *pages, 197 illustrations.* Price £16.50.
ISBN 0-8018-5130-0 (paperback).

This is the paperback edition of the 1995 revision of Casson's classic work, originally published in 1971.

SOURCES OF LONDON ENGLISH: Medieval Thames Vocabulary.
By LAURA WRIGHT.
Clarendon Press, Oxford, 1996.
245 *pages.* Price £30.00.
ISBN 0-19-823909-2 (hardback).

Dr Wright examines the development of a London dialect during the Middle English and early Early Modern period. A large part of her investigation is concerned with the technical vocabulary relating to life on the Thames; accordingly, there are sections in the vocabulary survey on constructions, fishing, and objects in the river, states of the river, and shipping and trade names of people working on the river.

THE JOURNAL OF A VOYAGE TO LONDON.
By HENRY FIELDING.
Edited with an Introduction and Notes by TOM KEYMER.
Penguin Classics, 1996.
xxxix + 142 *pages, map.* Price £6.99.
ISBN 0-14-043487-9.

In 1754 Henry Fielding departed for Lisbon in the *Queen of Hungary* in an attempt to restore his health in the mild Portuguese climate. Though he died from 'a complication of disorders' soon after his arrival, Fielding completed an account of the voyage replete with unflinching humour and pathos. This version of the *Journal*, now made popularly available by Penguin, includes an interesting appendix on the career of Captain Richard Veale, a notable privateer commander in the 1739-1748 war.

FIGHTING SHIPS: Ships of the Line 1793-1815.
By DAVID DAVIES.
Constable Publishers, London, 1996.
201 *pages*, 8 *plates*, 8 *figures*, 12 *diagrams*, 4 *maps*.
Price £19.95.
ISBN 0-09-476020-9 (hardback).

In terms a layman can understand, David Davies describes the activities of the battleships that took part in the world wars of the Napoleonic era. He focuses on the ships themselves, on the crews who served in them, and on the great battles of the period, chiefly from a British perspective.

FEW SURVIVED: A History of Submarine Disasters.
By EDWYN GRAY.
Pen & Sword Books, Leo Cooper, London, 1996.
288 *pages*, 31 *black and white illustrations, diagrams*. Price £14.95.
ISBN 0-850524-99-7 (hardback).

A comprehensive account of every submarine loss by accident or error in peace and war since 1774. Mr Gray examines the important sinkings in some detail, analysing what went wrong and describing the attempts made at rescuing the crew and vessel.

OOOH, YOU NEW YORK GIRLS! The Urban Pastorale in Ballads and Songs about Sailors Ashore in the Big City.
By STUART M. FRANK.
The Kendall Whaling Museum and the Australian Association for Maritime History, 1996.
24 *pages, illustrated*. Price not stated.
ISBN 0-937854-34-4.

On 11 November 1995 Stuart Frank delivered the Vaughan Evans Memorial Lecture at the Western Australian Maritime Museum in Fremantle. This is the text of the lecture, adorned by scrimshaw and other illustrations from the collections of the Kendall Whaling Museum, Sharon, Massachusetts. It concerns the evolution of sailor ballads and includes much interesting material on the sailortowns of the Anglo-American maritime world of the nineteenth century.

POLSKIE SZKUTNICTWO LUDOWE XX WIEKU.
By JERZY LITWIN.
Gdánsk Maritime Museum's Proceedings, Vol. X, Gdánsk, Poland, 1995.
376 *pages*, 248 *photographs* and *drawings*, 12 *maps*, English language *summary*, *bibliography*, list of *contents* in English. Price not stated.
ISBN 83-85349-41-3.

Jerzy Litwin is Deputy Director of the Polish National Maritime Museum at Gdánsk. With its English summary and list of contents and with every one of its 248 captions to illustrations in English as well as Polish this well produced, lavishly illustrated, report on his exhaustive study over many years of the working boats of Poland's coasts and great rivers is a major contribution to European maritime ethnographic studies.

The Polish rivers present a profusion of boat types which is perhaps the richest in Europe and the traditions of wooden construction are still very much alive as part of the normal working life of the countryside. Even log boats have been made and used in commercial fisheries in recent years. I have had the advantage of travelling the length and breadth of Poland with the author and of watching him at work, and appreciating his thoroughness and his immense knowledge of his subject, but even to readers without a word of Polish this book conveys the richness and strength of Poland's boat culture.

And, for those who still like to argue the old subject of independent invention versus diffusion, the similarity of the Troki Lake boat illustrated in Figure 247 to the Fleet trows in use in Dorset today is surely interesting. Compare also with the flat äska of Gotland's southwest coast. [Basil Greenhill]

SEA FEVER.
By JOHN CALDECOTT LITTLER.
Jan Drent, 1720 Rockland Avenue, Victoria B.C., Canada V8S 1W8, 1995.
316 *pages, illustrated*. Price £17.00.
ISBN 0-9680370-0-3 (paperback).

An autobiographical account of life in the British merchant service and the Royal Canadian Navy. Captain John Littler became a master mariner in the Far East where he served the Jardine Matheson Company. He joined the Canadian Navy in 1940, commanded a corvette and served in the cruisers H.M.S. *Belfast* and H.M.C.S.

Uganda. After the war he commanded two destroyers and the cruiser *Ontario.*

CANADA'S NAVAL STRATEGY: Rooted in Experience.
By NICHOLAS TRACY.
Centre for Foreign Policy Studies, Dalhousie University, Halifax, Nova Scotia, Canada B3H 4H6, 1995.
x + 82 *pages*, 4 *maps.* Price not stated.
ISBN 1-896440-00-2 (paperback)

The first of the Maritime Security Occasional Paper series, this brief study examines thematically the strategic motives for national investment in a Canadian navy. A chronological approach is adopted to sustain the argument that, although there has been growth, the underlying objectives determining the Canadian naval establishment have been enduring.

THE SEA OUR HERITAGE.
By JEAN CANTLIE STEWART.
Rowan Books, Keith, Banffshire AB55 3QB, 1995.
304 *pages, illustrated.* Price £8.95.
ISBN 0-9509932-3-9 (paperback).

This is a revised, paperback edition of Jean Cantlie Smith's 1993 work in which she traces the rise and fall of British sea power and argues that government action is urgently needed to revive the nation's maritime interests.

SEA TRANSPORT: Operation and Economics.
By PATRICK M. ALDERTON.
Thomas Reed Publications, 1995.
292 *pages*, 140 *graphs, drawings* and *illustrations.*
Price £19.50.
ISBN 0-901281-63-8 (paperback).

This is the fourth edition of a book first published in 1973. Its purpose is to give a complete picture of the maritime transport industry so that those concerned with shipping can see their own specific field of activity in perspective and understand the basic model of the business.

LEADING LIGHTS: The Journal of Pharology, Pilotage and Seamarks. Vol. 1, No. 1 (1995).
60 *pages, illustrated.*
Available from Peter Williams Associates, Haven Lightship, Milford Marina, Milford Haven, Pembrokeshire SA73 3AF, U.K. Subscriptions: £24.50 for 6 issues; £12.25 for 3 issues; £5 per copy.

The first issue of a bi-monthly journal concerned with pharology, pilotage and seamarks. Contents include: 'Cinque Ports Pilots' (Roy S. Humphreys); 'Approaches to the Port of Liverpool, 1845' (Bob MacAlinden); 'Lights of the Tagus' (Gillian Williams).

SJAEK'LEN 1995: Årbog for Fiskeri- og Søfartsmuseet Saltvandsakvariet i Esbjerg.
Edited by MORTEN HAHN-PEDERSEN.
Fiskeri- og Søfartsmuseet, Esbjerg, Denmark, 1996.
160 *pages, illustrated.* Price not stated.
ISBN 87-87453-84-3.

Contents include: 'De fattige strandmaend' (Hanne Mathisen); 'Hjerting 1763' (Mette Guldberg); 'Tre foretagere på Esbjerg Havn: Firmaet C Breinholt 1875-1953' (Poul Holm); 'Strukturer under forandring? Udviklingen i danske trafikhavne siden 1960' (Morten Hahn-Pedersen). With English summaries.

510

G.L. GREEN, NAVAL AND MARITIME BOOKSELLER

18 ALDENHAM AVENUE, RADLETT, HERTFORDSHIRE WD7 8HX. TEL/FAX: 01923 857077

Stock may be viewed by appontment only. All items are in reasonable condition and are subject to availability. More details on content and condition can be provided. Orders can be made by telephone, fax or letter. CREDIT CARDS ACCEPTED (not American Express). *Postage up to £3.00 extra for UK Customers. Overseas Customers' Sea Mail Postage at Cost.*

ALBION Square Riggers on Schedule. New York Sailing Packets to England, France & Cotton Ports £75. **ANDREWS** Elizabethan Privateering £15. **ANONYMOUS** Life & Glorious Actions of the Right Honourable Sir George Rook 1707 £150. **ANONYMOUS** Instructions for the Management of Harveys Sea Torpedo 1871 43p. Illus. £100. **BARNES** Naval Actions of the War of 1812 £25. **BAXTER** Introduction to the Ironclad Warship 1968 £30. **BLOOMSTER** Sailing & Small Craft Down the Ages 1st Ed.1940 £75. **BOUND SHIPPING MAGAZINES ALL V/G** in Publisher's Binding with Indexes Marine Engineer & Naval Architect 1960-1976, Motorship 1960-1973, Shipbuilder & Marine Engine Builder 1954-1964, Shipbuilding & Shipping Record 1962-1973, Shipping World 1962-1975, Syren & Shipping 1960-1967 Prices from £15.00. **BOYNTON** History of the Navy During the Rebellion 1868 2 vols £125. **BRITISH ORTHOPAEDIC ASSOC.** Clinical Session at RN Hospital Haslar. Its history, building & past Medical Officers £35. **BYRN** Crime & Punishment in the RN 1784-1812 £25. **CHARNOCK** Biographia Navalis 5 vols £400. **CLARK** Naval Documents of the American Revolution 9 vols £300. **CONNELL** Jacks War WW2 Ordinary Seamen £9. **CORNWALLIS-WEST** Life & Letters of Admiral Cornwallis £30. **CRAIG/JARVIS** Liverpool Registry of Merchant Ships £15. **CRADOCK** Whispers from the Fleet 2nd Ed. £15. **CRAWFORD** Sailor Whom England Feared Story Paul Jones £20. **CROWHURST** French War on Trade 1793-1815 £25. **CRUTCHLEY** My Life at Sea £7. **CUNNINGHAM** Dock Engineering £25. **DIRECTORY OF SHIPOWNERS, SHIPBUILDERS & MARINE ENGINEERS 1949** £35. **DOUGHTY** Merchant Shipping & War £15. **DOW** Slave Ships & Slaving £100. **FOX** British Admirals & Chinese pirates 1832-69 £40. **FRENCH** Martyrdom of Admiral Byng £25. **GARITEE** Republic's Private Navy Privateering during war of 1812 £30. **GATES** City of Portsmouth Records of the Corporation 1918, 1929, 1930 bound together £25. **GIBSON** Marine Transportation in War the US Army Experience 1775-1860 £30. **GOLDENBERG** Shipbuilding in Colonial America £30. **GOUGH** RN & NW Coast of North America 1810-1914 £25. **GREEN G.L.** RN & Anglo-Jewry 1740-1820 £14.95. **GUIDE ARMSTRONG** Gallery of the Naval Exhibition Modern Naval Artillery 1891 £60. **HAKLUYT** Gaunches of Teneriff 2nd Series No. 21 £50. War of Chupas 2nd series No. 42 £50. New Light on Drake 2nd Series No. 34 £50. **HAULTAIN NAVY LIST** Feb, May 1943 £40 each. **HAMMERSLY** Naval Encyclopaedia. Dictionary of Nautical Worlds, Biographical Notices & Records of US Naval Officers £95. **HICKLING** One Minute of Time. Melborne Voyage Collision £12. **HUMBLE** Fraser of North Cape £15. **JOURNAL RNLI Vol. 18 Feb 1901- Nov 1903** Illus. Plans £75. Services by the Lifeboats of the RNLI 1939-46 £150. **JAMES NAVAL HISTORY** 6 vols + Index (Richard Bentley) decorative cloth 1860 New Ed. £150. **JONES** Civil War at Sea 3 vols £75. **KELSHAL** U Boat War in the Caribbean £35. **KEMP** Oxford Companion to Ships & the Sea £20. **LANGENSIEPEN/GULERYUZ** Ottoman Steam Navy 1828-1923 New £35. **LEANS** RN Navy List 1887, 1892, 1894 £40 each. **LEES** Masting & Rigging of English Ships of War 1625-1860 £30. **LEWIS** Welsh Port Books 1550-1603 £40. **LEWIS** Napoleon & British Captives £25. **LUBBOCK** Down Easters 2nd Ed. £30. **MACINNES** Bristol A Gateway of Empire £20. **MACKANESS** Fresh Light on Bligh £45. **MACKANESS** Blue Bloods of Botany Bay £10. **MACKENZIE** Life of Lord Collingwood £95. **MAHAN** From Sail to Steam £10. Types of Naval Officers £15. **MARCUS** Age of Nelson £40. **MARRYAT** Jacob Faithful 2 vols £30. **MARSHALL LT J.** RN Biography 1823-35 or Memoirs of the Services of all Flag Officers, Superannuated Rear Admirals, Retired Captains, Post Captains & Cdrs With typed index £1000. **MEIGS** Story ofthe Seaman from Earliest times until 1924 2 vols £25. **MELTON. MITCHELL** Every Kind Shipwork Todds Shipyard £20. **MORRIS** Captains Lady £20. **NAVY LEAGUE ANNUAL** 1910-1, 1911-2, 1913-4 £15 each. **NAVY LISTS** (corrected to previous month) Oct 1839 £35. Feb 1884 £20. July 1861 £30. July 1870 £30. Aug 1880 £25. Oct 1892 £25. Jan 1915 £60. **NAVAL REVIEW BOUND** 1913, 1921, 1922, 1923, 1924, 1933, 1934 £10 each. **NAVY RECORDS SOCIETY** First Dutch War 5 vols £75. Old Scots Navy £25. Russian War 1855 Black Sea £25. Life of Sir John Leake Vol. 1 & 2 Saumarez Papers Baltic £10 each. Sandwich Papers 1771-82 Vol. 1, 2, 3 £25 each. Jellicoe Papers Vol. 1 & 2 £12 each. Keyes Papers Vol. 1, 2, 3 Pollen Papers, Sergison Papers £5 each. **NICHOLSON** Shipping Arrivals & Departures Tasmania 1803-33 £25. 1803-42 £25. Log of Logs (Paper covers) £30. **OFFICE OF NAVAL INTELLIGENCE APRIL 1898** Discussion of Questions in Naval Tactics £65. **POLLOCK** Modern Shipbuilding & the Men engaged in it £35. **POWLEY** Naval side of King Williams War £25. **PUTNAM** Sailing Vessels & their Voyages Vol. 1 & 2 £30. **RASOR** Reform in the RN 1850-1880 £25. **RICE** British Oceanographic Vessels 1800-1950 £20. **RODGERS** Naval Warfare Under Oars £20. **ROMME** Dictionnaire de la Marine Francaise 1813 £100. **SCHOMBERG** Naval Chronology 5 vols 1815 £600. **SMOUT** Scottish Trade on th Eve of the Union 1660-1707 £15. **STEEL D.** Shipmasters Assistant & Owners Manual 10th Ed. 1803 £85. **SEA BREEZES Old Series (P.S.N.C) Vol. 1 Dec 1919 to Vol. 24 Oct 1939** Bound in blue & gilt cloth all with indexes except the last volume possibly not published Good 24 vols £600. **SEA BREEZES New Series** all in publisher's binding with Indexes Jan 1946 to Dec 1962 sold individually. Vol. 1, 2 £25 each. Vol. 3, 4, 5 £20 each. Vol. 6, 7, 8, 9, 10, 11, 12 Vol. 13, 14, 15, 16, 17, 18, 19, 20, 21, 22, 23, 24, 25, 26, 27, 28 £15 each. Vol. 29, 30, 31, 32, 33, 34 £10 each. **SNOW** New England Sea Tragedies, Tales of Sea & Shore, Mysterious Tales of the New England Coast (other titles in stock) £7 each. **SPURLING/LUBBOCK** SAIL 3 vols Good £700. **STEELS NAVY LISTS ALL BOUND BLUE CLOTH WITH GILT TITLE** £65 each. 1799: May, July, Aug, Sept, Oct 1800: March, May, June, July, Aug, Sept, Oct, Nov 1801 Mar, Apr, May, Aug, Sept, Oct, Nov 1802 Mar, Apr, May, Sept, Nov 1803 Jan, Mar, Apr, May, Oct, Nov 1804: Jan, Feb, Mar, Apr, May, June, July, Aug, Sept 1805: May, Apr, July 1806 Feb, Apr, June, Sept, Oct. **SYME** Shipping Arrivals & departures Victorian Ports Vol. 1 & 2 1846-55 £65. **SYRETT** Shipping & the American Waters 1775-83 £20. **THOMAS** Companion to the RN £20. **TUCKER** Arming the Fleet US Naval Ordnance £30. **UDEN** Dictionary of Ships & Seamen £15. **WEIGHTMAN** Heraldry in the RN Crests Badges of HM Ships £40. **WHITEHEAD** Gaspard De Coligny Admiral of France £30. **WILLLIAMS** Maritime Trade the East Anglian Ports 1550-90 £25. **YEXLEY** Our Fighting Seamen £25.

THIS LIST IS A SMALL SELECTION OF CURRENT STOCK. PLEASE LET ME KNOW YOUR SPECIFIC REQUIREMENTS & INTERESTS. COMPUTERISED PRINT-OUTS AVAILABLE
BOOKS PURCHASED THROUGHOUT THE WORLD
NAVAL & MARITIME BOOKSELLERS FOR OVER 20 YEARS